WHY WE OCCUPY

WHY WE OCCUPY

LIBERTY PLAZA 2011

INTERVIEWS BY OLIVIA SCHANZER

Matchlock Press
New York

Why We Occupy: Liberty Plaza 2011
Interviews by Olivia Schanzer

Library of Congress Control Number: 2012951985
ISBN: 978-1-939333-00-1

Published by Matchlock Press
PO Box 90606
Brooklyn, NY 11209
matchlock.com

Contents

Abbreviations

A.A.	Alcoholics Anonymous
A.C.L.U.	American Civil Liberties Union
A.E.D.	automatic external defibrillator
AIDS	acquired immune deficiency syndrome
a.k.a.	also known as
a.m.	*ante meridiem*
B.A.	Bachelor of Arts
B.C.	British Columbia
C.C.U.	critical care unit
C.D.	compact disc
C.E.O.	chief executive officer
C.I.A.	Central Intelligence Agency
C.P.R.	cardiopulmonary resuscitation
D.A.	Direct Action
D.C.	District of Columbia
D.O.E.	Department of Education
D.V.D.	digital videodisc
E.M.S.	emergency medical services

E.M.T.	emergency medical technician
E.T.A.	estimated time of arrival
F.D.A.	Food and Drug Administration
F.D.N.Y.	Fire Department of the City of New York
F.D.R.	Franklin Delano Roosevelt
FERC	Federal Energy Regulatory Commission
F.I.T.	Fashion Institute of Technology
G.A.	General Assembly
G.M.O.	genetically modified organism
H.E.R.E.I.U.	Hotel Employees & Restaurant Employees International Union
H.I.V.	human immunodeficiency virus
HVAC	heating, ventilation and air conditioning
I.R.S.	Internal Revenue Service
I.V.	intravenous
I.W.W.	Industrial Workers of the World
J.F.K.	John Fitzgerald Kennedy
L.A.	Los Angeles
LETS	local exchange trading system
M.B.A.	Master of Business Administration
M.I.T.	Massachusetts Institute of Technology
MoMA	Museum of Modern Art
M.T.A.	Metropolitan Transportation Authority
M.T.V.	Music Television

NASA	National Aeronautics and Space Administration
N.P.R.	National Public Radio
N.V.C.	Nonviolent Communication
N.Y.C.G.A.	New York City General Assembly
N.Y.P.D.	New York Police Department
N.Y.U.	New York University
O.C.D.	obsessive-compulsive disorder
O.W.S.	Occupy Wall Street
PAC	political action committee
P.C.	politically correct
P.D.F.	portable document format
Ph.D.	Doctor of Philosophy
p.m.	*post meridiem*
P.R.	public relations
P.S.	public school
P.T.S.D.	post-traumatic stress disorder
P.V.C.	polyvinyl chloride
R.E.I.	Recreational Equipment Inc.
RISD	Rhode Island School of Design
R.N.	registered nurse
S.I.S.	Shipping, Inventory and Storage
T.V.	television
T.W.U.	Transport Workers Union of America

Why We Occupy

U.C.   University of California

U.F.C.W. United Food and Commercial Workers

U.F.T.   United Federation of Teachers

U.S.   United States

U.S.A.   United States of America

v.   versus

vs.   versus

WOW   Women Occupying Wall Street

X.L.   export limited

A Note on the Interviews

The seventy-one interviews collected in this volume were conducted by Olivia Schanzer in downtown Manhattan during the fall of 2011. The first interview took place on October 22, when Occupy Wall Street was thirty-six days old. On day sixty the people were evicted, and the last interview took place, barricaded, the day after that.

Except where otherwise noted, these conversations were recorded in and around Liberty Plaza a.k.a. Zuccotti Park. The atmosphere in the park during the day was turbulent: busy with occupiers, and rippling with wave after wave of reporters, photographers, tourists, panhandlers and hecklers. The roaring wind and the beating of the drums were relentless. Adding to the challenge, Olivia was carrying an energetic one-year-old on her back most of the time. These factors all contributed to a certain spontaneity evident in the body of the recordings which bears some resemblance to the occupation at that time, and which is largely preserved in this volume by presenting the interviews in chronological order.

Many more people agreed to be interviewed for this book, but the eviction was carried out before they had a chance to go on the record. We miss their contributions, and it is our sincere desire to see all of those suspended conversations—indeed, all suspended conversations everywhere—resume. ❖

Introduction

To a passer-by drilled in the formations of twenty-first-century America, an occupier is a stranger. All of her traits are alien; they might even be cause for alarm. She carries herself well. Her handshake is very firm. She maintains eye contact without wavering. She is confident and easy when engaged in conversation. Her voice—how it resounds! All of this resembles the people of twenty-first-century America not at all. We have only to peer into the nearest reflective surface to see it: "This is the impression I get from looking in the television set."

When faced with occupiers *en masse*, our disturbance only grows. Their arrival is always preceded by a great noise. Before they appear, they are announced by shouts and cacophony. The sound reverberates from the office buildings and jars us at our desks. What kind of voices are these rattling the windows? Who are they?

Are they perhaps not people at all? But they must be people: They abhor wet socks. Just like people, they need peanut butter sandwiches at regular intervals in order to survive. If not people, then why do they have a beer at the end of a stressful day, or stamp their books for circulation? The little things add up quickly, and the first idea must be discarded. Even a casual observer can see that they are in fact people.

A disturbing second choice now asserts itself. A wild aberration in the laws of physics has occurred at a location somewhat to the northwest of the Stock Exchange. A greased slide of dark matter has manifested—though maybe it was a fold, or better call it a ripple; it could even have been a flexing of string. Perhaps a cæsura in the fabric of space-time. If we want something more specific, we should call the university and get an expert on the phone! But even without an expert, the layman is forced to see the sense before his nose. All signs point to it directly: Occupiers are people from the future.

It is obvious, irrefutable. People from the present are complacent, while occupiers face pepper-spray and cuffs and go willingly to jail.

They march though every step is dogged by their faithful chaperones the police, though every time ten people and a sign step out onto pavement, the mayor calls for troops in phalanx. In the park, they shelled and ate their peanuts under the unblinking eye of a guard tower that saw and strained to hear not just their lawful assemblies, but every clicking of their teeth. They blew on their coffee and browsed for books ten feet from a line of police vehicles that sat empty, ready to take them away. To meet their ends, they lay down outside in rain and sleet, under tarps or whatever else they could find. Tapped phones didn't deter them, neither did the surveillance of their meetings, nor did the provocateurs who showed up so diligently it seemed that they, like everyone else, had no sick leave from their jobs.

In twenty-first-century America, we work hard to maintain a status quo that doesn't serve us. Perhaps we do it from a sense of brotherhood: It is a democratic status quo and diminishes poor and rich alike. Our lives are predetermined by our material circumstances. The roles we are forced to play based on accidents of birth limit and constrict our growth. The space the present has sold us to live in is so small that it leaves no room for air.

But the occupier exhorts us to step out of our cells. It must be that men and women from the future are not subject to the rigors of closed doors. They claim we do not even need a key to open them; the doors have always stood ajar. In the park, people took on jobs and roles according to need and not duress. They worked at the jobs they wanted to work at, in the fashion they wanted to work at them. Occupiers relate organically to time; an occupier is alive in all the moments of her life, not only those times when she is off the clock.

However, their virtues are not only inward-directed; occupiers are also compassionate. Occupiers fight negligence in all its forms. They take care of the homeless and indigent within their ranks even when it is difficult to do so. They work to bring health and safety to people who have none. Even the chronically ill were looked after in the park, in spite of those who said that this work compromised the movement.

The occupation countered America's false sense of scarcity with the truth of plenty. We are a very rich country, they remind us, and no one has to suffer from want. Occupiers amassed enough food and clothing and housing for groups of great numbers, and they showed us that we might continue indefinitely, if only we care to. There is enough, in fact, for everyone, and by everyone an occupier has the brass to mean the whole planet. They challenge us with the question: What reason can we find not to be generous, when we can afford to be so easily?

But it is easy to see that an occupier would be generous even if he couldn't afford it. Kindness is a primary occupier virtue; kindness is a political platform. Though the people of twenty-first-century America might flinch at the sound of this idealism, an occupier shows us by his actions a practical implementation.

Of course we flinch! We've been led to believe that bamboozlement is inevitable when we offer our help. Everyone knows there is a vulnerability on both sides of that kind of transaction, but when an occupier offers a stranger ice cream, poisoning is not a foregone conclusion. In fact, the stranger finds that the ice cream tastes very good. But even when his generosity is badly received, the occupier himself will tell us that the impulse to be generous wasn't wrong. Occupiers show us that generosity is not a synonym for weakness. To offer of oneself, whether the offer is accepted or rebuffed, is to be strong.

Moreover, security doesn't come from pathological self-protection. An occupier is a good judge of character because her business is conducted eye-to-eye. She cannot put institutions over individuals because for an occupier, there are only people, there are no institutions. An institution cannot stand in front of you. You cannot have coffee with the Federal Reserve. The knuckling under to endless bureaucracy has stifled our ability to make decisions and our ability to protect ourselves. It is this that has made us timid and gullible. An occupier is neither timid nor gullible.

Occupiers have no truck with bullshit; they neither give it nor receive it. Over the present hangs a miasma of euphemisms, lies and prevarications. Words are garbled and contorted by political parties, corporations, and the full spectrum of the media. In fact, anyone who can get a hand on language puts screws to the idea of meaning itself. "Natural" is the vague term used when you want to pack your product with chemicals. Corporations claim to sponsor human emotions and human relations. The reading level of the newspaper drops a grade every few years.

That vaporous substance inside us—however you would describe the soul—is in danger of being blown away entirely by the squall of modern life. An onslaught of products and false responsibilities, the unrelenting drudgery of our jobs, and the speed at which we are forced to travel through our days—all this threatens to disperse us. Whatever our heart has to offer is drugged away, and just as it is with the presence of our physical bodies, the expression of emotions is considered barbaric. To feel pain and heartache and to suffer in consequence, to be sentimental, to want things that are not material, to age, to be mortal—all these things are barbarisms. To mourn the death of your own beloved for too long is mental illness. But an occupier mourns the death of his beloved.

When will our present America age to meet these virtues and these people who embody them? At what point—what specific year—will we be in hailing distance of this future spot in time?

Past the crises of a parboiled globe, nuclear meltdown, economic chaos and depravity. Past starvation, public libraries and hospitals gone. Past children educated not into freedom but only into slavishness. Past the whine and hum of a capitalism that grinds up the bones of the third world and sells the grindings back for bread. Past American workers left in towns whose only product is meth. Past permanent eternal war, on the other side of apocalypse and misery. This is the future from which they come. In their time, people rebuild with the planks and detritus left to them and find that it is plenty. They need bravery and resilience, and so they have it. They need camaraderie and patience, and they have that, too.

But why wait to rebuild until then? Why not cross over now, immediately, through this perforation in time, bypassing calamity and despair?

This future America . . . here it is. Somehow it has slipped back to us, filled with its free people, blithe within their new bones and new blood, new sinew, new synapses, like our own in form, but somehow entirely different. Unbent where we are bent, poured full with hope where we are empty of it. They would have us rebuild not later but now.

Is their future distant or near? The fact that they are here at all tells us that it is easy to get to. The gulf is narrow. It is nothing to cross, and if you look, they are holding out their hands to us.

—Olivia Schanzer

The hope of a secure and livable world lies
with disciplined nonconformists who are
dedicated to justice, peace and brotherhood.

—Martin Luther King, Jr.

Peace and friendship with all mankind is our wisest
policy, and I wish we may be permitted to pursue it.

—Thomas Jefferson

WHY WE OCCUPY

October 22

Rafael

So if you could just, for the record, tell me your name, age—

Rafael, forty-seven years old.

Occupation?

Occupation? Occupying Wall Street—oh! [Laughs.]

Right, that's the problem with calling it that.

Okay, okay, occupation . . . uh, computer technician.

And are you occupying?

Um, yes, I'm—yeah, I'm employed.

And how—no, are you occupying?

Am I occupying? Yes, I am occupying Wall Street. [Laughs.]

[Laughs.] I've got to pick a different word for that. So you're occupying. How long have you been here for?

Sixteen days I've been here today.

Sixteen days?

Yeah, but I was gone for two days.

How has your experience of the occupation been?

I absolutely love this place. There is so much love here. I've been able to find other people that feel and think the same way that I do. For a

1

long time I thought I was crazy, and in my house, everybody thinks I'm crazy. Every time someone comes over and I try to start talking about it, my wife goes, "Oh, God! I'm sorry, Mary. Uh, Ralph, please stop. Come on, come on. She didn't come over here to hear that!"

But here there's so many people that I can talk to that it's great. I really feel comfortable, and I think we may be able to wind up doing something, eventually. It might take some time, but . . .

What's your average day like?

I get up probably about seven. Six thirty, seven o'clock depending on whether it rains or not, or how cold it is. [Laughs.] And, uh—

Wait, you sleep in if it's raining, or you have to get up earlier?

No, I have to get up earlier because I don't have a tent. We're not allowed to put up tents, even though some people have. I don't want to go to jail, so I'm trying to, you know, minimize. As soon as it starts raining, I've got to get up. Then I walk around for a little bit. I talk to people. And about one o'clock, I leave and go to work. And then I get home about maybe eight, nine o'clock in Staten Island, and I see my wife, my kids—

Take a little shit . . .

Yeah, you know, [laughs], take care of the basics. And then I come back out here about ten-thirty, eleven—come back and occupy.

And it's been rough. I mean, the first night I didn't plan on staying here. It was just me and what I have on. They told me, "Go to Comfort and get a blanket." They gave me, like, a baby-sized blanket that basically could cover my chest. [Laughs.]

Oh, geez.

And I laid on the floor with it and froze and shook, but by the next day . . . I went home to get some blankets and my wife was furious. She was like, "You're not taking anything out the house!" So I was like, "Okay." Then I came back here and they gave me a sleeping bag. By then they had more stuff, so . . .

So you were here a little bit at the beginning?

Yeah, yeah, but it's all right now. I have a tarp. I have a blanket, sleeping bag. I've made a pillow. I have a bucket to put my stuff in, nice and neat at night, and I have a spot right next to Medical there. So I'm all right, you know? Like I told them: If I freeze in my sleep, I'm right next to Medical, so I'll be all right. [Laughs.]

[Laughs.] They can resuscitate you.

Yeah, they can bring me back.

"Um, heat up the frozen guy . . . bumsicle." Oh, that's not a nice term.

You have a great personality.

Oh, thanks. That's nice.

◆

So the name of the book is *Why We Occupy*.

Right.

Can you tell me something about—

I occupy because I feel that the corporations rule the world. I feel that the corporations control everything: from the food supply, to our politics and our officials, to what jobs are going to be in what area. They decide to impoverish a community or enrich it, and that's too much power for any one entity to have. And I feel that by being here, we can do something.

For example, the taxes. Personally, I pay so much more taxes than a corporation does. Even though they pay more, you know, they pay less percentage-wise compared to what I pay, and that's not fair. I don't think it's fair that when a corporation runs out of money, they can get bailed out, but when I run out of money and I can't pay my mortgage, the bank decides to take my house and put me and my kids out in the street. It's so unfair!

So I feel that by my being here . . . I don't know what it's going to fix or whether it's going to fix anything, but I know that I've been doing nothing for a long time, and I'm tired of doing nothing. I'm hoping that being here—even if it's just sleeping here—might make a difference.

Someone was telling me last night: "It's too cold to be sleeping here." I said, "Well, this is a sacrifice." I mean, we weren't expecting room service and nice, big, fluffy down pillows. It's a sacrifice that we're making—hopefully, for a better future for our children. ❖

Kent

I'm Kent, from New York.

Are you occupying?

Sometimes I stay over here and sometimes I go back home. And I'm here for this cause—their movement—but I'm here with the troops. Yeah, I want to get him home.

You want to bring the troops home?

Yeah.

How long have you been involved with the movement?

Couple of weeks. On and off, you know? I've got to do my thing.

Okay.

So I may be not the best person to talk to.

I'm trying to hear from everybody, including visitors. Anyway, if you're coming frequently, that counts as an occupier.

Right, right. Yeah, you could say that, yeah.

Where are you from originally?

I'm born in Sweden, but I growed up here in Manhattan.

I think the movement's been good, you know, for the economy. I've been in bad situations. I've been homeless. I've done that, been there. I've seen how bad it is. This city is now closing down shelters—all kinds of stuff—because of economic interests.

And to try to get some money for the poor.

Is that the primary reason why you're occupying?

Yeah, you could say that, yeah.

How did you first hear about the movement?

Well, I just turned on the T.V. at home. They were talking it over. And then it started.

What did you think when you first saw something about it?

Well, I think it was awesome. Yeah, because I've been follow this, with all the taxes and something like that, you know? They need to tax the wealthy people. Like Warren Buffett said: "I need to pay more taxes." Russell Simmons was here another day and said: "I need to pay more taxes." Warren Buffett's secretary—he present this—pay more taxes than what he do, and he's a fifty-five-billion-dollar man. And she have, just . . . it don't make sense, you know?

We need to tax Wall Street. All the greed's going on down there; set their own bonuses, and all the paychecks. They have to change.

How have you been finding the occupation itself?

When first I come here there was not that much, but it's getting bigger and bigger, and they go for more and more. Every day it's a new cause or something like that coming down. You can see here every day, if you walk around, a different union coming down and ask for our help here and get the boost from all this. Yeah, mm-hmm.

It does seem like it's growing every day.

It does.

We were down here with the kids who slept over[1]—

Oh, yeah. That corner here was a lot of kids and families. Parents and whole families . . .

Was there a lot of crying in the night?

No, no. They were sleeping. It was pretty quiet during the night. There's nothing much happen.

And also, parents just taking their kids down here. I talked to a family yesterday who took his son down here, too. You can see because he had no idea what was going on and he had no idea why. They took him down so he could see for himself. And he was stunned. He said, "Wow." He was about ten, eleven years old.

Just for him to see what the movement was like?

Right, right, because he had no clue what this is about.

I think it's good, you know? Just growing and growing for every day. See how long time you can hang out.

---

[1]Parents for Occupy Wall Street hosted a family sleepover on October 21–22.

Are you in it for the long haul?

Yeah.

Pretty much?

Yeah, until something get changed, you know? I mean, I don't make any money. I don't work any more, been retired. But I don't get nothing. Everything I do is paying my rent, and then I don't have anything else because they have taken everything from me.

But Mayor Bloomberg—he don't like people who don't make two hundred thousand dollars a year. They not worth nothing for him.

Yeah, he does not, it's true.

That's why, since he come in office, he close seven shelters, and gave that money to the wealthy.

Well, my mother-in-law goes to the senior centers, and that's the other thing.

Right.

I mean, that's where people go to get dinner, lunch . . .

Yeah, and the lunch and the dinner get poorer and poorer, less and less. You can see if people go to the soup kitchens. Sometimes I drop by there and see. Places that are usually really very good for you, now it's almost nothing. They don't have nothing.

Economy goes down, everybody goes, and that's not good. They have to change that. ❖

Charlie

My name's Charlie. I'm twenty, and I was a student in Little Rock, Arkansas. I've been following the movement very closely, and the day the first union joined—the Transport Workers Union[2]—I dropped out and headed up here.

---

[2] The Transport Workers Union of America marched with Occupy Wall Street for the first time on October 5.

Really.

Yeah.

That's fucking baller! [Laughs.]

[Laughs.]

You were in the middle of the semester?

Yeah, I was six weeks in. It was like, "Fuck it! What good is a creative writing / philosophy degree going to be?"

That's what I have. It's not good! [Laughs.]

[Laughs.] So I'm basically a year away from graduating, but I'm here learning much more than I ever did in college. I came for a variety of reasons. Corporate greed destroys the planet is the biggest reason, but it also has a lot to do with how we oppress other people, how we fuel wars, how we poison ourselves and other countries and the environment. There's a lot of fucked-up shit.

How are you finding the experience?

Every day it gets better, while simultaneously I get more exhausted.

Are you getting any sleep?

I barely get any. It's cold and I'm sleeping on the ground, but there *is* free coffee.

Always important.

Yeah, that helps a lot.
    I love it. I'm working with the Sustainability Working Group.

What's that?

What is it?

Yeah. What do you guys do?

We realize that the sustainability of the movement has everything to do with how "sustainable" the movement is. So we built our booth and booth chair out of up-cycled lumber that we found in dumpsters. We have a pedal-powered bike that a New York organization called Time's Up! brought here, and we're working on getting more. We've got a greywater system for removing toxins from the dishwater and mop water. We're trying to start some gardens and green spaces in the area, with or without permission. We do recycling and compost, and we're encouraging all the other working groups to reduce their waste or completely get rid of it.

Which means what, to completely get rid of it? All of it's used?

Yeah, or just stop using things like Styrofoam and bleach and stuff that's wasteful. Like, somebody from one of our groups encouraged the kitchen to get teacups instead of using Styrofoam cups.

More elegant also.

Yeah. And as soon as all the bleach is gone, we've already bought the apple cider vinegar to replace it, so we don't continue to pollute the environment in the same manner that the corporations do. So yeah, that's exciting. In the spring we're going to go out to community gardens, but it's almost November now; it's not very practical.

Are you in this for the winter? You're going to be out here?

I'm in this for . . .

Forever.

Forever, yeah.

What are your winter plans?

Uh, I live under the Sustainability Booth table.

[Laughs.]

It's four by eight by forty inches tall, and it's insulated with cardboard, and I've got a nice sleeping bag from my experiences backpacking.

What do your parents think of this?

They're proud.

They're old lefties?

Yeah. Not this far left, but . . .

Somewhere.

Yeah.

Do you have anything else that you would like to say, for the historical record?

I think it's hilarious when the journalists come in and try to ask us what are our demands. They clearly just don't get it, not even a little bit. One sign I saw put it most eloquently: "The movement is the message." ❖

Wicked

If you would just tell me your name . . .

My name is Wicked.

And your age, profession?

Twenty-five. I'm a hair stylist but I'm currently unemployed, and I'm from Jersey.

When did you first hear about the movement?

I first heard about it a couple weeks before it started—through a Facebook invite, actually—but I didn't know it was going to be like this. I thought it was just going to be, like, a one-day thing, because it's New York City. You would figure they wouldn't let anybody stay in a park. So in the beginning, I didn't come. And then I came . . . I would say about three weeks ago, and we checked it out during the day. And we started coming every single day, me and my husband. We're—actually, we were in a shelter. We're homeless.

We would come every day, and we would have to leave to get back to Queens by ten o'clock. Then we ended up getting found ineligible in the shelter, and they kicked us out. We didn't have nowhere to go, so we came here. This is actually a safe place for you to sleep. You don't have to worry about cops yelling at you to leave and blah, blah, blah.

So that's originally why I came, but it started to be much more than that for me. I think in the beginning, the message was that people are displeased with the bailout of the bankers while, you know, everybody else is kind of suffering. There really isn't a middle class anymore.

It's either you got money and, you know, you're living good, or you're broke and you're barely making ends meet.

As I came here, I started realizing that this is something important. This is making history. And I mean, I'm young. I'm twenty-five, so to me, this is the first time I've been involved in something or actually really given a shit about something. I have two kids, so I'm sitting here thinking about, like, you know what? It is about time that somebody does take a stand for stuff, because if I don't, by the time my kids grow up and they're my age, this world's going to be in way worse condition.

Me personally—the reason why I'm here is because there's no jobs. I've been homeless for four months. I've been trying to find work since January. I used to work for a corporation, so I know how corporations are. They basically treat you like a number and a statistic. I used to manage a salon. Then I got demoted only because I didn't turn a profit. Not because my customers weren't happy with my work, not because the staff didn't think I treated them well, just because I didn't bring them in money. So that's why I'm here.

This country needs change, you know? There's no jobs, and these bankers and all their politicians are bringing in millions of dollars a year. You know what? If every single one of you just put a hundred thousand dollars . . .

And then they complain about getting taxed more, but you guys have it to spare. You guys could go drop money on the most useless shit that's not even necessary, while there's people out here starving and homeless.

Like twenty-five-thousand-dollar sunglasses.

Exactly. You could buy that, but you can't help somebody out, you know what I'm saying?

And in New York City . . . this is the best place to start the movement, because I was reading in the newspaper this is where a good chunk of this country's rich people live. This is the one percent right here.

I think a lot of people are blaming it on Obama—that he's not doing anything—but it's not really him. I think he's trying to do stuff, but he's meeting a lot of opposition. People want to make him look bad, the same way Fox News and different people come in here and want to make us look like we're socialists and we're trying to destroy the country. That's not what it is. We're just taking a stand, same way people took a stand in the sixties, same way they took a stand in Egypt. Just showing you we're not happy, because if we all sit on our asses and act like nothing's wrong, then nothing is going to change.

And that's pretty much it.

All right, what was that again?

¡Viva la Revolución! [Laughs.] ❖

Christopher

Go.

All right, my name's Christopher. I was an industrial union painter for fifteen years. I worked on bridge contracts, mega steel structures. I worked at the Hanford Site out in Richland, Washington. I worked on missile launch towers in Lompoc, California, for the space center. And I endangered my health. I do lead abatement/removal. The stuff gets in my blood. I watch it dump into rivers all around the country, you know? Nobody cares. So I decided—after my father died—that I'm going to hit the road, and I'm going to see what the real world is like.

The last three years I've been riding freight trains, going around. I got forty-six states. I got thirty-one national parks. I paid to go to a lot of these places. Now I realize that, you know, being a hobo, I can actually see America for free.

I was coming out of retirement, actually, for this. I hadn't ridden a train since, like, March earlier this year.

I have lifelong friends in Florida. I was sitting there watching the news, and . . . I'm a native New Yorker. I grew up out on Long Island. Moved to Florida as a child—my dad retired, you know? So next thing you know, I'm, like, so upset about what's going on. Now I mean, I was doing just fine out at my friend's property, doing some tree work. He doesn't ask for any money, and we're out in the country, just enjoying life. But we get cable T.V., you know, satellite . . .

So it's, like, now I watch Robin Meade, *Express in the Morning*, and—

[Laughs.]

But then I started getting more into the protesting thing. Like, you know, "What's *really* going on?" Well, I decided: I'm going to come out of retirement.

Last week, I jumped on a freight train. A thousand miles; I walked fifty. It cost me twenty-two dollars to get here. I got here last Saturday, and I've been here, and I've been sleeping here, and I've been knee-deep in the trenches with the revolutionaries. I'm totally down with it. I'm totally down with this cause. And I was sitting on the chair saying, "Can I make a difference if I come here and tell my story?"

I believe that I am a red-blooded American. I don't believe in public transportation. I don't think that people should pay to get on the bus. You know, I drove a taxi for three and a half years in South Florida. I used to give rides away, when I had single mothers that were coming back with all the groceries and the three screaming kids, and she's like, "I only have seven dollars." I ate the rest of it because I knew that I was giving something back.

But really what I was doing is: I was paying four dollars a gallon for gas—during the horrible reign of George Bush—and I'm paying into this money machine, like, you know, gas taxes and stuff. I remember when gas—when I started driving—was a dollar forty-eight. Now it's over four dollars a gallon.

I'm sitting there, like, okay, Obama came in and he's going to make a change. Nah, the gas went down a little bit, and then it went back up. Who's controlling that? It definitely ain't Obama! He's getting his share, but it's the bankers. I'm totally against the bankers.

We don't make decisions to go to war and all kinds of things through the one mind of the president. You know, Congress acts on it. So when you think about it like that, everybody says, "Oh, it's a good idea to go to war." Yeah, that's because they're back-dooring the Afghan people for the lithium mines!

It was a personal thing to get Saddam Hussein. Not saying he wasn't a terrible, terrible person, but it was all, like, a personal vendetta from family crap, as far as I'm concerned.

When Hillary was going to run for government—yeah, I think a lady should go to office, but at the same time, when you look at it, I don't want two families in the last twenty-eight years, possibly, reigning and running this country. That's why I didn't go with Hillary, you know what I mean?

So looking at all the politics, sitting on the couch, my head's going to explode, and what can I do? I walked outside. I walked down the railroad tracks and I caught a ride here, and that's my story.

And I'm here just to make sure that . . . you know, I police myself. I don't believe in "New York Police Department." I think that these guys are all crooks over here. I think they're eyeballing, they're looking to mace people. I'm totally not for that.

If we policed ourselves and we lived in a peaceful world, we'd watch out for the other, you know what I'm saying? And I don't see that. I see these guys; I says, "How much money do you make? My friend says you start at twenty-two thousand, and you're getting shot at and everything. You know, that's not a lot of money. You can't raise a family on that."

I think they're tax collectors. I think they should do another job, you know what I'm saying? I don't think that they should walk around with guns. I think that they should turn around and help the people in other ways. Not say, "Hey, you did something wrong," and tax you. That's really all it is, and I don't even know where this money goes. I don't know where the money goes.

I'm not on food stamps. I depend on my brothers and sisters to help me. I don't believe in the government, I'm sorry.

Okay, so you're full-on anarchist.

No, I'm not.

Oh, okay.

No. They're more of a violent kind of group, you know? Like, throw a monkey wrench in and confuse people and stuff. I'm not about that.

Okay.

I want to hear the truth. I want you to say, you know, straightforward, so that the common American . . .

I was in Small-Town America. I woke up to a sign that had a thumb with a circle and a slash—I'll show you a picture if you want to see.

Yeah.

You get discouraged when you wake up in the morning and you see something like that. I mean, I was in the middle of nowhere, dying of thirst. So then—get this—I walk up to a church in the middle of nowhere, and they took the faucet spindle off the spigot! So in the middle of nowhere, the church—even established religion—wasn't worried about somebody maybe, like, needing water. Like, they were going to control how much water they're going to give as a church!

I'm against a lot of established things, you know? Somewhere along the line, the government decided that we're going to make up a bunch of these signs and post them around. I mean, how much you think that sign's worth? Twenty bucks?

Yeah.

Yeah, so how many do you think there are?

Oh—it was, like, a serious *sign* sign? Like, a road sign?

Yeah.

That's fucked up.

This is coming right off of I-95—where I-95 meets 301—in the middle of nowhere.

Wow.

And, like, so does that make me a criminal if I do that? Would the local sheriff show up and be like, "You can't hitchhike?" What happened to carpooling? What happened to ride-share programs? Oh, no, I have to have my own gas, my own insurance.

Insurance companies last year profited twenty-five thousand dollars a second.

[Laughs.]

You tell me, who's getting this money, man?

Yeah, "Where is that going?" is a good question.

It's going to the rich people, you know? It bothered me! Yesterday, I read in an article that there's, like, seven thousand families that are worth more than thirty million dollars right here in New York City.

Really.

Yeah, we happen to have more rich people here . . . the second runner-up was L.A. at forty-two hundred families with thirty million dollars or more. That bothers me because, like, if everybody came down here and chipped in, man, we wouldn't have shitty tarps and tents, you know what I'm saying?

Right, absolutely.

So, uh, I broke the law, like I said, the whole way here, and I don't feel bad about it.

[Laughs.]

Um, I'll just give you a quick—

[Christopher brings up photographs on his cell phone.]

Oh, that's beautiful.

Yeah, there's me taking one step forward right there . . . small town . . . I ran into a sandblaster . . . some more trains . . . there I am hiding from the people, you know? I've got to hide in this dingy spot. So I mean, that's beautiful America. Now I start coming into D.C., and you can see it in the background. See it? The monument?

Yep.

Now, if I was Al Qaeda . . . I mean, the infrastructure . . . look how close I got to that, riding through on a freight train. All I'd have to do: jump on in Richmond with a bomb, and I could take out the city! ❖

Tamber

If you could just tell me your name?

Tamber.

And for the record, you know, age, place of birth?

Uh, I am thirty-two today.

Oh, happy birthday!

[Laughs.] Thank you.

Bystander: Happy birthday!

Tamber: Thank you, sir.

I was born in Wichita, Kansas. After living other places, I live in Wichita, Kansas, again. I'm here kind of because it's my birthday. I was like, "I'm going to get a plane ticket. I'm going to come out to Occupy." We have an Occupy Wichita.

Oh, you do.

Yeah, we heard what was going on here, and researched, and we were like, "We've got to get on this, too. This is very important." Everybody in Wichita that is doing it is like, "Finally!"

You know, there's so many people out there that were just waiting, right under the surface, ready to go anytime anybody was willing to stand up and do something. It's happening in Wichita; it's happening across the world. This tugged on a lot of strings, for sure.

I'm here, also, just to get some experience—see what they're doing so as to take it back to my community.

They're really together here.

Yeah. I found it interesting—and this is just an outside perspective, but it happened in Wichita, too: It started very much as a communal, everybody-is-getting-together type of thing, but the General Assemblies have gotten so big that they have started taking the work groups out, just to make sure that, you know, stuff is getting done.

People have a forum. People come to General Assembly and have a forum, and they definitely discuss major issues there, but other proposals that are needing to get made? People meet and have their own general consensus before they take it to the General Assembly.

That's interesting.

And that's what has happened in Wichita, too. Having a democracy—a giant democracy—would be ideal, but it's difficult, you know, to formulate. It would take forever to have everyone's opinion. So people come together and make a proposal. If it doesn't work, people add amendments, and then the group gets to decide. Even in the time that we've been in Wichita, that's happened. It's almost like the government that we grew up with . . . we do want to have this government. It's starting to form on its own, naturally. Coming up with different democratic ideas and views, and everybody's still working together but you see the different camps and groups . . . it's very interesting to me.

The name of the book is *Why We Occupy*. Maybe you could talk a little bit about your reasons for doing it.

You know, I have been watching for a long time—even before 9/11—and seeing . . . like . . . things just weren't quite right. They're not really giving us the information. Starting back when I was a kid, I don't even remember being as inundated with advertisements and movies and all of these things to kind of . . . dumb us down a little, I guess.

Yeah.

And it's just really, really happened. And then after 9/11, it was just a media blitz of "Look, this is what happened. We're going to give this report, and everything's going to be fine." Just washed it over, and it wasn't the truth, you know? I don't know what the truth is, but it defi- nitely—what the government told us is not the truth, and with further research, you see that everything is corrupt. The war machines are funding both sides. There's evidence that even back to World War I, America joined the war and every war after that under false pretenses.

The Gulf of Tonkin didn't even happen. Our reason for getting into the Vietnam War didn't even happen, you know.

And, um, I don't even want to get into 9/11 conspiracy theory.

[Laughs.]

Trust me, I could go for days. But there's just unrest, and you saw peo- ple getting richer and richer, and you saw other people getting poorer and poorer and having to struggle. For me, now, the time is right. Other people are standing up and saying this is not okay.

All the politicking and everything that we've seen in the past cou- ple of years, where it's just been this red herring of Democrat versus Republican and we're supposed to focus on this side and that side . . . really it's all the same politics. It's all just kind of like a sham to have us not see what's really going on.

I grew up in Kansas. The Electoral College and voting and all that stuff—I wouldn't call myself a Democrat and I'm certainly not a Repub- lican, but it's a red state. So many times, in Kansas, you hear from the more left-thinking people, "Well, we're not going to vote because it's not even worth it. We've been a red state for fifty years. Why are we even going to vote?" That to me was completely flawed. There's so many reasons, so many things that add up to "Enough is enough!"

We're not getting a voice. I hear all the time: "Going around occupying and holding signs—that's not going to do anything." You know, "It's not going to change any policies. You need to worry about changing policies," and all this. Honestly, it is doing something, because whether this right now is changing policies or not—whether there are specific solutions or anything like that—people who have never talked about it before are talking about it. People are getting educated, where before, they just took whatever they saw in the media and believed it. They believed that their country wasn't lying to them.

So I think that why I occupy is that I want to help bring awareness to this stuff. Do I have solutions? No. Am I, you know, a political science major? No. I don't have any background like that, but just being here is getting people talking and wondering what's going on.

♦

For the record, I just want to say: There's this idea that everybody here is a jobless hippie, or doesn't have anything going on. I work full-time for a social-services government agency, and I'm going to school full-time for a master's in teaching for Early Childhood Unified Education. So I'm doing all that, and I still feel like it's not enough. That's all. ❖

Maria I

My name is Maria, and I am an R.N. I have been helping here at the First Aid station, delivering health care to people who otherwise would not have any other option.

Are you staying over, or do you just come in for the day?

I'm here about sixteen, eighteen hours a day, so . . . twenty years ago, I could have spent the night out here. I just can't do that, but I am dedicated to being here for people. The medics are the ones who cover the night shift. My nurses come in and cover mostly during the day, to give them a break.

Why did you decide to help out here and work here?

Because I'm a nurse! [Laughs.] I take care of people, and there's a great need here. Since I started here, I have come across . . . I've lost count of how many people who do not have health insurance, and who have not spoken to nor seen a health care professional or provider in five, six, seven years.

It's very important that people have access to health care, and I absolutely embrace the fact that there needs to be health care for all. There needs to be a single-payer system. It works in other countries; it can work here as well.

So you're coming in sympathy with the movement?

In sympathy? I am here to provide health care.

Okay.

Needed health care for everybody, and I guess if I'm going to stand behind anything, like I said, it's the fact that everybody deserves to have health care.

Is this something that you have done before?

Yes I have. In my daily work; also in disaster relief.

So you basically come to these impromptu kind of situations.

Sure, sure. Wherever the greatest need is, you know? I like to be there, and like I said, everybody deserves that. I have the skills and the ability to do so, and I'd like to pay it forward.

Where are you from?

I live in Las Vegas.

Did you come out here just for this?

Yes.

You're taking a leave from work?

Yes.

How long are you planning on staying?

A total of three weeks. ❖

Celia

Celia was accompanied by her four-year-old daughter.

So if I could just ask you your name?

Celia.

And where are you from?

We live in Central New York, outside of Ithaca.

Did you come here for this specifically?

Yeah.

So you're planning on staying over?

We're staying tonight. We have a ride back home tomorrow which we need to catch, but we might come back later on.

How are you finding the experience of being down here?

Well, we've only been here for a little while, but I've found it really positive. I've been to demonstrations before, and have always felt really comfortable and safe with the people that I was doing it with.

My husband was a little bit nervous letting us come down here. I don't think he's ever taken part in a big demonstration; he didn't really know what to expect. But it feels good to me. I'm impressed. I've heard mixed reports, but it seems pretty organized to me.

[Celia's daughter obtains permission to play with a dog, Calvin, who is camped nearby.]

What made you decide to come down?

Well . . . I believe that we live in a country and a world that is controlled by great powers, and that we've forgotten as a society how to take care of what's important. I'm really fearful for the future of our world.

My family and I live in a really simple way. We live without electricity and we do composting toilets and all that because I feel like it's what we can do as individuals to take personal responsibility for our lives. This [Occupy Wall Street] is a great chance to tie into something, to get to the source of it, in a way.

And I want to bring [my daughter] down to have the experience. I want her to understand that there's other people, and I want her to understand that what we do, we do for a reason.

What I'm so scared about is nuclear energy. It's a huge issue that people somehow made peripheral. I mean, I think that the main driving force is the strength of corporations and the reach of corporate power. Without a doubt, that's what all of the threatening issues right now really stem from. But it's amazing to me how nuclear energy is on the periphery of our consciousness.

I just saw Helen Caldicott speak—I don't know if you know who she is. She's a doctor who founded a few big organizations about doctors against nuclear energy. She was just explaining how the reactors in Fukushima are basically bombs, waiting to explode. I don't know if you know about that, but I guess there's something about the hydrogen mixing within them.

Or there's another scenario in which the lava could percolate down into the water. And then the seas rise, and—we can't take care of those freaking reactors! That's really what's going to change the shape of our Earth and life on Earth, and I think that's a huge threat. ❖

Marie & Ann

This interview took place at Au Bon Pain, 222 Broadway.

Tell me a little bit about the book club.

Marie: Oh, okay. We're a group of twelve. Well, actually, there are thirteen members, and there are eleven of us here today, right?

Ann: Yeah.

Marie: And we were celebrating our hundredth book that we've read together as a group.

Wow!

Marie: We've been together for several years, and a few years ago, we read Eleanor Roosevelt's biography. Then we went up to Hyde Park and we did a tour.

So we recently read this book called *Someone Knows My Name*.[3]

I have not read that.

Ann: It's written by a Canadian author, and it's the story of an African woman who's captured as a . . . I think an eleven-year-old, and brought to South Carolina to work as a slave in an indigo plantation. And then through one of her owners, she ends up in New York City during the Revolutionary War, and manages to become free by working for the British. Then at the end of the war, she is brought with the British loyalists to Nova Scotia. I happened to to be in Nova Scotia and saw the book in a bookstore. I thought, "Wow, this sounds fascinating!" So, brought it back to the club and said, "Let's read this!"

Marie: And so we read it, and we got fascinated with her story. During her stay in New York, the British came over, and they were actually hunting people down. She was hiding out and sleeping in a park, and also, someone at Fraunces Tavern was hiding some of these slaves.

Ann: Well, Sam Fraunces—which I didn't know—was black.

Marie: Right.

Ann: And I never knew that.

I didn't know that, either.

Ann: You know, I've lived in New York and seen Fraunces Tavern, but he was actually a black restaurateur.

Marie: So then we said, "Oh, we need an outing!" We had our hundredth book to celebrate, so we said, "Why don't we go on a walking tour of Lower Manhattan during the Revolutionary War time, and we'll end up at Fraunces Tavern." So we called Patriot Tours, and they were able to arrange it. They said they'd do a private tour, whatever time we wanted. So then we thought, "Well, let's go do Occupy Wall Street." Ann's son and my son have been occupying.

Oh, they have?

---

[3]Lawrence Hill, *Someone Knows My Name: A Novel* (New York: Norton, 2007).

Marie: Yeah. This is a very mixed group politically, although we're very like-minded. So we have some independents, some Democrats, and maybe even some Republicans here, but we all just checked out Occupy Wall Street. Although Sue and Gloria . . . Sue is a former newspaper editor of a small-town paper in Durham, Connecticut. She just retired. And Gloria has been an elementary school teacher. So they came down a week ago and spent the entire day and evening here, and said, "You guys! You know, we all had said we wanted to go check this out, so . . ."

Actually, on the train here from Connecticut—from Durham, where we live—we met a whole group of social workers.

Ann: Students.

Marie: From the University of Connecticut. And we just met up with them at the park, too! They're here! We didn't know them, so we just thought, "Well, this is really interesting!" And we just can't believe . . .

Ann: We're just . . .

Marie: We're all blown away at how incredibly clean, organized, civil and caring all these occupiers are toward one another. We also thought there were some Native American Indians who had a really interesting table, and we would've just walked by them on the street corner. But I think this movement is giving voices to so many disenfranchised.

Ann: Yeah. We were talking about the diversity of people there.

Absolutely. It's fascinating, right? Who knew that that diverse a group could have anything in common?

Ann: Yes.

Marie: Unbelievable.

I'm not sure what Peter is doing now—is that who's here?

Ann: Yes.

Marie: Yes, Peter is here. Ann's son and my son met up last week at the Times Square thing.[4] My son actually has a job on Wall Street, but he's been occupying before and after work.

Oh, my God! Really?

---

[4] A storied march through Manhattan that took place on October 15 culminated with an assembly in Times Square.

Marie: And on some of the weekends, yeah.

Wow.

Marie: But you know, there's a lot of young adults that are working, and they are just watching their bosses spend millions of dollars hiring people to get them out of paying any taxes at all. So the interesting comment that Robert made was that, you know, he can see his grandparents—in their eighties—worry about Social Security and all these things, and sort of say, "Well, if these corporations aren't paying their fair taxes, how are my parents going to be supported?"

And they're all trying to earn a fair wage. He's been a freelancer and unemployed. You know, it's just a really difficult time for a lot of young people.

It's fascinating that both of your sons are occupying.

Marie: Yeah.

Ann: Yeah.

What's the story with *your* son? How did he get involved?

Ann: Oh, well, my son was working for a corporation, and has left his job and is investigating being an artist. While he's doing that, he's staying with friends who live in Brooklyn. So because he's in the city, and this is . . . you know, he's committed to a sustainable lifestyle. Well, he studied engineering at Rensselaer, and one of the things that his professors said he worked with really emphasized sustainability in developing new products.

I was talking to another guy who was in the Sustainability Working Group. Is your son in that group?

Marie: He might be, yeah. I'm not sure.

Ann: I know he was there the Thursday night that they cleaned the park. He spent the night that night, yeah.

But they're not sleeping there all the time?

Ann: No.

Marie: Robert's been sleeping there a couple of times, yeah. He has a degree in neuroscience from Oberlin, but couldn't find work. He just kept getting jobs science editing—freelance work—and finally got this offer from a friend's father who happens to own a Wall Street firm. It was the only job he could get with benefits, so he had to take it. And he's doing editing and stuff for them, but it's not something that he really would love to be doing. He feels very conflicted, because he feels like this is not a corporation that works for social justice, you know?

[To Ann.] Like you're saying, sort of having a sustainable living, and really looking out for others.

What I think is interesting is that they grew up in a small town where they saw people really looking out for each other. One of the feelings my son had when he came to New York was that you're seeing all these people, but he found it hard to make connections with groups of people that were like-minded in terms of issues. And this [Occupy Wall Street] is something that I think is unifying a lot of people.

He had restaurant jobs, and I mean, he would . . . he's saying that this is insane, you know? Fourteen hours a day people are chopping vegetables. They're paying them under the table, and these restaurateurs are just . . . He's in the restaurant union. He's gone to Washington to represent workers' rights.

But he's just very conflicted about his parents' role in this. I think these young adults—it's a different world and we have to sort of change to that, but they can just see this incredible injustice to people that work hard and are making this economy hum for a very small group of people that are taking advantage of them. That's how they feel.

I think a lot of people are feeling like that.

Marie: Well, this is great.

Ann: My son had been going to planning meetings since the early summer. I couldn't believe how the national media was not . . . I mean, they were just pretending it would go away. It was just shocking to me.

Marie: Even N.P.R. took nine days.

Ann: I mean, it's shocking. ❖

October 24

Terry

Why I occupy I can explain.

Can you give me just, like, any kind of a name, nickname, or—

CommonTerry.

Okay.

That's my tree name.

Okay, tree name.

I believe—well, I know—that the Earth is sick. You can feel it. Thirty thousand children starve to death every day on Earth. I also know that desperate, hungry people work cheap, and Wall Street profits from that. And it could end so easily. It could end so easily. We need a world based on compassion, and not a world based on greed.

I occupy because this is a demonstration of compassion. I cook food and I do outreach—trying to recruit people into the movement. I do my work and I don't even participate in G.A. We need to get people fed. We need to clean up. We need to get people to join us. And then we can worry about the kind of democracy we have. We can't make demands because we're not everybody yet. Not everybody's with us yet.

So my demand is: "Step up!" I go out in the streets. I tell people "Step up!" because I think they've already woken up. They might not have rubbed the crud out of their eyes; or maybe they just choose to, like, not see. I call those people not-sees. That's N-O-T S-E-E.

Yeah.

And I think the day's going to come—soon—when a billionaire's going to flip to our side.

That would be helpful.

Then people are like, "Whoa, a billionaire has flipped! A billionaire bought those people a building. A billionaire went and gave a quarter of her money to save Somalia, and then put the rest to G.A." People decide, "Oh, my! Maybe I should join Occupy!"

And in the future, after the Revolution, how cool you will be. It'll be like, "What day did you start occupying?" And I'll be October fifth. And people will be like, "Oh, wow! You're really cool! October fifth!"

[Laughs.]

Because most people will be: "Oh, I started occupying a week before the Revolution."

Right.

That will be what most people say, because there'll be this hockey stick: [makes slap shot sound]. It'll be very sudden. But you can see now that it looks like exponential growth. It looks like zero, zero, zero for a long time. It isn't, but looks like zero for a long time. But now you can start to feel it. The curve is starting to move up a little bit.

What are you feeling? What's the change that's coming?

People are stepping up. More people. I'm talking about the number of people stepping up is now starting to be perceptively geometric. Exponential. I mean, still at the fairly flat stage, but it's happening. I can feel it happening.

And we have no choice but to make it quick and nonviolent and compassionate. We have no choice, because even if the compassionate world starts next week, and we start living based on compassion and love and caring and not on greed, and we stop driving cars because we realize, "Oh, yeah, that's causing asthma. That's running over squirrels. That's running over children. It's causing more deaths in a month than 9/11. Gee, why aren't we having a war against car driving?" *Et cetera.* I can go on and on about different things we do that destroy the Earth. That *we* do, not just the billionaire's do.

Right, right, sure, because they're not the only ones doing it.

Right, of course. Especially in America. The rest of the world looks at us as the ten percent. Almost all of us, unless you've been homeless a long time—they're not in the ten percent—but we're all in the ten percent here. Like, I work part-time, ten hours a week, and I'm definitely in the ten percent of the world's population.

Half the world's people don't have running water. Half the world's people don't have electricity. They don't have phones. They certainly don't have Internet access. Their children die of diarrhea. Five thousand children die of diarrhea every single day, and that would cost much less to fix than the Iraq war. Much, much, much less. But the powers that be don't want that. They want people suffering.

We import food from Africa. We import coffee from Africa. You know, we here are drinking coffee from Africa while African children are starving to death. I'm Irish, so that really bugs me. It really bugs me that Ireland imports food from nations with starvation. We sell their leaders arms to keep the poor down, and then we say, "Oh, you've collected debts. You owe us debts." And they're paying for arms that were used to keep them down!

The interest payments on debts in the poor part of the world, across the board, total, is greater than all aid going to the poor world. So money flow is actually—people don't realize this—money flow is not from us to them; it's from them to us, from them to our bankers, to our rich people. It trickles down for us, you know. That's why we're in the top ten percent. You live in Manhattan, you get more trickle-down than people in Kansas, but . . .

We need to wake up and realize that America is not the all-great, all . . . like, everybody waving American flags here? I want to see more Earth flags here, personally.

Do you have an Earth flag?

I do not have any flag, but I love the Australian guy with the Earth flag and all the other flags.

I didn't see that guy.

He has a display of, like, light blue sort of flags with rainbowy colors on them. All different flags. Very beautiful.

I've got to look out for that.

He has a big, long smock. He wears a, like, gas mask.

Oh, the gas mask? That sort of freaked me out a little, I've got to be honest. The minute I see a gas mask, I'm like, "Should I be running? Is there gas?"

No, that's like . . .

It's his political thing.

He's saying, "Look! The world is poisoned! Wake up! We are poisoning the world!" So even if we change next week, my point is that we're going to have a lot of work to do. And shit is going to be hitting the fan, anyway.

Well, it's objectively the case that shit has been hitting the fan.

Oh, it's going to be much worse. Even if we get together this week, it's going to be much worse. We don't realize it yet, but Fukushima is the worst disaster of all time, by far the worst disaster of all time. I'm sure they know that in Fukushima. They're just, like . . .

"Let's not talk about it."

Yeah, don't want people to think about it. Do you know how you spell Fukushima? F-U-K . . . U-S . . . fuck us . . .

[Laughs.]

H-I-M-A . . . hi, Ma! So my theory is: Mother Earth looked at the human race and was like, "Don't they realize all those nuclear plants are going to melt down some day? That something could happen where they all melt down at once?" If there's some solar flare or something and all electricity gets kicked out, all the nuclear plants could melt down at once. Maybe some of them will be saved because people were really on the ball at that nuclear plant, but other ones won't be, and we'll have Fukushimas all over, all at once.

That's a terrifying image.

So Mother Earth said, "You know, I'm going to make one of those nuclear plants melt down right now, because they're all going to melt down eventually. So let's show the people who are benefitting from it now, with their Sony products and their cameras and their high-tech equipment that we've all bought with Fukushima power. I'm going to kick the human race in the nuclear nuts!"

And the human race went, "Fuck us!" And then we look, and we see that it's Mother Earth, and we go, "I give up!"

That's my cartoon. I can't draw those, so . . . not very well.

You've got to get someone to draw that.

I know. This one would be really hard. I have another one I got somebody to start drawing, but that one I could sort of do.

The one I can't do—that takes some skill to draw—is: "How do you succeed in the corporate world?" You go to school; you cheat. You get high grades. You don't get caught. *Do not get caught.*

Right, you can't get caught.

You get a high-paid job because you got high grades, and then instead of climbing the rungs of the corporate ladder like you're supposed to, you back-stab your way up from behind your co-employees, stabbing them in the back. And the C.E.O. on top of the corporate ladder looks down and says, "That's a real go-getter!"

[Laughs.]

And that's my cartoon for that. That one would really take skill. The new, young guy in a suit, stabbing other people in suits, and clearly just, like, lifting himself up. And another knife, ready to stab. And other people down there falling off the corporate ladder, dead. And another guy, a little bit below, like, "Ugh!" blood coming out of his mouth. And the C.E.O. on top with the nicest possible suit, sitting up there in his leather chair and being like, "Hmm."

Seriously, get somebody to draw that and we'll put it in.

I had someone, like, start it. She started it. I'll talk to more cartoonists. She looked too sweet to draw that, though. The guy I had drawing was like, "Oh, yeah!" He's like, "Dark humor, awesome."

I have all kinds of jokes. I'm all about jokes.

I like jokes, too.

How about this one: You know we see "Eat the rich!" signs?

Yeah.

The people with the "Eat the rich!" signs think this is really funny because, well, they have "Eat the rich!" signs, right?

Right, sure. Yeah.

Other people don't think it's so funny because they think the "Eat the rich!" sign is bad. I think the "Eat the rich!" sign is funny.

"Eat the rich!" is funny. It's objectively funny.

Yeah, it's funny. It's not . . . literal.

Right, right.

So I say, "Yeah, parenthetically . . . eat the rich—parenthetically—who shop at Whole Foods."

Heh.

And the "Eat the rich!" people think that's just hilarious, because you don't want to eat the rich person who doesn't shop at Whole Foods! You could die! But a nice, free-range . . .

[Laughs.]

The free-range rich! Who live in the suburbs, with trees around their mansions.

But people in the city do the Whole Foods thing, too.

Yeah, but I want one that lives in the suburbs.

Right. Clean air—

Clean air, shops at Whole Foods, sure. Unpolluted, nice, healthy rich person. [Laughs.]
    Now my rich friend who puts me up when I go to Boston—if he ever hears this, he'll be like, "Terry, were you thinking of me?" And I'll be like, "Yes. Yes, Chuck, I was."

[Laughs.] Does he use Whole Foods?

Oh, yeah. Oh, yeah. I visit them, and their Whole Foods budget is, like, more than I spend . . .
    I went to the first Whole Foods.

Where was that, California?

Austin, Texas. Cheap!

Really? Because it's not cheap now.

There was only one. It was cool! It wasn't so corporate yet.

That's interesting. It was, like, just an organic store?

It was . . . it was unique. It was the only thing like it. There was no co-op in Austin at the time. This is in the eighties—a long time ago. Fantastic store.

Is that where you're from originally?

No. I lived there, though. I lived there for three years, when I was a yuppie.

You were a yuppie? Really?

I used to be. I used to be a software engineer.

What flipped you?

Well, you know, when I was young, I wasn't what I call an in-activist. I did some activism when I was a yuppie. I worked for Jesse Jackson for President in '84 and '88. When I was really young, I worked for Mo Udall in '76, running in the primaries against Jimmy Carter. In 1980, for our high school, I ran with the proto-Green Party campaign. You know: I was a liberal.

This guy is too mean! [Points.]

Who, that singing guy?

We need the women talking to guys, being like, "Be nice!" I'm not trying to censor what he says, but just be nice about it.

Which guy? The guy singing there?

No, that guy right there in the purple. He's too mean. And there's other people who—there's other white men that are too mean. It's all white men.

Is it?

It's all white men.

Wait, point out to me who you're talking about.

The guy with the purple thing on his head.

Oh, yeah.

But he's not the meanest one at all. Usually, he's nice, so . . . but we have to be. We have no choice. My sign is, "Let's be nice!" I'm making them, and I'm also trying to get the shirt people to start making them.

I agree. I talked to the Catholic Workers about that, actually.

I hear someone said that before me, though.

Yeah.

That's a joke. I think every teacher says that. I hold it up, and kids look at it, and I go, "This is for the adults."

[Laughs.]

It's for the white men. I have, actually, a movement now: I'm trying to get all the white men over thirty-five to shut up. Shut up and clean dishes.

How's that going?

Well, you know progressive stack? The idea of a progressive stack?

Uh-uh.

That's in a direct general assembly, and you want to speak next. You get the stack person to say, "Oh, I'm next to speak." Three other people on the stack? I become the fourth person. They say they prioritize it by people who have been oppressed—traditionally oppressed minorities.

Well, I just say, "Get the white man to shut up." No progressive stack, just racist.

[Laughs.]

White men shut up, because, like, we fucked things up. We are part of the privileged class who fucked things up, even if you were homeless and stuff. It should not be a rule, but something that white men decide to do, that becomes the cool thing for white men to do.

To shut up.

To shut up and do the dishes, and let the kids run things, and, like, the sixty-year-old black women, and the . . . you know, the people who have not had a voice their whole lives. Let them run things, because we fucked things up. And I don't mean me—*I* fucked things up—although

I did. I mean, I was a yuppie. I flew planes all over the world. I've gone skiing many times. Now I live in poverty, but I've got a huge carbon footprint debt from my life before I flipped, which happened when I got beaten by a police officer, by the way. That's what flipped me. That's what made me an activist.

When did that happen?

Um, 1989. I was beaten in a party at Halloween, actually. The twenty-second anniversary of my becoming a hard-core activist is coming up.

Halloween. I was at a party. We had parties across the street from a cop—state police—and he had his Boston cop friends come and raid the party. Someone spilled a beer on one of them—some cute girl spilled a beer on one of them—and they turned around and dragged the ugly six-foot-four guy down the stairs and beat the hell out of him, and started beating other people. Thirteen people got arrested, and spent a month in jail for assault and battery of a police officer. Actually, seventeen people got arrested. Four pled out, and thirteen went to trial.

And then they manipulated us into waiving our right to a jury trial. I got convinced to go along with that, but I shouldn't have. They're pissed off at me to this day that I fought that. But they should have listened to me, because a jury trial we could've won. In a judge trial, the judge was just going to find us guilty no matter what. And they gave us thirty days in jail. Thirty days in jail!

And then my third day in jail, hepatitis A hit me that I'd contracted in Nicaragua.

I had that when I was in seventh grade, and that's horrible.

It hits you hard and fast, right? Brutal.

That's bad stuff.

I was in Nicaragua for the election when the Sandinistas lost power. I contracted it there, came to trial, lost, went to jail. Third day in jail, it hit me.

So you were sick . . . with hepatitis . . . in jail.

In jail.

That's terrifying.

And you know how hard it is to eat?

Yeah, you can't eat.

But you *can* eat. No, you can eat. I could eat applesauce.

I couldn't really eat anything.

I could only eat applesauce, and not very much, but they wouldn't serve me applesauce every day. They were like, "Oh, we serve a big can. I'm not going to just open one for you." I'm like, "Yeah, but I'm freaking dying!"

I can't believe they didn't send you to the infirmary.

After a week, they sent me to the hospital—once I turned yellow. They didn't believe me at first. They just thought I was lying. Because you're in jail, they think you're lying. And I'm like, "I'm sick, nigger! I'm sick! I've never been sick like this!" And I was really sick in Nicaragua, too. But, "I've never been sick like this!" In Nicaragua, I knew it was, like, a flu or a bug, you know? It's a stomach thing. And this—I was like, "What the fuck is this?" I never felt anything like it.

Yeah.

I don't know about you, but my stomach felt like it was wrapped around a brick.

Yes, it was the worst feeling.

And then my liver started puffing out.

It was puffing out. Totally.

My stomach felt terrible. My liver was puffing out. I could only eat the applesauce. Nothing else they fed me could I possibly eat, and then I only ate a few bites of it. So twice a week, for two weeks, I had a couple bites of applesauce. Then they put me in the infirmary, and that was the fucking worst thing ever.

Really?

I would've way preferred to just be back in the cell, because in the infirmary, I didn't get to talk to anybody. No one did my laundry. I wasn't allowed to take a shower. I was in medical isolation. I was in the medical isolation cell. No one would touch my laundry. I had two pairs of clothes, and I just kept alternating them for, like, ten days, whatever it was. It was, like, ten days I was there. And there was a big window outside my cell where guys would line up for the drugs, and they could stare at me. It was freaking disturbing.

I had a huge cell, though. I had a gargantuan cell with pipes, and I would play on the pipes like a monkey when they were staring at me, which I couldn't do very well because I was really tired.

Right, because you're weak.

I slept, like, twelve hours a day for six months after that. My mommy came and picked me up a couple of days after I got out of jail. Brought me home and took care of me for three months in Ohio.

Yeah, that's the way.

My mom and my sister. But I was much, much sicker before that. By that time I was okay, but I was still really tired.

You're tired for a really long time.

Very long time. And I couldn't drink alcohol for years and years. Years and years. And I just recently started drinking again for the second time. I started drinking once, then started getting hangovers, stopped. I started drinking again, and now, finally, my liver is at the point where I can drink again. And even then, if I drink too much, I get terrible hangovers. But at least it's only a one-day terrible hangover. When I first started drinking again when I shouldn't have, I would get four-day hangovers. Now I'm just kind of like a normal person who has a somewhat destroyed liver. Not too bad. Your liver comes back! It's amazing! It's an amazing organ.

I don't think my liver really had long-term—

But you were young.

Yeah, I was young.

Makes a big difference. And you weren't in jail.

I was not in jail. I was at home. My mom took care of me, too.

In jail made it much worse. I mean, I had visions. My body was eating myself alive. I looked like I was in Auschwitz at the end of it. I didn't weigh myself in jail, but I weighed, when I got out, a hundred and thirty-five. So I had been down to about a hundred twenty-five, and I went in at a hundred eighty-five, so I'd lost a third of my weight in jail. I just looked horrible. My body was just eating the muscle alive.

They said, "Oh, you have a heart murmur." But then I got brought back another time and the doctor said, "Oh, that's just a *flow* murmur." That's your body working so hard that it *sounds* like a heart murmur. It's just your body going, "Ba-boom! Ba-boom! Ba-boom!" trying to cure you, trying to cure you.

And then I had two friends die of hepatitis B and C a couple of years after that. I knew all about hepatitis when they got it. They were hemophiliacs; that's why they got it. They already had AIDS, but they didn't die of the AIDS. It wasn't for any reason because of the AIDS. It was because they got blood transfusions. They got dirty blood. They both were hemophiliacs. Brothers.

You turn orange before you die if you have hepatitis and you die from it. You got yellow, orange, yellow, yellow, orange, orange, dark orange, dead. And that's, like, the shit in your blood, because your liver takes the shit out of your blood. That's the shit in your blood, and you stink when you have hepatitis. I know I stank. I know I stank.

You do stink. You're sweating out. The whole thing's disgusting.

It's very gross. And painful.

[The baby screeches.]

Oh, no! You're very mad!

Babies like to grab hair. That's also evolutionary. Like, grabbing onto the hair to ride the back. You've got to talk to a baby, though. You've got to interview your baby.

I know. We actually use this [recorder] for that, too.

Well, hopefully a little of that got into my interview.

Yeah, I think it did.
Let me just ask you: You said your name was CommonTerry?

CommonTerry.

It's your tree name?

Yeah.

What does that mean?

Oh, that's a line used at the Berkeley Tree-Sit. We had an occupation at U.C. Berkeley in December 2006 until . . . September whatever it was, 2008. Six hundred sixty-six days, ironically.

And you stayed up?

I wasn't living in the tree, but I'm, like, spoken-word guy. I'm the guy on the ground. I was the town crier, as it were, of the Tree-Sit, who explains why. People always were like, "Why are you trying to protect forty-two trees? Why do you care about forty-two trees?" And my line was, "Well, if you can't save trees in Berkeley, where are you going to save any trees?"

Right.

We need to stop cutting down. What we need is to *plant* trees! Now! Massive campaign to plant trees, not cut down trees. Like, New York City brags about how many trees they plant. Well, that's good, but it has to be done worldwide and massively.

And what's there needs to be protected.

And what's there can't be cut down, absolutely. Zero. Unless they're invasive. If they're invasive, that's different. But then you replace invasives with trees that provide food.

We need to do a lot more fruit-tree planting. I don't understand why we don't plant more fruit trees everywhere. That's because cities are like, "Ah, it'll fall off the tree and get rotten." Well, that's—okay, good point. Let's not let it fall off the tree and get rotten, but . . .

I live in Berkeley, and there's food trees everywhere. Some of it does get wasted, it's true . . .

But people eat it, in general?

But people eat it for sure. You just pick it off the tree. There's, like, plums everywhere. When it's plum season? Oh, my God!

I live in Bay Ridge. A lot of people planted fig trees there.

I'm amazed you can grow figs here.

I don't know how they taste.

I was in Palestine and I ate figs there. They were freaking delicious. I thought they were a Mediterranean fruit, but . . .

I mean, there are tons of trees, so I don't know.

They must just be small. Probably they don't get very big.

Probably. There are even peach trees. That can't be good.

Peach trees work if you're south of the real bad winter line. Southern Ohio you can grow peaches, but Northern Ohio you can't.

Interesting.

It's getting warmer. The peach line's going north. There'll be years when your peaches get wiped out, though. In California, even, there's years where the peaches don't do as well. But that's the thing: If there's a frost at the wrong time, your peaches get wiped out. Or if it's too cold too early in the year, you won't get very good peaches.

Right.

But yeah, it's amazing: global warming will allow us to grow more things, but then when it kicks in fast, it's going to be a disaster. People are going to be starving.

It depends where you are, I guess, in the world.

Yes. Luckily, my family is from the Great Lakes, and there's going to be plenty of water there for a long time. They have a huge aquifer underground.

[The baby babbles.]

Yeah.

Indeed.

I know.

I agree with the children. My line for, like, you know how they say, "No leaders, no spokesperson?" I say we need, like, a six-year-old girl spokesperson.

I love that.

Super cute.

They talk a lot, though.

Yeah, I know.

They talk a *lot*.

You have to train them how to say, "I don't know." Like, when they don't know.

I don't think you'd get that.

Well, a lot of times kids will do this: "I don't know," and then say what they know. You have to train them to pause, and then think about it, and then if you still don't know, say, "I don't know." They would be adorable at a press conference. Can you see it at a press conference?

That would be magical.

And if they don't know, train them to be able to say, "You know, I'm not as highly educated as I should be." Teach them a few facts, you know?

Xìnbù: Hànwèi rénlèi hépíng zìyóu mínzhǔ![1]

Terry: This here is the longest-lasting sign of the demonstration.

Xìnbù: Chénjìe![2] Chénjìe!

Terry: This sign—he's re-lettered it. It was fading...

Xìnbù: Hànwèi rénlèi hépíng zìyóu mínzhǔ! Rèn zhòng dào yuǎn.[3]

Yeah.

Terry: It's a great sign.

It is a great sign.

Terry: [To Xìnbù.] Unite! All people!

Xìnbù: My name is Xìnbù.[4] Xìnbù.

Terry: Qíbù.

Xìnbù: Yeah.

---

[1] 捍卫人类和平自由民主! [Protect humanity's peace, freedom, democracy!]
[2] 尘芥! [Dust!]
[3] 任重道远. [A long way to go.]
[4] 信步. ["Be the march."]

Terry: Want to interview him?

Sure.

Terry: [To Xìnbù.] You want to interview?

Wait, can you just tell me—you said you haven't been here from the beginning?

Well, no. I wasn't here from the beginning, but I've known about it since long before it started. I mean, I'm one of the few hard-core, long-time activists here. There's very few of us here, and it's great! It's great. I just step back, and I do my outreach, and I just go try to bring my people in. I do outreach, and I cook on Fridays for the Friday meal. And I clean once in a while. I've got to do more dishes. I haven't done enough dishes.

But a couple of my friends from Berkeley are, you know, main organizers here.

Did you guys come from Berkeley with this?

No, we're just . . . one guy from Berkeley was coming out here to work with the War Resisters League when this started, and so he was already here from day one because he was already here. He had graduated at Berkeley. And then another guy from Berkeley involved in the Tree-Sit was a brand-new activist when the Tree-Sit was ending. He was only in the Tree-Sit for, like, three months. My friend John. You should find him and talk to him. I don't even know his full activist history, but I'm pretty sure he was not an activist at all, and he was certainly not one of the main organizers at Berkeley. But he came here for this. He knew this was happening, and he came across.

I don't know his story about how he came across the country, if he was already traveling or whatnot. I was already traveling. I usually stay in California for years at a time, and I leave once in a while for the summer—so I can experience summer again, because we don't really have summer there. And then I house-sat for my parents, and they left to Russia on the fifteenth. Yeah, right at the same time this started, they went to Russia. I was house-sitting for them, and I fattened up.

Psychologically or literally?

No, literally, because I'm gluten-intolerant, so I can't eat much here. Like, all the time, I just can't eat here. I came out here on the morning of the fifth, so yeah, I'll have to say 10/5. But it was perfect, because that's when the weather got great.

Yeah, totally.

The day I got here, the weather got great. So I was like, "Good timing!" And I brought my energy in, like, I'm like, "Voom!" I had my energy. I helped really lift people's spirits again.

Has that been an issue? Are people getting bummed out?

No, no. I wouldn't say bummed out at all, no.

I mean, it seems like—how could you be?

No. You're up here, but I try to lift it higher, you know?

Right.

You can always go higher.

Right, right.

My friend John, who I told you about?

Yeah.

Who was a brand-new activist at the Berkeley Tree-Sit? The first step I took into the plaza at one o'clock on the morning of the fifth—the night before the big rally—first step I take into the plaza, John jumps out of a working group and goes, "Terry's here!"

Awesome.

I'm like, "*You're* here, man. What are *you* doing here?"

You didn't know he was going to be here?

No! He was a—I didn't think of that guy as a hard-core activist.

Really? That's interesting.

Although he was at the Tree-Sit, so he was. And when the Tree-Sit ended, I kept doing my activism, and then he would sit and listen to me. He was, like, one of my people who'd sit and listen to me doing public speaking at Berkeley. So I'm really psyched! And, like, he works so hard—much harder than me. I think outreach is easy. I know it's hard for most people.

Right. Well, it depends on your personality.

It's hard for most people. Most people can't even start to do outreach. They can't lift themselves out of this park. They're intimidated by it.

I get that, I get that.

They can do outreach here, but the people coming here—they're already here.

Right, they're already on board.

Well, they might not be on board—there needs to be outreach going on here, I don't deny that. Everybody—every single person here—should do outreach, and you should do it a lot, when you don't have anything else to do. If you're one of the people who just sweeps all the time, obviously I respect that. I totally respect that.

That's Michael, right? Every time I see him, he's busting his ass.

He's hard-core. The Sanitation people are hard-core. I respect that. I tremendously respect that. Like, I only do sanitation when somebody spills stuff by my camp. And then I clean it up because it's my camp. I do sanitation where I live, but . . . I don't really do sanitation at all. I do outreach. I train people to do outreach, if they want it. I encourage them to do outreach, give them lines. And I recruit. It's not that hard to go out and get people interested in coming to Occupy Wall Street.

[The baby screams.]

This is her thing. Don't take it personally.
   [To the baby.] Are you getting bored?

Maybe a little bit above you, huh?

[Terry distracts the baby by waving his hands in the air.]

A little bit older, they go, "What is that?"

It's sort of magical, but at least someone's paying attention!

Jesse Jackson taught me this.

Really? To do to kids? Mesmerize them?

No, no, just . . . that's a way to wave. It's finger dexterity when you speak and talk.

Just to sort of communicate energy?

You can feel the magical energies around you. Jedi mind tricks. [To the baby.] "You will not use death sticks! You will reconsider your life!"[5]

I'm finding that incredibly relaxing, actually.

When I speak, I'm doing Jedi mind tricks. I used to have a photographer in Boston follow me around. Not to take *my* picture, but to take pictures of people reacting to me, because I say some really . . . before, when everybody was still asleep. Now people are starting to wake up; I'm a little bit nicer now. I used to be really brutal.

What did you say?

Well, I mean, like what I said to you. "We're importing food from nations with starvation."

Why is that brutal? That's the fucking truth.

It's brutally true. Brutal truth.

Yes, I guess people don't like that.

"You're driving a car, you're killing your own children!" That's not very nice.

Sure, I guess that's not the nicest.

It's nice to the children, but not nice to the person I'm saying it to.

Right, it's not conciliatory. It's not like, "Yeah, we're all fine."

It's not like, "Oh, it's okay that you're killing the planet. Let's all just get together and we'll kill the planet, then we'll be nice to each other before we die." That's not nice. To me, that is not nice.
I call it nice-ism.

You're into nice-ism in general.

I am a nice-ist. I'm not the nicest nice-ist. Far from it.

[Laughs.]

---

[5] *Star Wars Episode II: Attack of the Clones*, directed by George Lucas (Beverly Hills: Twentieth Century Fox, 2002).

Far from it. The guy who's sweeping all day and doesn't complain and doesn't yell at anybody—he's a nice-ist.

That guy's fucking awesome. He's a total nice-ist.

The guy over here who does dishes all the time—he's a nice-ist. When I show my sign, all women agree with it. And I explain nice-ism and what nice-ism is—nice-o-anarchism, if you want. It's an anarchist belief, but it's to differentiate myself from the mean-o-anarchists who want to burn all the buildings down and live in the woods. I'm not into that at all, although I like living in the woods. I'm okay with that part of it. Like, I admire Ted Kaczynski, not because he killed people, but because he actually lived in the woods.

Because he got off the grid.

And he got off the grid. He made enough money at Berkeley. From a very young age, he was a hard-core environmentalist. That man is going to be a hero in the future, not because he killed people, which we're against, but because he shocked people. He was shocking. He didn't kill very many people; he wasn't doing mass murder. And I'm certainly not for that at all, but he was desperate. He was like, "Oh, my God!" People were so asleep then. So asleep, and refusing to wake up.

And it's only because people don't have jobs that people are waking up. How many people would take a job, go destroying the Earth, and quit this movement in an instant? I worry about that. ❖

Steve

Tell me a little bit about yourself.

Well, I'm a long-time activist. I got involved in the anti-globalization movement. That was really inspiring because everyone came together. You had convergent spaces—I don't know if you know about that—in D.C. So I got involved in that, but that movement pretty much just came to an end after 9/11. We were on the defensive, trying to stop this war and that war, and failing to stop them even.

And things just got worse over the years. It was really looking grim. I got so burned out, I stopped even doing political activism. I tried doing Green Party stuff. We were playing their game, up against their money. We were losing again, and everybody was getting burned out. All the old methods were failing, and I didn't want to waste my energy on stuff that wasn't working. I withdrew, like a lot of people.

So this was just, like, a spark, you know? This thing came out of nowhere. It didn't really come out of nowhere because it happened in Tunisia and Egypt, but just like that, one little thing happened and everybody congealed around it and started it. I guess the potential was always there, you know? Everybody, at any moment, everybody could come out and just do this.

So you've been here for two weeks?

Oh, two weeks, yeah. I was here for six days and I went away for five days, so . . . yeah, it's been about two weeks.

And how are you finding the experience here?

It's pretty good. I mean, there's problems. Like, if you work. I think I finally have a secure sleeping situation, but up until today, I had this problem where I'd go off in a working group—and I'll work until nine in the evening sometimes, ten in the evening—and come back, and you know, my sleeping space is taken by someone else. So it was, like, the more you work—kind of like a reverse incentive—the more you work, the more someone who isn't working can take your sleeping spot.

Actually, it was Terry who got me connected with some people who, you know . . . and now I have a secure spot. I don't have to worry about that anymore, so that's good. And I don't know, things are coming together. I feel like I'm starting to get more involved in the community, more connected. Just the last couple days, I feel like I've gone through another step in development of getting into the community.

For the first couple days, I just spun around. I didn't know what I was doing. Then I got into a working group and I got more focused on that. And it's just developing, slowly developing. I guess the longer it goes, the more connected I'll feel. Hopefully it'll go long enough.

It's hard to figure out how to get connected. The first couple days that I came down here, I just sort of wandered around.

Well, yeah. And it's even harder because we can't talk to each other. The G.A. is too big, and the Web site doesn't really work. They're getting a new one. There's a different Web site called N-Y-C-G-A. I think it's called N-Y-C-G-A dot net or dot com or something, but anyway, that's an actual Web site. Didn't occur to me until the other day how odd it was that in this day of, you know, everything is about computers, this group were doing all these things so, so right, but yet we actually didn't have a way to communicate online, really. We didn't have a Web site. We did but we didn't, which is even worse, because then we have one that wasn't really working because it wasn't really us. Occupy Wall Street Web site isn't really us. It's run by someone.

Adbusters?

I don't really understand what it is, but N-Y-C-G-A I just heard about yesterday, and that's going to actually function. People are getting on board real fast. We're making up for lost time every day. It's developing really fast. The working groups are up on it now, and everything's happening, so hopefully, that'll make things easier, somewhat.

When did you first hear about the movement?

I heard about it before it started. My friend told me it was going to happen—my friend in Boston. I'm from Pittsburgh. My friend in Boston told me they were going to do it, and I thought, "Well, that sounds good, but . . ." You know, it just sounds like . . . who knows? It's just some other attempt, you know? But when they pepper-sprayed those three girls,[6] I said, "Oh, I have to! I should go!" But I kind of lost my enthusiasm over the next couple days.

Then when they arrested the seven hundred people on the bridge,[7] I said, "Now I really have to go!" And I did.

Did you feel like it was maybe more real because of that?

It was just kind of like, "Well, if they're going to arrest seven hundred people . . ." It's like a chess game. If someone moves, you have to make your move. That was their move; they arrested seven hundred people. That's them saying, "You can bring a big crowd, and we're just going to

---

[6]N.Y.P.D. Deputy Inspector Anthony Bologna was videotaped using pepper spray on immobile protesters during a march to Union Square that took place on September 24.

[7]More than 700 protesters were arrested on the Brooklyn Bridge on October 1.

arrest them." The next response is, "Okay, well, now it's going to be a bigger crowd. Are you going to arrest *them*? Now it's going to be three thousand people. Are you going to arrest all of us?" And then if they do, then hopefully it will be next time ten thousand people.

So if you give up at that moment . . . it's a crucial moment. It's an opportunity, actually. It's a good opportunity. As a matter of fact, it played into our hands perfectly. It really turned out really great that they arrested seven hundred people. But if you don't take that opportunity, then it's a huge defeat. It just ups the ante. It's either a big victory or a big defeat, so at that point, I had to stop what I was doing; but I wasn't doing anything anyway, so it was good. ❖

Ben

My name's Ben, and I'm from California. Graduated college two years ago, and now I'm out here occupying because this is where I see we need to go. Corporations destroyed the environment, destroyed everybody's ability to use the land—the great wealth—for themselves. It's just been so centralized.

How did you get involved in coming out here?

I heard about it two months before it started. The *Adbusters* thing—I saw that. There was a whole bunch of discussion on this reddit dot com. I was on there—on the Web forum—discussing what was going to happen, and organization things. And I had been traveling around the East Coast, just by buses, checking out the different cities beforehand. So I was like, "Oh, I know I'm going to be there."

Were you an activist before this?

No. I went down to the Keystone X.L. Pipeline Protest in D.C.—that was just before Labor Day weekend.[8] Then I went to Shale Gas Outrage in Philadelphia,[9] against hydrofracking. But before that, I was definitely not really an activist. So it's been, like, these last couple of months.

---

[8] The Keystone X.L. Pipeline Protest began on August 20.
[9] Shale Gas Outrage took place on September 7-8.

I guess there was one more thing before that. I went to this May Day rally in San Francisco, and we marched probably twenty blocks with a few thousand people. I signed up on all these email lists. And then, so all summer I was getting these emails about different events and things. I would get an email every couple weeks, and then at some point, it was just, like, "Tar Sands is coming up in a week![10] Get out here! We're doing it!" And so I was like, "Yeah, I've got to be out there for that," because it seemed like it was that important.

How has your experience of the actual occupation been?

This one here?

Yes.

Yeah, it's been great! Everybody's so nice! I mean, I can't even walk halfway across the park without getting stopped every fifteen feet, especially if I'm carrying my fracking sign! [Laughs.]

Are you involved in any particular committees?

No, I haven't joined any groups yet. I don't know … I've been here since Wednesday, but I'm going down to D.C. for a couple days, so I feel like I'm kind of moving around. Once I get more settled in, I think that's something I'd like to do, because I definitely feel like that's the way to get involved. ❖

Balance

I'm a person who goes to India and helps with the "Free Tibet" cause. I got upset after 9/11, because I didn't think nobody was going to ever get to this point where we'd have a revolution.

This isn't occupation, this is revolution—a revolution of consciousness, a revolution that people want change. They don't know exactly what it is they want to change to. There's many architectural designs.

---

[10] International Stop the Tar Sands Day of Action was June 18.

If you look up a movie on YouTube called *Zeitgeist*,[11] you're going to see a whole thing, and they're even doing it in Dubai. M.I.T. is doing the Venus Project in Dubai. But most of us know: with G.M.O.'s, with chemical seeding above our planet that's affecting your baby and you, and NASA said, "Yes, it's not a conspiracy. We *are* doing this. We *are* doing this. We're doing it for your protection."

They want to take nutrients off the market, too. They don't want you to have vitamins. There's always a big deal in Congress about this.

So some of us are saying, "Okay, how far is it going to go?" And, "Why should we keep producing babies if we're just bringing them into a world where there's no work, but there's sickness, and there's disease, and new types of cancers, and new kinds of tuberculins?" My ex was a C.C.U. nurse. She says, "Viruses just keep changing. No one can get a handle on it."

And these big guys know—the chemical companies: the DuPonts, the Dows, the Monsantos—all these people know how to genetically modify chemicals. Just think of how many ideas the human populace is going to come up with, in our type of life in America where we have the ability to think, and go to schools to help us to think critically. And don't you think that the government knows that they're going to affect some of the populace like that?

So before the government comes in on all of us activists against dumping toxic waste into the Colorado River and cutting down redwood trees—which is illegal but the government lets it because there's money involved—and all this stuff, some of us are saying, "Enough is enough! I'm willing to go up against the wall! I'm willing to go to an internment camp! I'm willing to do whatever it is to stand up and be counted at this time!" I think that's what's motivating most people.

But also this idea of 11-11-11 and December twenty-first, 2012.[12] All the prophecies—the Hopi, the Lakota Sioux, the Huna from Hawaii, the Vedas—all talked about the twenty-six-thousand-year cycle,[13] where the Earth is going to go through tsunamis, earthquakes, flooding, the whole thing.

It seems like that's happening already.

---

[11] *Zeitgeist: The Movie*, directed by Peter Joseph (New York: Gentle Machine Productions, 2007).

[12] The 2012 phenomenon predicts cataclysmic events for December 21.

[13] In Milankovitch theory, Earth completes one precessional cycle every 26,000 years.

No, no. It's happening, but some of it is made by the government. The government has a machine that can create some of that stuff, too.

But when that happens—when the planets line up, which they do every twenty-six thousand years—that means a huge pull. That's why, in the Bible, it says it's not good to be married or having babies at this time. You're going to be more, "Oh, where's the baby?" and all that stuff. It's better to think critically: to show consideration and love towards all those that are compassionate about things, and to not enable the ones of us that are neurotic and hurting right now, because we don't have time.

We need time to get stronger, to become warriors, to get ready for whatever it is. We need time to get through the conspiracies and get to the real constructive stuff—the things we can do to make a real conscious change, whatever destruction happens, if there is destruction. We hope that there isn't, or that it's limited, but I believe there is going to be a huge amount of destruction on Planet Earth.

So that's why I'm occupying.

Can you tell me a little bit about yourself?

I'm a divorcé. I've had two children and two grandchildren, and I didn't make a good . . . I couldn't live in a square box. It was hard. I wasn't into making money, so of course, women don't want to stay with someone that doesn't provide the American conspicuous lifestyle of shopping at Walmart every week, and "Where's the credit card?" and "Can I have a hundred dollars?" and all this stuff. I wasn't into that.

And so they found out—after they were in lust or passion with me or whatever they saw—they realized they've got to find a guy that's going to bow down to the system and be stressful and pissed off about his job, but still bring home the paycheck to give to mama.

The majority of people are like that. And they say, "Okay, well, China . . ." Before, we said, "No, no, no! We don't want China involved with our stuff." But now they own Walmart! Now they own all of our manufacturing—R.E.I. and all this stuff. They make everything! Our sleeping bags, our military gear, everything! And they're doing such human rights violations . . . it's atrocities. So it must be that America doesn't care, because maybe America is going to start doing human rights violations, too!

You said you go to India?

I go to India just because . . . there, the life is: I can live on a hundred dollars a month. And also, I can be with *babas* that don't care about money, that are living naked up in the wilderness. And you learn so much from these people who believe that none of this really matters. What matters is the letting go—surrender—of the soul, of consciousness. Not to a Jesus, not to an Allah, but to the . . . just the is-ness. But you find it only when you go within, only when you go within. It's not from books. It's not from moderators. It's not from the television set. And so that was a possibility.

Yoga yokes body, mind, and spirit. That's the whole purpose. It's not a religion, it's a philosophy. Hinduism is a philosophy.

In America, we have empirical religion. We have all these different groups. None of them really agree with each other, but they're all making money from their parishioners.

I went to India to get away from the idea of money and malls. But now, America is coming to them. Starbucks, McDonald's, Domino's Pizza—it's all coming to them. ❖

Recai

I show you my name sign if you want, because I'm Turkish from Turkey, so my name is kind of . . .

I can spell it out.

Yeah, spelling is easier. My name is here: R-E-C-A-I. I'm from Turkey, and I'm here because of my two injustices I endured, one in Turkey, one in here. In Turkey, I was blacklisted by the C.I.A. / Turkish *kontrgerilla* [counter-guerrilla] military takeovers in 1980. I was blacklisted as a political dissident.

I was in the high school, and then I studied political science. I entered the foreign ministry as career diplomat to become ambassador, but because of my blacklisting—

What was the reason they gave for blacklisting you?

It's secret. They don't give reasons. Because of your political opinions. Because of your political standing. They blacklist you, and they never have to explain to you anything. They have to keep it secret from you because that's the power of blacklisting. When it's a secret, they can hit you sneakily. Otherwise, when it is open, then there is no reason to blacklist. They lose the power. There's no ground to blacklist anybody.

It's against human rights. It's a crime against humanity.

The civil war they created—C.I.A. and Turkish *kontrgerilla* together created, before 1980, a military takeover—was a war crime. And then after the military takeover . . . military takeover itself is unconstitutional and a crime, and the tortures and killings and disappearances and everything . . . imprisoning people and canceling so many people's citizenships and stuff like this . . . firing them and blacklisting millions of people—all crimes against human rights, crimes against humanity.

In the foreign ministry, they fire me six times. The real reason was the high school blacklisting, but they always find some stupid excuse, like, "You printed your opinion on the flyer," or, "We saw you without a tie," because you know, they have to find something. If they can't find it, then they find, like, something wrong with your eyebrows.

That's their constitution—that's 1982 constitution—is military constitution, which was installed right after the military takeover. And then it's still in force in Turkey. That's the country we are talking about. They cannot, still, change that constitution. The legal framework—the human rights, according to that military constitution—is nothing. And it is, still, in Turkey.

They forced me to move . . . run away from my country with my own will. I couldn't get anything, any future. I couldn't work in any place there, or all over. They have control, military government.

I'm here [at Occupy Wall Street] because I'm not a citizen. I couldn't go to college, like, masters or anything. So what I did is: I start driving. And then finally, I bought my bus—motor coach—and I drove for Tropicana Casino in Atlantic City. As driver, I was their slave. I worked for them like a driver, and they gave me thirty-thousand-dollar checks. Bad checks didn't clear, and then I lost everything. I'm bankrupt. I lost my car. I'm losing my house. And I'm not paying anybody any bills for the last one year. So actually, on two fronts, in Turkey and in United States, I'm burned. You know, that's capitalism, and C.I.A., and here, one-percent Tropicana.

That's why I'm here and I'm part of the protest, because this is all about changing the system, fighting the one percent, and get rid of the capitalism. Actually, if you have a minute, I'll tell you what's going to happen. This capitalist system—this world—is like putting a million people in a small room which can fit only fifty people. If you put a million people in a small room which is only for fifty people, what's going to happen? Layers and layers of people on top of each other. That's capitalism in this world, which cannot sustain. This is going to destroy our planet because our planet cannot sustain this kind of seven billion population, and everybody has right and wants luxury, you know? Everybody has right and wants luxury, like luxury houses, luxury cars. You can't say only rich can have them and the poor don't have them, cannot have them. That's not fair.

So as you see, capitalism is, like, broke. Capitalism cannot bring any solution. This system is down. That's why we are here, and this is really important because it's not like the past protests—like in Woodstock, which was out in the wild and far away from people; it was all disconnected from the world. This is right in the middle of the biggest city, right in the Wall Street, right in the global financial center, and this is all connected with the world. This is, like, global moment—global Occupy Wall Street—over maybe eighty, eighty-three countries. This is all connected, and they are all protesting together. So this is very different from the past, okay? We count very good moment. Very good strong moment. ❖

October 25

James

James, originally from Washington State, but I've lived in New York for four years now.

How did you get involved?

I just came down here. I was walking around, and I started talking to people, and then . . . I just moved into the De-Escalation/Security role.

What does that entail?

Just kind of keeping the peace in the park. Making sure nobody steals anything from the area. Recognizing faces in this spot.

In this spot . . . to see that people are coming in who should be?

Yeah.

Is that a full-time job?

Yeah.

Do you sleep right here? You have to sleep near the equipment?

Yeah. Here, at night, usually.

I take it there have been some problems with theft.

Yeah, there have been.

Do you think it's from within or from without?

Uh, I think it's from without. We've kind of gotten rid of the sketchy people in the group.

How have you done that? You kicked them out?

We kicked them out, yeah. There's people that work in here who say that they recognize people that have kind of taken something.

When you kick them out, you kick them out of the park, or you kick them out of this area?

Just the immediate area.

So then they move somewhere else?

Mm-hmm.

I guess you can't actually kick them out of the park.

No.

Are there problems in general with that, or just basically with the equipment?

With the equipment, like laptops, cameras, stuff like that. Electronics, backpacks.

When was the first time you heard about Occupy Wall Street?

It was the pepper-spray incident. And then I watched Chris Hedges being interviewed here. He's been a war correspondent for a long time, and he's been supporting this movement from the beginning. I was watching this on my computer—YouTube video—and he said this line: "People need to wake up from their digital hallucinations." And then something kind of clicked in my head. That's when I started coming down more, started getting a little more involved.

You were not an activist before.

I was not. Not at all.

What was your old life? What were you doing before?

Just going to school. Kind of just milling around, not knowing what to do with myself, with my time.

Sum up your reasons for occupying.

The environment is definitely one, because I think we're at the cusp of environmental disaster with all the natural resources being taken out. Weather's getting weird. And then, corruption. Politicians. Lobbyists in Washington writing the laws and stuff like that. ❖

Dan

Do you work here at Media, too?

No, I work in Info, and I'm in the band.

What's the band?

It's called the Pulse. We do drumming every day.

Oh, the drummers.

Bystander: It's an actual working group.

Is it really? I didn't know that.

Dan: Yeah. Come down at twelve o'clock. You'll see it.

Okay.

We're, like, the heartbeat of the movement.

I heard you guys got kind of shafted with the money?

I don't know if that passed. I sat on the original proposal, and they wanted more input and stuff. I didn't stick around. Myself, I carry my own drums, and I don't worry about people funding me. I got my stuff, you know? Some of the others . . . I guess they had a proposal in. They wanted the occupation—you know, the organization—to kick in eight thousand dollars to replace some of the drums.

What did you think of that?

Ah, I thought it was a little excessive. I think there's enough drums down there. We don't have to spend more money, you know? They never asked me, so I never told them. I just keep quiet. I go down there and drum whether they get the money or not, you know?

What kind of drum do you play?

Djembé. African drum. And I play the cowbell.

How did you get involved with Occupy Wall Street?

Well, I've been an activist all my life, and I thought it was a really good strategy of coming to Wall Street with our peeps. I think that as long as we're underfoot, we can call attention to what's going on. And we're getting a lot of press. For the amount of work we're doing individually, we're getting a lot of press nationally, you know? We're actually accomplishing something. What the final outcome is I'm not sure, but I like the momentum.

Have you been occupying since the beginning?

No, I got here about two weeks ago.

And are you here? [Points.] Is this your sleeping spot?

Yeah, I'm in Info. One day I manned one of the—I person-ed one of the tables, and they seen that I was helpful. And so one thing led to another. They kept on giving me more stuff to do, more stuff to do.

And one night we got rained on real bad, and I met some girl that I'm particularly fond of. We got stuck in the rain together. The rain actually brought us together, you know? So the next day, we went to the laundromat. We went to my house—we took a run up to Beacon and back—and we've just been really good friends ever since.

That's wonderful.

Yeah, it's funny how tragedies bring people together, you know? In a good way, it was a nice rainstorm. We got stuck in rain, and the rain was coming down so hard, but we helped each other stay dry. We went to McDonald's after work, and we've been close friends ever since.

When was that?

When was it? I think it was Tuesday or Wednesday night. It really rained hard that night.

How's the preparations for the weather going?

Well, you see, it's kind of rag tag. But the city don't want us making anything really constructed. You know, we could really do a lot down here if they allowed us, but we're just doing a little more than they allow. But yeah, we'll get to it no matter what. I'm kind of interested to see how it's going to be in the wintertime. But, ah, I'm kind of prepared for it. I have a big van that I've been parking across the street, and I can park there twenty-three hours a day.

Except when they're cleaning?

Yeah, one hour I've got to move so they can clean, but so far, I didn't have to move it yet. I took it home the other day, and I left it there and took the train down, but I'm getting ready to go back up there—back home—because I ran out of medicine. I have Parkinson's disease. I'm going to be out of medicine in about four or five hours, so I've got to get my butt going home. It's a hassle that I've got to stop and head up north. I might be able to make a phone call and have someone come down here.

It's one of these things where you have to pick it up yourself?

It's kind of one of these things where I didn't bring enough, so I've got to pay for it. In other words, I've been down here three or four days, and I underestimate how much I need. When I put them in my bottle it seems like a lot, but you know, as much as I'm taking, it goes quick. I'm putting a lot of hours in down here, so I need to take more medicine.

They take care of me well down here. They got a medic tent over there, so I do the herbs and I do acupuncture. It's for free.

They do acupuncture over there?

It's really neat. They don't have much room over there, so they do acupuncture that's performed on the ears. Ever hear of that? They say every part of your ear goes to every part of your body, so if you've got a bad—like, I've got a bad upper and lower back. You can actually see some of the things in my ear. Can you see them things?

Uh-huh.

They leave them in there. So in other words, I'm getting acupuncture. These'll last up to forty-eight hours, and I had them put in the day before yesterday.

So you find that helpful, the acupuncture?

I got so much wrong on me, I can't really notice the little things. I got a really bad back and I hurt all the time. So right now I'm kind of pain-free, but if it's not one thing it's another, yeah. That's what you get for getting old, you know?

I know. I'm trying to avoid that, but so far it's not working.

Yeah. I don't know how to stop it myself, but I'm going to have a good time doing it, you know? I've been waiting for these days for the last forty years. I've been a leftist my entire life. My brother turned me on to it when I was in high school, you know, and I've been reading this left-wing literature all my life.

What was the first thing he turned you on to?

Just some political party called the Socialist Labor Party that was a revolutionary organization way back then. I think at the time they were the third-oldest political party in the United States. They were around since 1905 or 1895 or something. Pretty dogmatic group. I learned a lot from them. They since have disbanded, but they had a lot of good ideas. Probably a little ahead of their time, I guess.

Maybe now the times are changing?

When the time is ripe, it will happen, you know? Can't force anything. It'll happen when it happens. You've just got to stick around, that's all.

I'm not sure what it's going to be. I'm looking for some type of collaborative or cooperative society that's not based on profit. In other words, this country is run just for profit, where I think we should be producing for human needs rather than this anarchy of production.

Would you say that your primary reason for coming down is to hasten that?

To help out any way I can, yeah. I'm just happy to be around to witness it and to be a part of it. I go to a lot of Rainbow Gatherings, you know what that is? That offers some kind of glimpse of future society as well, and I see a lot of the same kind of people at Rainbows that I see here—very helpful, very friendly, outgoing, willing to give their all.

When I was leaving the subway yesterday, I met a couple of people. Normally, I wouldn't talk on the subway with people, but we engaged in a great conversation just for a few minutes. Then I was getting off the subway, and I left my phone on the seat because I was doing something and I totally spaced out. And these two attentive kids down here ran up and said, "Hey is this your phone?" They got off the subway; they missed their train.

You can tell, really, that people have been here. After they've been here, they're simply changed. I get the same feeling when I go to Rainbow Gatherings. You see people after they've been to the gathering, they're very helpful, very mellow. Just nice people, you know? ❖

Jacquel

Well, my name is Jacquel. I'm from Brooklyn, and I'm an occupant. That's pretty much it.

How long have you been here for?

The days start to blend together. I can't say correctly. I'll say two weeks and a half. Yeah, about two weeks and a half I've been here. Been long.

It's turned into something like a residential building. You have your good neighbors, your bad neighbors, your friendly neighbors, your neighbors willing to help, your neighbors who ignore. So it's a community within a community, and we're working the kinks on how to better deal with each other. The issues of economics can only be dealt with once we learn how to deal with the issues of social, because economics affect our social interactions. Once we learn how to build the social—which we are doing—we can work on the economic. So I think that's the problem here, the whole residential-building analogy.

So some people are not getting along very well?

Well, people you wouldn't see together for the most part are working with each other. People are genuinely trying to understand that they're not the only people that need help; there are other people out there who are in positions of despair. One person's situation may not be as dire as the other, but we all are in a bind. We all need to lock arms in protest, and help each other out. So there's a general consensus.

Yeah, we may have disagreements. There may be arguments. There may even be in-house fighting. This is a movement, and there are different energies. Abundance of energies! For the most part, people get along a lot better than outside the park, relatively. So it's pretty good.

What is this desk?

Well, this is the Info desk. It's sort of like a host, but I don't involve myself too much with things. I'm actually trying to get a paper going. I am a writer—a poet-slash-writer—so I'm trying to get involved with generating the identity. Like how with the Great Depression, they came out with some products that became the staple of the community not so much because they were great products, but because the products were thoughtful and considerate of the consumer.

So you know, the occupation is a platform for those people who truly want to go into the next stage of our culture. What happens is: This won't be here forever, and once it reaches its pinnacle and change does come about, there has to be something that we can bring out of it, something that can remind us of the reason it happened, so we won't forget. There's definitely a need for that.

◆

I do everything. I sweep. I help if someone's falling. I do whatever's necessary to maintain the overall occupation. Whatever's necessary.

What made you decide to come down for the first time?

Well, I'd like to give a shout-out to my son.

Okay.

I came down because I have a three-year-old son, and I have a nephew. It was something that I'd heard of; I can't remember exactly where. But there's a sense that the generations which come after us . . . if we are not fighting for their freedoms and their abilities to dream and their abilities to have an opportunity, we are committing suicide by mass neglect. We are allowing our children's future to be but a measuring stick—something which we can barter—just so our present can be a little bit more comfortable.

I am here because I believe, as Whitney Houston said, that "the children are our future." I don't want to be sixty-seven years old and there's only two doctors in New York, you know? I want there to be a consistency in the growth of our country, and we have kids going to school to be doctors, and they're able to find jobs as doctors, and the hospitals are not closed.

I'm concerned about the future of my baby, too.

Very important. By fighting for them now, it also instills in them the idea that we have the right to fight. It's not just because we don't like what's going on, we also have the right to say so.

We want to be heard. As an African American, our voices have been suppressed for so long. Our voices have been but images on T.V., or a radio song. Whether it be the golden oldies or today's hip hop, we only have a select amount of images. When powerful images come up, people feel empowered. So if we continue to give our kids images which they can fight for and live for, then we become a much stronger nation in the future. That is the reason I'm here.

◆

My winter game plan is just to stay in motion, because a body in motion stays in motion, and motion generates heat. So I mean, as long as you dress warm, you stay in motion . . . and enjoy the sun. Don't hide, but let the sun heat us.

Do you have good gear? Do you have a sleeping bag and stuff?

I have a sleeping bag, but I haven't had outside gear. I never really went camping, so I'm going to make do with what I have, and what I have will make do. I have no choice.

Where's your spot?

I don't sleep. I just rest on a bench and close my eyes for a little bit.

You're sleeping at home?

I sleep at home, yes, because I work two jobs. I need to be home to get back into the world. Well, I quit my other job, but I have to be in the world to take care of my son. Although this *is* taking care of his future.

What does he think about it? Have you talked to him?

Well, he's three years old, so I just tell him Daddy's working. But there will come a point where he will ask me because I've been interviewed by a few people. Underground people have spoken to me, and there will be a story somewhere that I've told, so it will come out. I don't know what I'll tell him because I don't know where it's going yet. And if the story comes out bad, I'll tell him that I wasn't in my right mind.

[Laughs.] "I was young . . ."

I was young. It was the thing of the time.

But if it comes out well, "I was there from the beginning."

I was there from the beginning. I had the belief, the faith. You know, we don't want to be passive-aggressive when we lose, so we set that up.

You've got to have—what's the expression?—plausible deniability.

Plausible deniability, yeah. "It was cool." ❖

Laura I

You don't have to give me your full name.

Great. If you're happy to go with Laura, I'm happy to work with that.

May I ask what the danger is?

Um, I work in media and journalism.

Do you think it would be a problem?

No, I just think that I am here on my own personal activities. I don't want to mix business and work, especially when I'm supposed to be unbiased in my work.

Sure, that makes sense. Are you occupying?

Yep, I'm occupying. I work in the kitchen—that's the working group I work for. I was living in New York City for about a year before this happened. I found it very hard to make ends meet, frankly, doing freelance work. A lot of my friends were working in the financial system. I thought it was pretty frustrating that so quickly, a great social and cultural divide had opened up between very close friends of mine. I also was frustrated to see a lot of the smartest and most passionate people of my generation going into the financial system because it felt like the only option for many to make a really good life.

I'd like to see a system in which we value work that contributes to the community. I'd like to see us value that more highly, both monetarily and respect-wise. Obviously, the debates over the teachers' unions this past summer and this whole past year made me very frustrated. The way we treat teachers, the way we treat unions . . . I think we're starting to devalue hard and important work in this country, and I want to start valuing it more.

I also think that right now, the financial regulation rules get written by the people who work at the top of the financial pyramid. That's not the way that we run any other sector of our society. That to me doesn't feel fair. I'm all for a high-functioning capitalist system, but regulation doesn't mean internal regulation. Obviously, that didn't work very well for the last forty years.

And how have you been finding the experience of occupying?

Really inspiring and really frustrating at the same time. Right now, the fact is that we have gotten really wrapped up in park politics, because we're trying to bring a lot of different people into a very small area, and get them to get along and live together.

For a lot of people, they consider that we're trying to create a model society, and use this as a microcosm of what could happen in the rest of the world. I'm not interested in that. I'm not interested in changing the republic. ❖

Cam

Well, my name's Cam. I'm a resident of Texas. I actually just got here on August twenty-seventh. I moved here, and then this happened, like, two and a half weeks later, so I just came at the right time, I guess.

What am I doing here? I've always been involved in social issues, like in my schools and things like that. My major was social justice. I've always been proactive, and concerned about my future. That's the biggest reason why I'm here. Finally, people have woken up and said, "We see what you're doing, and we're going to say something about it."

It bothers me that people are gambling with my future who are not going to be around, you know? The lawmakers—the Congress—have us trapped in the two-party system. All the decisions that they're making, and they're not even going to be around in twenty, twenty-five years. This is my future that they're gambling with, and I don't like that.

The biggest thing that has me moved and inspired is that I always felt that the people of our generation didn't really care. We were more concerned with labels and things like that, or with the next electronic thing that's going to come out, without actually caring about our future, being proactive in it. So the fact that this is mostly young people saying, "We see what you're doing and we're not standing for it!" just really inspired me.

It took me a week before I actually came down here. I was just seeing what was going on, and then hearing from people I knew that were here, and then the stuff that I was seeing on T.V., and it not matching up, you know what I mean?

What was the discrepancy?

Well, I had no idea that it was a sense of community here. The first day I walked in, this guy that worked with me—his name is Chris; he's somewhere around here—he was like, "You want something to eat?" So I was like, "Sure! Where are we going?" But he said, "No, come to the kitchen!" I asked how much it cost, and he was like, "No, it's paid for. Everything is free. You don't have to pay for anything."

And then it was a rainy day. I didn't have rain boots, so I went over to Comfort and I got rain boots. And I just saw how organized it is, with Medical and all that.

On T.V. they're making it like it's a bunch of crazy hippies that don't know why they're here, or they're getting arrested—they're, like, loud. It's totally not what's going on. So I was like, "You know what? I've got to stay there."

So that day I stayed. I didn't have anything with me. I got clothes from Comfort. I got a sleeping bag, dry socks, so . . . so I've been staying ever since, with the exception of the last three days because of being sick, whatever.

You said that people sometimes take your sleeping bag?

Well, I didn't say that; I don't know. I haven't been over there, so I don't know if my camp is still there. But I didn't buy it, anyway. The Comfort station gave me a big bag—a potato sack—and it had, like, a pack of socks; two hoodies—not this one, but another one; a sleeping bag; basic hygiene stuff like mouthwash, baby wipes; shoes.

Really?

Yeah, in a potato sack. They gave it to me from the Comfort station over there. A side product of all this is the fact that we're proving our point by the little social micro-community system—whatever you want to put on it—that we have going on here. Everyone's donating, pouring out. Before we run out of stuff, people bring more stuff. Each day I get more and more inspired by the sense of community.

It's proving the point that you don't have to hoard. You don't have to take from people to be okay, to survive. Everyone's taking care of people that they don't know. Like, someone set me up with a soft place to sleep that night. It's just amazing, the outpouring. It's proving the point that we're standing here for, as a by-product—I don't really like that word, but for lack of a better word—of the literal society that we've got going on here.

◆

I don't like the fact that you have to be careful what you say because you may lose your job, you know what I mean? That type of stuff really bothers me, just in general. We can't say anything because we're controlled by these powers-that-be that *we* put into power. We're kind of stuck in not being able to have a voice, when we outnumber the people that are speaking for us!

We are one of the most developed nations—if not *the* most—but yet, we have such high unemployment. We don't have health care and this and that. It's just a lot of shit wrong, and no one's really brave enough to [act], for whatever reason: because they're going to lose their job, or they have a family, or whatever the case may be. The fact that we're finally coming together and doing it—I just had to be a part of it.

Are you comfortable sleeping here? How are you finding it?

It's surprisingly comfortable. Well, I kind of have a really awesome setup. I don't know what these things are called, but I got it from my friend. She was in the Marines; it was what she used in Iraq or whatever. It's, like, this little ... what are those things called? It's like if a tent had a baby with a sleeping bag. It's a one-person tent-style thing, but it folds up, and then it pops out. And it zips up, so it protects you. It's enough for one body, and it has, like, a little arch.

I use that, and then I put a sleeping bag inside of it so it's really warm, and then I put a tarp over that. So I'm living as though I'm, like, the Upper East Side of Zuccotti. I've been finding it pretty peaceful, for the most part. I don't really go to sleep that much since I've been here, but I usually go to sleep around two.

What is the system? How are you guys feeding everyone?

Well, it's pretty much all donations, is that what you mean? You don't have to pay for anything here. Whenever we have meals, people come with food donations. I don't know if you saw right there, but we just got three donations. That's what people do. They say, "What can I do? What can I bring you?" Or they'll come take an order, and then they'll go bring it back. And people have been sending lots of pizza, especially at lunch- and dinnertime. I don't know if it's that OccuPie Web site—I haven't been around a computer in, like, three weeks—but people from all over the world have been sending us pizzas. Yeah, everything is donation-based, and like I said, it's amazing the by-product.

I don't think any of us anticipated this happening, this sense of community and giving. People from different states! I keep getting close to people, and then I realize that they're from a different state. They're like, "Oh, I've got to go," and I'm like, "Are you going to work?" They say, "No, I've got to go home," and when I ask them what they mean, they're like, "I live in Oregon," or, "I live in Michigan." He's not here now, but there's a guy, Warren, who lives in Michigan. And the other guy who was sitting with me—oh, there's Warren.

How many people work at doing the meals?

In the kitchen? It's not a set number. There's people that are here regularly, like myself, but then there's also people that just help. There'll be people that are in line, eating, that are like, "Can I help you? I'll eat first, and I'll come back here." A lot of people may help one day, you know what I mean? There's not a staff, so to speak. If I had to guess . . . I don't know, twelve to twenty people, give or take, that rotate. There's a core of people that have been helping coordinate stuff, but I mean, there's no leaders or anything like that at all. ❖

Warren

Right now, the security issue is possibly our top priority as a collective. I personally don't know how we're going to handle it. As soon as we start trying to police people, then that is a nasty aspect that will make things fall apart. People will start pointing fingers, and go, "Oh, you're an elitist!" And then our whole little community that we've built starts having hierarchy, and that's not a good thing. If people could just respect the cause . . . unfortunately, some of the people here do not, and those are the people that are taking advantage of it.

Is it that area? [Points.]

I don't disagree, but . . . you can walk around and tell what's what.

Well, I can tell by who is really hostile about talking to me.

Unfortunately, there are definitely a couple of people, I personally believe, who are agitating strictly for the sake of agitating.

Do you think that they're agitating in a technical sense, or do you think that they're just assholes?

Well, that's what is in question. These are just my personal beliefs. I can't speak for everyone. I'm a little bit more conspiratorial, maybe, but I do believe that police are sending drunk people off the street, saying, "Hey, you can't drink in public, so you go to Zuccotti Park." And then they're standing out there, and that gives them an excuse to come in, because there's people drinking in public and they're agitating, causing problems. Not just that, but I do believe that there are people that are being asked—or are very willing—to come in and directly cause issues and spread rumors.

What kind of things?

Just . . .

There was a guy the other day who was shouting that the cops were about to come in, and people were like, "What are you talking about?" Is that the kind of thing you mean?

No, like, with the kitchen, people are saying—not everyone, but only a couple of people . . . almost exclusively one man—but they're saying that we're taking all the best food and hiding it. We're eating high-class, five-star meals. We have the kitchen shut down, and we're hiding under here and eating all the best food that comes in.

We on the line—when there's food out, there is none left, so if we don't . . . what we do: We take a bowl and we set it under the counter, and if there's something we like, we throw it under there real quick. And so after four hours of serving, all our food is cold, and you know, maybe a little dirty, and then we go back there and we eat. Everybody else we've served, and yet there are people coming up and going, "Look at all that food right there! We want that now!" But that is food to prepare for lunch and dinner, indefinitely, for everyone, forever.

So you can't win, even though you're totally busting your ass.

Yes! Yes! Obviously, a lot of people here are very appreciative and understanding, but when certain people aren't, it is very, very hard and frustrating to me. Still, it kind of makes it easy to understand who's here for what reason.

What do you think the percentage is of who's here for movement reasons versus who's here to do whatever else?

I'd probably say seventy/thirty.

Seventy movement?

Yes.

That's actually pretty good.

Yeah. That may be a little generous, but I would like to be optimistic.

So how long have you been here?

I flew out a couple weeks ago. I was here for, I think, five days, and then I had to go back home and work. I go to school, too, so I had to catch back up on that stuff. That got me enough money to come back out, so I used my vacation days, and called in a couple days.

You're in college now?

Yes.

What's your field?

Photography and philosophy.

How are you keeping up with your coursework?

Carefully. [Laughs.]

Do you have friends taking notes and stuff?

No.

You just have a syllabus?

I've got a syllabus, and I hope that they follow by it!

So you just make sure to be in for papers or whatever?

Yep, yeah.

That seems a little stressful.

A little bit. I have to—what day is today? Is today Tuesday? Okay, tomorrow morning, I have to get on a plane back to Michigan, go do all my homework, and then go to class.

◆

How did you first hear about the movement?

Well, I don't get on the T.V. or the Internet very much, but I heard that a band that is my favorite band ever was playing here.

You're not talking about the Radiohead incident,[1] are you?

No, they're a band called Kayo Dot.

What are they called?

Kayo Dot.

I haven't heard of them.

Not many people have. I heard that they were playing out here, so I was like, "Okay, I've never seen them in my life. They're my favorite band. I'm going to go out there." And then I'm the kind of guy that really likes to travel a lot, and it's like, "If I'm going to go to New York, I might as well stay for a while and bum around, whatever," because I don't have a problem with that too much. I've been just about everywhere.

Really? Like, in the States?

I'm working on going overseas. I've only been in the U.S., but I've been just about everywhere in the U.S., camping.

How do you get around?

Motorcycle. Last summer I had a motorcycle. I usually have a car, but I was trying something different, and I took my bike out for a while.

---

[1] Radiohead was rumored to be playing a concert for protestors on September 30.

So what was that like?

Uh, the most amazing summer of my life.

Really? That sounds wonderful. That's the kind of thing I'd love to do, but now I'm a fogy, so . . .

You can always do it. You can always do it.

So you camped your way around the country. Where do you camp?

In the woods or on the streets.

Do you run into a lot of trouble doing that?

I'm really discreet. I don't want to brag, but I'm very resourceful. I have a lot of logic, and a little bit of street smarts. I'm also a country kid, so I can take care of myself without too many resources. And I'm very minimalist, so if I have a tarp and a cot, I should be good to go.

That's awesome. You grew up in Michigan?

Yes, and Montana.

Are you going to be here for the winter?

Yeah, I especially want to come back during the winter because that is when we're going to need the core people here, the people who actually support the cause. We need to show the world that we believe in this cause. We believe in this, and we're not going to dissipate just because it's cold out. In the world's eyes, we're still just a bunch of kids who are hanging out, essentially. Because a lot of people don't come down here and see what's happening, they get one certain news, and it's portrayed very badly. They show people the negative side.

Which *is* here . . .

It's here, but there's more to it than they're portraying. On the news, it does look like just kids hanging out—up here and down there—because that's what it is. They're not getting in here and looking at these several different functional groups that are keeping this place going, and keeping the cops out, and keeping everyone . . . peaceful.

According to where you go and who you talk to, it is a slightly different vision.

Yeah, because *everybody's* here for it! *Everybody's* been slighted by our government and our current economic structure. *Everybody.* And in different ways. So if you go over there, you're going to hear a completely different story from over here. I'm a union member, so I might have something to bitch about, you know? They're hurting our unions.

What's your union?

U.F.C.W.

U.F.C.W. Federal Communications Workers?[2]

It's very convoluted right now. We've been having a lot of changes. We actually just changed our entire contract and everything. We lost our pension.

What did they do with it?

They changed it to a 401(k). We were told, "It is a good thing, because pensions are run on stocks," and then they said that the 401(k) is a solid plan. But that is a blatant lie; it is the other way around. If the economy collapses, the pension should be solid, standing firm, and then the 401(k) is contingent on the stock market.

So we got blatantly lied to, but unfortunately, us warehouse workers have the same contract as the people in the store, and the people in the store outnumber us greatly. They kind of got offered a better deal, and since they're the greatest number, we lost the vote. I respect the vote, but part of the reason why we lost the vote was simply because people weren't informed. Certain people got blatantly lied to. It's really unfortunate.

I digressed on a whole different train of thought there. We were talking about how I got here.

Oh, yeah. How you decided to come down here.

I heard this rumor that my band was playing. Not *my* band, but . . .

The band you like.

Yes. So I looked it up on the Internet—went somewhere and got on there—and sure enough, they were playing. And I was like, "Well, I'm going to be in New York for about five days. I better find things to do."

---

[2]United Food and Commercial Workers.

And one of the first hits when I type in "New York" was this Occupy Wall Street. I hadn't heard anything about it on the news. Nothing. Not . . . nothing, which is, in retrospect now, really bizarre.

This is how many weeks ago?

Two. So it had already been going for two weeks. I was like, "Wow! This is really awesome! It's about time!" And I came here. The first day, got off the train, did the stereotypical walk through Manhattan, Central Park, took a couple pictures, and rushed down here; tried to get here as fast I could. And I loved this so much that I came back again for it. Coming back again during the winter.

What's your sleeping situation?

Well, after we get done serving people . . .

Which is, like, what? Two in the morning?

The last couple nights, we've been closing at eleven. We used to stay . . . I remember one night, we were serving food until three or four o'clock, and it was just outrageous. We can't do that, you know? So we're trying to set up a structured time, and I believe dinner now is going to be from seven to nine, nine thirty. And then after that, I might have enough time to go grab a beer. And then when I try to find a spot to sleep, I . . . you know, well, there's a spot right there. I could lay down right there.

You have stuff you carry around?

I have a sleeping bag.

You were already saying you're used to rough-and-tumble.

Yep, I'm pretty used to it. But like I said, I'm a country kid, so the urban camping-type thing is a little different to me. I mean, I've never seen this amount of people. I'm from Michigan, so when I came up to New York and walked around, I was like, "Wow!" I've been to big cities. I've been to Chicago, but when people say "big city," they mean New York, New York. And it is what it is.

And strangers—complete strangers—are laying down shoulder-to-shoulder with no room in between. It's like that.

That seems a little intense.

It's pretty intense. It's beautiful, but also a little ... because I really like to be isolated. Noise I can't handle.

Does that disturb your sleep? I mean, it's pretty noisy down here.

Massively. I've learned, when I travel, to carry earplugs, and a bandanna or something to put over my eyes. That helps a little bit, but I mean, this is New York. Right now it's quiet, but it's still loud as hell to me. It's loud as hell. The generators aren't even on.

[Mohammad interrupts the conversation and hassles Warren about the kitchen being closed. After shouting obscenities for a few moments, he moves off.]

Yeah, and that. You know, set up a structured meal time, which I personally do not think is outrageous. I think it's a very good idea. A peaceful way to clean up the camp, probably, is by restricting meals, because when we're feeding 24/7, honestly, drunk people are coming in off the streets, you know? "Hey, I heard there's food up here!" Sometimes they cause problems because they don't care about this. They're just here because they're drunk and want food, and a whole array of situations like that.

[A passer-by donates a box of energy bars.]

A lot of people do that. These are just individuals, and that box of things right there probably cost at least thirteen bucks.

Do you take pre-made food? Like, if somebody made you chili or something?

It depends.

If it's a creep?

Uh ...

You use your judgment.

It is kind of a judgment call. I mean, if it's one of the people that has been openly agitating and has been very, very suspicious, and they come up: "Eat this, man!" You know, we're probably going to go, "Hey, okay, let's look at it." We look at all the food. If it is homemade, we look at it. We might taste it first, honestly. We've had people that are, like,

"Uh, I don't know. Who wants to try a bite?" But none of the food is rotten. We inspect all of it as thoroughly as we can.

We're obviously not . . . actually, we have some people who work in soup kitchens and gourmet restaurants here. They're our go-to guys when us more unintelligent, uneducated kitchen folk are in doubt, so we rely on them a little bit. That almost never happens. They make it, they bring it out, it gets sent down, it gets put out, and then it's gone.

It seems like you run a pretty tight ship. The first time I was down here, there was some dumpster food.

We at no point ever served it. Some people did try to bring it out; it was good intentions, but misguided because we are not homeless people. I'm not saying that homeless people need food from the dumpster.

That's something you do when you have to.

When you have to, and we don't have to. And we don't want to. We don't want to give our people food from a dumpster. It's unsanitary, unsafe, and we have to keep everything as clean and orderly, and I don't want to say it, but looking as good as possible, because really, this is the epicenter for all the Occupys. The eyes of the world are on this spot mainly. If we're putting trash out on the table, and again, those certain news crews come in: "Look at this garbage that they're putting out! Look at all these people getting sick!" That would be detrimental to what we're trying to build.

We're trying to make something really nice here. So far it's working. There are always some negative elements to anything, but overall, it is going pretty well.

It really is looking pretty good.
Let me just ask you before I forget: The book is called *Why We Occupy*, so we're just trying to get that part of it down, too.

Um, a lot of people aren't, but I consider myself an ideal capitalist, or even a communist, which kind of sounds contradictory, but . . .

Well, they meet around.

Yeah. I do thoroughly believe that when a person works and earns for something, they deserve their rights to it. I'm a union member. That's the union in me. And the communal idea—this [kitchen] is that aspect of it. We're serving everybody, even if they're coming up and they're yelling at us. We serve them. We say, "Please, just . . . you can argue with us over here. You can yell at us over here, but don't hold the line up. We've got eight hundred more people to serve. Just yell over there." But, uh . . . oh, shit! I got deterred.

Why was I here? A major thing: the bailouts. That's the capitalist in me. It is simply outrageous. Outrageous! A business, when it does not do well, should fail, move over, and make room for another business. That is what keeps the economy and society stimulated: continuous growth. Unfortunately, everything at some point will come to an end. These banks are hemorrhaging money, and then our government is taking our money that we earned, and putting billions into this bank that is hemorrhaging money. Bleeding out.

And we lose that money because that money really doesn't exist. Unfortunately, we stopped backing our money by gold and precious metals in . . . what? 1913? I'm not sure of the year. But we have so much imaginary money, and everybody's in debt to everyone.

A child knows that when we have five dollars and we go to the store and spend that five dollars, we don't have it anymore. We don't say, "Go ahead and give it to me on credit." It's outrageous.

They have our economic system set up to where we are indentured servants. Education is a beautiful thing, but they're making students pay tens of thousands of dollars to go to school. And how are we doing it? Middle-class people can't afford it, so we have to take out loans. They give people loans that they know they cannot repay until they're sixty-five, making their wage as a doctor or whatever they're trying to be. And media and society are saying, "We don't have enough doctors." I don't want to say it's untrue, but—uh, what was it? The pharmacists push. They pushed pharmacy massively a couple years ago . . .

As a degree?

Yes, as a profession. All over the U.S., they were saying, "We're short pharmacists! Pharmacists are making thirty dollars an hour! Everyone become a pharmacist!" So all these people were like, "Oh! Jobs are in need! I'll do that!" They went and did it, and they went in debt. They found out that there were really no pharmacist jobs. And again, because I'm a little conspiratorial, it is a construct: Tell people what to get into, and then there's no market for it but they're in debt.

Everybody's drifting away from knowing how to take care of themselves. If this all collapsed, all these people would be done. Nobody knows how to grow anything—very few people do. No one knows basic survival skills without Walmart, and it's scary. It is so scary. When the government controls the food, they control the people. The government controls the food and the media.

The media concept of all this is scary to me, because people don't have a will to learn for themselves. They watch the T.V., and the news tells them, "This group is stupid." The news is telling them that these kids want more welfare. That is obviously not what this is about. I've heard that from several different extremist Republicans that see just a group of kids that want more welfare and disability and free money from the government. That is so outrageous!

That's just a lie.

Yes! And you can watch the news channels go around and specifically pick people out who are obviously not really part of this group—people who have no political intelligence. And then they display it and say, "This is the face of the occupation!"

Right. Like a crazy guy who's shouting in your face.

Yes, and they have done it.

I've seen it.

Yeah, media's terrified of me, and it comes back to the people. So many people just don't care. They don't even have a drive for themselves to live, anymore. They have no will of their own. Everything's kind of, I think, turned a shade of gray for them. And it's just, "Well, I'm told to do this." I think things are getting very Orwellian. I love George Orwell.

I do, too.

I think things are going that way. That's what this is about, you know? Wake up! Please! It is work, but work has to be done for things to happen. We can't go to the metaphorical grocery store and just get whatever we want. We have to cultivate it, work on it, and say, "This is possible, people! Open up your mind just a little bit. Please don't just accept what this news channel's telling you. If you have a doubt, or even if you agree with it, look into it to see if it is true. Try, at least.

At least try, because there's always going to be disinformation. You're never going to get the full story, even if you are here." There's aspects of this place that I haven't touched on because I just don't know.

Like what?

Um, you know, I can't tell you exactly how Media works.

Yeah, I feel like there's something mysterious going on in there.

This might be a psychological thing, but these people that run the tech—I don't want to use a cliché word, but I mean, they're tech kids, and they're usually more secluded people, a little bit.

That's true. It's probably not some Machiavellian thing.

Yeah, I would not believe that. I think that they just are maybe a little bit nerdy.

Okay, maybe you're right, yeah. You're right. I immediately assumed something scary and diabolical.

Sometimes it's hard not to. It really is. But Media have to deal with a lot of people who just want to get on camera. We have a LiveStream; you can actually see it right over there. People come up and talk just for the sake of talking. People are saying, "Hey, man! You have to tell the people about this, man! I got shut down when I was playing guitar!" Well, that's unfortunate, but this is not about playing guitar.

[Just as the interview draws to a close, Joshua belatedly tries to interrupt it, decrying "the media" and shooing Olivia away.] ❖

Ian

This is my second night. I'm staying here for four nights.

And you're from Occupy Toronto, you said?

Yes, I am.

So how are you finding this, as opposed to Toronto?

Ah, it's different. It's interesting to see that each city has it's own problems. They have different setups, and different ways of dealing with things. There's definitely some things that I want to bring back to Toronto. I see some problems here that I see can be prevented, such as the panhandling thing.

Do you guys have a problem with that?

Not at all. I just want to tell them that it is a possibility. And I want to make sure that in Toronto, money is donated only to the logistical tent. It's interesting here because I think there's a lot less support from local businesses.

There's, like, none, right?

Well, there's food—I think that's donated from local businesses. And there's a couple other things donated, but in Toronto, we constantly have food and resources, and a small Internet provider donated Wi-Fi for the whole park, like, public. The Media tent has their own line.

Are you involved in the media side in Toronto?

Not really. I'm involved with the Info and Welcome centers in Toronto. I'm a full-time student and work two jobs, so I don't have a hundred percent free time to commit to the movement. But when I have time, I'm out there.

What are you studying?

I'm studying sociology and cultural studies.

So you're sleeping over there sometimes, and doing your school-work there?

Yes. When there's some downtime during the day, I usually take out my textbooks and read them and stuff like that. I'm originally from Toronto, but I go to school an hour and a half outside of Toronto, so that makes it a little extra hard to be there.

I'm looking to spread the Occupy movement to schools. We need to get students more organized. The press stopped coming to Occupy Toronto because they realized, "Hey, this is organized! We can't just rag on them anymore," which they did for a really long time. There's been media blackouts at certain newspapers and television stations, so now there's a movement for protesters to interview media.

That's a good one.

And if this media outlet refuses to be interviewed, they get blacklisted. It creates a level playing field.

What are some of the good things you're seeing here in New York?

Lots of people.

More so?

Due to New York just being bigger, I think there's more flux of people coming in and out.

It's interesting that Occupy Wall Street is not exactly on Wall Street. It's kind of impossible to occupy Wall Street, just like Occupy Toronto Market Exchange is not right in front of the Market Exchange. It's by a park, similar to this.

In a park, you can have a decent conversation, and you know, if somebody wants to discuss something beyond politics, most people are down for a little laugh here and there. Just keep things a little light-hearted. You can't be serious all the time; you'll burn out or get annoyed. You have to keep an open mind with everything, and laugh when it's appropriate.

Can you say a thing or two about your reasons for occupying?

Well, the division between the rich and the poor is just growing at an astonishing rate. It's reached a point higher than it was during the Great Depression, and that's not really okay.

The way things are going, they're not how I'd like to see them. People are not treated as individuals; they're treated as a number, and treated as profit. And Wall Street getting bonuses when their companies are failing? That's kind of ridiculous.

I think the Occupy movement around the world sees this. Although they're not directly going to change Wall Street, I think standing in solidarity with all of America is a great thing, and shows that they do care. They might not have a direct voice in the State's politics, but they can see that they too are not getting as much as they should.

The global economic situation sees no borders, so everyone needs to get out and have their voice heard. Every country has their own problems and their own solutions to stuff, and this is a great venue for all these minority voices to get out and say, "Hey! This is a problem!

You can listen to us! The media is not covering the story, but here's some legitimate information. Here's links, here's books, here's such and such!" I think it's a great venue for doing that.

Were you an activist before this?

I don't know if I would consider myself an activist before this. I did do other political things, and I do volunteer and stuff, but I've never been involved with something like this.

So what was the difference for you?

Well, I was following this online since the first or second week, and I just saw this growing and growing. As soon as I saw the videos of the protesters being arrested on Brooklyn Bridge, and the kettling, and the weird mesh thing they're putting around people to arrest them . . . it's absolutely bizarre and appalling that they treat people like this. I was in support of the movement, and then when it was expanding internationally, I was just like, "I'm on board a hundred percent."

Any political spectrum can walk through, and most people are going to start an intelligent conversation with them. You know, everyone can be engaged here. It's not an us versus them thing that I think many protests in the past have been. This isn't, "If you're in support of that, you can't be in support of us." This is, "You're a part of this, too." This is humanity. We're trying to get a voice out, and it's great. And it's being heard. The world's watching. The passion that some cities have put on, and the amount of support that other cities have gotten . . .

In Albany and L.A., the cops are refusing to arrest the protesters, whereas in Chicago, they're constantly being knocked down.

That's traditional, though, for Chicago.

But at the same time, there's huge riots and police brutality in Toronto.

I'm so surprised by that!

Canada is very conservative right now. The divide between the rich and the poor is growing at a faster rate than in the States, and they're thinking of introducing mandatory minimum sentences. I'm pretty sure only Texas and California think that's a good idea.

Well, we had the Rockefeller Laws here in New York. I don't know if that's exactly what you're talking about.

I don't know. I'm more involved in the Canadian perspective because I feel like I have more of a voice there. Yeah, Canada is not going the direction that I think it should. I don't think a lot of people are educated on what's happening. Large corporations are charging more and more for their services when they're making two thousand percent profit.

I'm talking about the telecommunications in Canada. It's in a sad state. The idea of having unlimited Internet access is not going to be a reality anymore. Most companies have started introducing bandwidth caps and charging exorbitant rates. And that's just computer Internet. Smart-phone Internet is also extremely expensive.

Yeah, it's kind of ridiculous. When our communications are mostly done online, I don't want to think, "Hey, is this YouTube video going to cost me five bucks? Is accessing this information that I need for school going to bankrupt me?" That's obviously an extreme, but it's a lot of money. If most politics and stuff are being discussed online now, it really leaves out a large segment of the population: people who can't afford to be a part of this Internet economy and Internet politics.

It's already been hugely stratifying.

Already, like with people who don't have the education on how to use it. They have another bar that they don't have the economic means to clear. That's terrible.

Yeah, and the crime bill is ridiculous in Canada, trying to introduce warrantless wireless spying on people so anybody in power can look at whatever you're looking at online. They can look at your love letters to your sweetheart. They can look at how you're spending your money. They can see who you're supporting. It's really not a good thing, and it's sad. Nonviolent offenders are seeing more jail time than violent offenders and pedophiles. It's kind of disgusting. And having a system where those who do not own property see more jail time than those who do own property . . . a crime's a crime.

The world's watching every moment of this. Everyone's going to be in support of this at some point. It just takes time. ❖

October 26

Walter I

My name is Walter. I am a building trades journeyman in Plumbers Local Union Number One, and I am a 9/11 first responder. I was at the World Trade Center from September twelfth to September sixteenth, 2001, as an unpaid volunteer. Unfortunately, I was diagnosed with autoimmune disease of the lungs, which is known as sarcoidosis, and I was also diagnosed with post-traumatic stress disorder. Both conditions and everything that's attached to them have put me out of work.

On the table in front of me, I have all my medications. All the medications that you see consist of steroids, painkillers, and cream for my leg because I get breakouts. You know what's called the World Trade Center Rash? I actually have that, and a myriad of other problems. I'm out here risking my health to support what goes on here.

I think people have gotten sick and tired of the system the way it exists at the moment. And it's not just here in the United States, it's around the world.

You know, people can walk by and be apathetic all they want. When it hits them and it hits their family, they'll be sleeping on this side of the fence, too. I used to be a hard-working guy. I used to go to work, but because of what I did for my country, I got sick. And now, that system which I went to go save is trying to throw me under the bus.

My compensation case happens to be this Friday. I also have a disability case—thanks to Congressman Crowley, by the way, who was able to get it pushed up—but my lawyers have a case that same day, so I got adjourned temporarily. I'm also signed up with the Victim Compensation Fund, so I have a huge legal battle in front of me.

It's because of that, and it's because of what I'd seen my father go through in the past when he was out of work. I'm watching everything that's going on: people fighting, these punk cops beating up on little kids the way they are, people losing their homes left and right, people having to sell their stuff on eBay just to put food on their table . . .

A lot of people in this country and all around the world are having to say, "Do I take whatever money I have right now and put a roof over my head, or do I feed myself and my family?" That's not a choice to make. Why are people being forced to make that choice? Especially here in America, the supposed greatest, most powerful nation on the planet? It might be worthy in Nintendo terms, but in real life, it's not the giant it claims to be anymore, and that's sad. It really is.

I'm very disappointed in my leaders. I'm disappointed in my government. I'm disappointed in people that I voted for. You know, I think a lot of people are starting to feel like that—I hope at the polls. Like when George Bush was our president, I hope this experience that people see all around them smacks them in the face. I hope they drink a hot cup of coffee, and say, "Hey, maybe after ten years . . ."

After the Trade Center came down, that was the main catalyst for what's going on right now. Maybe there'll finally be a learning curve if we turn off the *Jerry Springer* and the *Jersey Shore*, and the cooking competitions where people are fighting and committing suicide over who can make the best cupcake. That's the American culture for you. We have to change as a people and a culture, and start getting wise, and start paying attention to what's going on, and stop being asleep.

I made a sign here the other day, and people got insulted by it. You know they call New York the city that never sleeps? I crossed it out with a big red X and said, "Fell asleep." Essentially, it read, "New York: The City That Fell Asleep," because that's what happened. People fell asleep, and it's time to wake up.

What future do you envision for Occupy Wall Street? What would be your best-case scenario?

I don't want to call myself an old man, but I'm a New Yorker, a tough guy. I use harsh language for this interview, even though I'm trying to censor myself. I have that working-class attitude like everyone else does, man. I don't like to quit. I don't like to lose. Now the people behind me are much younger than myself, and they have a fighting spirit unlike anything I ever thought I had. For a time I disagreed with a lot of things they were doing. Then I started watching a few of them getting interviewed. Last night I seen one of the gentlemen that was standing here about an hour ago—I didn't have a chance to ask him his name. He was on New York One, and he put these guys in their place. He tore them apart, basically.

People have been accusing everybody of being hipsters here, and filthy and dirty. I mean, you know, you look at myself. I don't look like a hipster. I don't look filthy and dirty. I'm a construction worker. I'm an American. I'm a union man. I'm not a hipster. I'm not an artist. I'm none of that stuff. I would like to see these people try to come to a person like me and accuse me of being a hipster. But they won't do that because they're a bunch of cowards.

A lot of these young folk here are very intelligent. They are not stupid. Let me tell you, if I were to take a spelling test alongside with them, I bet you ten times out of ten I lose. I'm well-educated myself, but they make me look like a dummy. What does that say?

Not everybody here is as dumb as they may appear. They might look like they just got thrown off a bus in the middle of a hurricane, but a lot of them are very smart, and I think people underestimate that. The media have been saying that there's no single message. "Where's your message? Where's your message?" There can't be a single message because there's so much to be pissed off about.

I'm here because of health care. Just look at what's on the table. There's one, two, three, four . . . let's just say a round number: twelve. So there's twelve to fourteen medicines in front of me right now, plus I'm out of work because I got sick. I got thrown under the bus because of Christie Whitman and this corrupt government saying, you know, "First responders are not sick. They're making it up." Cancer, you know? They left cancer out of the Zadroga Bill. People are losing their homes. They can't afford to feed their families no more. They probably can't even afford *one* of these medications I have on the table. They can't put shoes on their feet. They can't put clothes on their back. There's so much to be pissed off at.

These stupid wars, like with George Bush sending our troops over to Iraq, which had nothing to do with what happened at the World Trade Center site. We all know that. We all know it was a bunch of crap, yet nobody did anything about it.

All of what I'm saying essentially boils down to: Why does it take so much bullshit to get Americans to wake up to do anything? They have to wait until two giant buildings come down. Three thousand people have to die for them to say, "Oh, man. It's time to do something." No, you should be like that every day. I'm not saying you're going to walk around in paranoia, but you should be on your toes every day to prevent stuff like this from happening. I can't stand it when people say, "I'll wait until tomorrow," and then they wait until the last minute.

It took almost four thousand American citizens dying overseas in Afghanistan and Iraq—fighting to defend us—and the three thousand plus people that died here, right in front of me at the World Trade Center site, and the people at Shanksville, Pennsylvania, for people to say, "Okay, now we have to do something." Bullshit! It should be happening every day. It should have happened then, it should happen now, and it should happen in the future.

What would you recommend? What should people be doing?

I think our culture seriously needs to change. People are too apathetic. I don't want to call them stupid and unintelligent, but they need to wake up right now. Stop watching your *Jersey Shore!* Stop eating your doughnuts and your pizza! It's enough! Change your attitude, man!

You know, it took people in our past like Rosa Parks and Martin Luther King and Mahatma Gandhi and John Lennon to shake people up and say, "No more, man! We're going to go sit in the front of the bus! We're going to go drink out of the white people's fountain! To hell with this! Let's go! Let's do something!"

Doing things is what gets things done. None of this "Okay, well, it doesn't concern me," you know? "It has nothing to do with me right now." Bullshit! Bullshit! I'm out here risking my health right now by sitting here telling you this message. I shouldn't even be outside for this long, but I'm going to be here as long as I can, until I can't stand up no more, because I believe in it.

Are you coming every day?

I've been trying to, but you know, recently, because the weather's gotten cold, my breathing hasn't been so good and all that kind of stuff. But when I have the strength, I'm out here with my fist. I'm out here ready to fight. If I get sick, I'll stay at home a couple days. I'll come right back again, as long as this thing is going.

I'm out here collecting money not just for myself, but for the orga-nizations that helped me out. There's a couple of organizations that help me with my rent. One in particular—John Feal, if you're listening to this—the FealGood Foundation donated seven hundred fifty dollars to me over the past two months to help me pay for my medications, my rent, my credit card bills, and for me to put food on my table and all that kind of stuff. It has also been a huge lobbyist to get the Zadroga Bill signed.

Tuesday's Children is another organization. Whatever I get here, I'm going to donate to them, also. They've been taking care of us with events over at Giants Stadium or at the Meadowlands Arena. I was over at Citi Field—on the field, as a matter of fact—carrying the flag out in the outfield on 9/11, which I was honored to do. They did the F.D.N.Y. versus the Russian firefighters over at Floyd Bennett Field in Brooklyn. So I've been proactive with those guys. I hope to help them out a little bit today.

And of course, Occupy Wall Street. It's a worthy cause, and I have to be a part of it. If I don't do it, I feel like I cheated on my girlfriend, basically. I have to be here. That's just the way it is. They have, like, this little financial system set up here.

I'm going to divide it up evenly amongst those four groups, includ-ing myself. I try to help out those who helped me, and that's what it's about, man. You know, our leaders aren't helping us. The people we voted for aren't helping us. And unfortunately, now we have to look to help ourselves.

◆

If my body won't cooperate, I just pick up and leave. I don't even tell anybody. What'll happen is: The longer I stay outside—I mean, I got my pain meds here, but my breathing will start getting screwed up, and my muscles will start to hurt. I'll probably go indoors for a little bit—at Burger King or something—but if I feel I can't handle it, I'm out of here, basically. But I try to stay here, you know? I mean, I'm armed: I got dust masks in there, I got my meds here, I got my seat. The only thing is the bathroom situation.

Somebody actually asked me—it was funny—it was like, "I see you're a plumber, why don't you hook up some bathrooms." [Laughs.] I'm like, "First off, I would get in trouble. I'm out of work." I can't do something like that, but I gave them a few suggestions, like Call-A-Head, for example, to get porta-johns here and all that kind of stuff. But the city is trying to fight this every which way they can. They sicced the Fire Department after them again.

What happened yesterday with the Fire Department?

Well, see, I kind of warned these young people here when this thing first started. I've been to rallies like this before. I know the system, and I know what they're going to try to pull. Sure enough, I proved right at every turn with everything. It just happens to be that I'm a certified fire watcher, which is what they need here. I could direct them in every which way, and tell them what to do.

See, you're not supposed to stack anything above a certain height; I think it's six feet. You're not supposed to have any kind of walkway blocked up, no less than three feet. This way, people can walk through, for hazards and all that. If you have a gas generator, you're supposed to have somebody on that thing 24/7, especially with something like this. You're supposed to have a guy taking a log of all the escape routes and all that kind of stuff. You have to have fire extinguishers all around.

I offered to help them with that, but they kind of frowned on me a little bit. Yeah, they got this strange thing. I guess, probably because they're young, they see an older person coming along and they think, "Oh, he's trying to tell us what to do." They have that thing a little bit.

I've gotten that a little bit.

They accused me of being a cop many times already. I've been accused of being a Fed, a C.I.A. agent. I've been accused of being a police officer, a detective. [Laughs.] I'm like, "Well, what's next, then?"

Bystander: I get that every time I get a haircut. And when I had a mustache, they were sure I was a cop.

Walter: It's amazing.

That level of paranoia is not helping anybody.

I can understand the fear of theirs. It's understandable because there are people that are trying to close this down. The mayor, no matter how much he tries to spin it, can't stand this. His business friends look at it and they're like, "It's an eyesore," and all that. I love it, though.

I'm trying to restrain myself from what I really want to say about why I'm here. I don't want to make myself look bad, but I like to be a thorn in people's sides and make them squirm around. Like, "Aw, man, did he just say that?" I love that. I love that this is an eyesore.

It's a beautiful eyesore.

There's really not a lot of bad people here. You've got to realize that a lot of the people that are getting high—doing whatever it is that they may be doing here—you've got to realize they don't have anything else. I get tired of hearing, "You're just a bunch of drunken yuppies and hipsters!" These people—a lot of them that are in here—are homeless. They've got nothing else, man. You see people begging out there in the subways and on the streets—begging for money, begging for change. Yeah, they might be going out there and getting drugs. So what? They might be going out there and getting beer and booze. That's because they've got nothing else. They've got nothing else.

I can't stand asshole people: "Oh, he's a fucking bum!" He's got no home. He's got no job. He's got barely any clothes. That's the reason why he's out there begging. If he goes and gets booze and weed, fine. So be it. Let him go get booze and weed. I've got no problem with that. That's because he's got no hope. He's lost his hope, so he's had to turn to that, unfortunately. If it makes him feel better temporarily . . . yeah, it sucks because he's inebriated, but at least his mind is not set on, "Oh, my God! What am I going to do?" I can't stand when people on this side of the fence say that kind of stuff about people here. I would love for them to accuse me of something like that.

Some idiot in my union actually called up my business agent to find out why I'm here. Imagine that.

That seems not very full of brotherhood, huh?

No, because there's an I in U-N-I-O-N, unfortunately, nowadays. And I get tired of that kind of stuff, man. You see, somebody like me, who comes out and brings it on the real . . . like, I told him to shut up and be quiet, you know? Whatever, so that ain't going to happen. That's why I'm out here—another reason why I'm out here.

Does your union support this?

I have spoken to the delegate that was here. In his roundabout way, he kind of said that as long as I stay out of trouble . . .

I'm older. I'm experienced. I'm not going to go out there and start lighting bonfires, dancing around with Indian garb on while beating a drum, and then smashing the drum like I'm in Iron Maiden. No, that's not going to happen. And go smoke a bowl of hash, no stuff like that.

I'm here just to get my point across, you know what I mean? Honestly, carrying this thing . . . as a first responder, it does come with a burden, you know. A lot of people—they look at that as they would look at soldiers or whoever it may be. It comes with responsibility behind it. I have to represent that. At the same time, I'm going to throw my comedy out there once in a while—poke fun at people—but it comes with responsibility.

When it comes to badmouthing and bashing certain individuals, most people here have been disenfranchised by the system. They have no home, no job. They have their dog and their green army gear and their knapsack. They have dreads. I know the type that everybody's judging. Leave them alone. They ask you for a few nickels and they go buy a pack of cigarettes with it, so be it. Leave them alone. They have no choice. Their parents threw them out on their ass because they themselves are struggling. They're out there trying to survive. I don't want to hear that they're all bums. That's where I stand. ❖

Rory

I totally understand why people don't want to talk to me.

The P.R. guy told us to stick to the facts and stay away from personal stories, but you know, he's wise in the ways of a world we're trying to change. That's very P.R.-savvy and very political-savvy, but it's not people-savvy. It's not human, really. It's enforcing programming on people, you know?

A lot of people really want to see an end goal and a structure to this place, but my opinion—I'm a Taoist before I'm anything else—is that life is a means unto itself. If that life is working—everybody's happy, everybody's fed, everybody's warm, everybody's sheltered—then none of this really matters to me.

We've introduced a new paradigm, I think. I mean, other people have thought of it first, but we timed it to the point where it can really take hold and stick, and you know, this is only the beginning. I'm very encouraged, and I hope that one day we have no need for politics or rules or anything like that. We can just—I don't mean to use an expletive on your tape . . .

Say whatever you want.

Okay, well, my one guiding rule—the one thing that I wish I could get out to the world, you know, spell it out in magnetic poetry on the refrigerator—is: "Don't be a dick!" That's it. It's so simple. Life is very simple. It's us that makes it complicated.

So I'm here to help things along, nurture a very, very good thing, and I don't have any overarching goals that I want to see accomplished or anything. You've got to accept what you have right now. You can't have your eyes cast on the horizon. As Buddha said: "One who walks with their eyes constantly on the horizon falls in many ditches." So right here, right now, we're doing good. We're happy. And right now is the only thing any human being has ever had, anyway. The past and the future are simply ideas.

You know, I think we've already succeeded, and will continue to succeed on a grander scale as it goes along.

I feel the same way. I go home at night because of the baby—

Fair enough.

But it's nice to know it's still going on.

Well, you're contributing a lot to the movement by what you're doing right now, so I appreciate that.

If people will talk to me. We'll see. More and more, people don't want to talk. Now I hear that the P.R. guys told you not to.

Yeah.

That's fucked up, though. That's so against the spirit of the movement that it's sort of blowing my mind.

He's coming from the right place, just the wrong time.

Well, also there is a difference between, for instance, me and Fox News. I mean, I'd like to think there is.

If Fox News were to interview me, I would just grin like an idiot, thank them for showing up, and invite them to join us. That would be it.

Well, that would be the way to go with them. Sort of like intellectual nonviolence. Passive resistance.

◆

Tell me about your day-to-day experience of being out here.

Day to day, I usually wake up pretty early-ish, get myself some coffee and some breakfast. I go around and see if there's any fires that need putting out.

Literal fires?

Metaphorically speaking.

So you're mediating?

Um, no. Basically, I'm just doing what needs doing, and sometimes, you know, if somebody's really stressed out, I'll tell them to just chill out, and I'll handle it for a second. My main goal here is to find the shit that nobody else wants to do and do that, because somebody's got to do it. I tried doing this gentleman's job [mediator], but I am not good at it because I am not emotionally connected in such a way that I could peacefully negotiate sanity out of people.

Wait! [Laughs.] What does that mean?

[Laughs.] The training that we receive basically states that we're supposed to recognize some kind of emotional need in ourselves in a given conflict situation, and then try to put ourselves in the other person's place. You know, I'm caring, but I guess I'm bad at empathy. [Laughs.] If I see somebody cold, I put a blanket on them, but if I see somebody drunk and making *themselves* suffer, I kind of get this . . . my dad kind of comes up in me, and I'm like, "Maybe you'll learn this time!" I work very hard on the face I put forward to the world, but at the end of the day, I really am a curmudgeon. Kind of a jerk.

[Laughs.] But you're a Taoist jerk.

Yeah.

They're not mutually exclusive.

No, they're not. As a matter of fact, before I was a Taoist, I practiced Zen, and we have a storied history of bitter, crotchety old men who like to hit people in the heads with sticks to instill enlightenment, so . . .

Like how all the kōans end with the guy giving a shitty answer?

He hits him with a stick, and suddenly he becomes enlightened. That's the end to pretty much all of them: "Suddenly he became enlightened." Some of them are just *non sequiturs*, though. You have to disengage the literal, linguistic part of your mind to understand them, and you have to sit with them for a long time. Basically, the unifying theme is that words don't necessarily indicate the phenomena they're meant to describe, so they're essentially nonsense. Once you dispense with them, then you can really start to get it. And sometimes, you know, Zen is just a slap to the face. It's not always, "How are you feeling right now?" Sometimes it doesn't matter how you're feeling right now. What matters is what needs doing.

Tell me if you think this is totally off, but in Jewish theology, there's a lot of jokes, you know what I mean? That's part of it. The irony undermines meaning, the calcification of meaning.

There's a great story about a young rabbi who's studying—I forget the word for it, but basically, it's somebody who's been studying the Torah so long that it starts to lose meaning for him. The younger rabbi comes to an older rabbi, and he's like, "I think I'm becoming this." And the older rabbi's like, "Oh, he's been studying the Torah for two years and all of a sudden he's this!"

◆

Tell me about how you decided to come down here.

Well, I decided to come down here because this is the focal point of a new way of being and thinking. It's still in it's infancy, and it hasn't reached anything near consensus, but it will, and I want to help it along in any way I can.

What do you think is going to help people to get on board?

"Relax."

Easier said than done. [Laughs.]

A major part of it is that people's egos get in the way. This isn't a movement until it's moving in their direction, you know? Until it's moving
towards the way *they* think it should be. But you share the planet with
seven billion other people. They might have some input, too.

And I think that once we get rid of the really oppressive forms of
structure, life will be able to organically take the shape that it's meant
to. And that's what I think this is, for good or ill. There's always going
to be a bad element here, and you know, without it there would be no
appreciation of the good element. It's just something that we always,
as human beings, will have to struggle with. It's part of what makes
us human, and it's part of what makes us better as human beings, and
pushes us to evolve.

**Well, somebody was saying to me that it needs to be worked out
here so then it can be worked out in the bigger world.**

Yeah, and the conclusions we come to here may not necessarily be the
same conclusions they come to everywhere. I don't know if they're
occupying Idaho right now, but let's just use that as an example. It's
completely different individuals there, completely different needs. ❖

October 27

Joshua

This interview was conducted at Charlotte's Place, 107 Greenwich Street.

I see that people are feeling pissed about getting burned. Can you tell me what the media's been up to?

There are narratives being created to affect public opinion; that's not my expertise. I have been so busy with the kitchen that I don't have time to brush up on the latest, current stories that are floating about. I just know personally, from working in the kitchen, some of the stories that have been written about us.

Our interaction with those media groups happens to coincide with the increase in some of the unwanted activity of drugs, violence, and assault in the rest of the park. The media has worked different ways of trying to smear us. There's been a lot of bullshit that's been said. They're spinning it out in such a way where, you know, we're a group of people who don't have any direction and goals. They keep trying to say that: "Well, what is this all about?" and this and that and the other.

It's an important discussion that needs to be had amongst ourselves, but we need to do P.R. It's going to take a coordinated effort. We're getting attacked at different angles related to the movement, and to our individuals who are activists and organizers. We've been attacked for how the Finance Working Group has been operating. We've also been attacked for serving good food!

I mean, the kitchen itself has really worked hard to do as best as we can in the situation we have. We're going above and beyond what I think is required of us, because we're not a "kitchen," you know? We're not a restaurant. It's more like . . . a potluck. So we often get catered food, or we outsource some of our meals to people who are passed by the health inspectors. And so for us, it's not something we should be worrying about. We don't need to have some sort of grade in our kitchen because we're in a unique situation. We're basically handing food out that's been given to us or catered.

We have also had some internal issues. An individual in the kitchen disseminated false information to the media, and it was negative information that caused a dust-up among conservatives.

What information?

This person said that a fifty-five hundred dollar computer was stolen from her personal belongings.

What kind of laptop would that be?

Well, right. Fifty-five hundred dollar laptop . . . does it exist? I mean, I don't know that much about the prices, but from what I hear, if you got the most expensive laptop that Apple offers, and you had it tricked out with all its bells and whistles, then maybe you're talking about a laptop that could cost that much. But right away, the bullshit detector goes on, you know? It's really sad that the *New York Post*—

Is that where it was?

Yeah.

Are you from New York originally?

No.

Oh, because they're the worst rag.

They're just gossip-mongers. My impression is that they don't know what to make of the movement. They like to create climates of opinion, but they're also a hop-on-the-bandwagon sort of newspaper. They'll like it if other people start to like it, but then they also like to be on the front lines of smearing and causing friction at the same time.

And also, the false information was that we had a certain amount of the kitchen's finances stolen from the kitchen, which was just total and utter falsehood.

Who said that?

The same person.

Could it possibly be that this person was purposefully spreading misinformation?

It is possible that there are people in the movement who could do something like that, but I don't believe that she is a provocateur. I just think that she has a problem of not speaking the truth. I mean, she's told me she has a psychology degree, and then she's told somebody else that she's a law student at N.Y.U., and that she's eighteen years old, and she speaks, like, forty-eight different languages. So you make your own assessment of that, you know? When someone starts saying stuff like that, I mean . . .

We can't stop that. We can't stop what people in the park say to the press. Reporters are going to be walking around, digging for information, looking for any lines they can put in their paper. They need to get the story. They need to find something that, basically, helps the bottom line for them, you know? There's a cynical saying in the newsroom: "Don't let the facts get in the way of a good story." So . . . I think that definitely applies to the *Post*.

What's your take on the whole strike thing? The workers' strike that people are talking about?

We're trying to simplify kitchen services, but we're not going to just completely stop serving food cold turkey. There's been lots of rumors swirling around about that.

All we're trying to do is cut back on the types of food and services we are offering, so that we as a group can reorganize, possibly winterize, and discuss future projects on how to make this thing better. We're trying to coordinate our efforts.

We're working on attitude, and on guidelines for the kitchen. It's a big issue that people who come in to help serve have core customer relations abilities. Basically, we're needing to train people to work in a food service situation, even though we're not an official kitchen or restaurant. We do have people here who have that experience, and so we need to be able to share knowledge. We need to take some time to rethink on how we can do this. Part of the problem is that the kitchen is a very fast-paced working group, where we're trying to feed a few thousand people a day.

How many?

A few thousand. I mean, we've gone through that many plates. We've gone over that many in a single dinner.

There are individuals who want to strike. They're upset about these negative elements destroying what people are working to build. I've been in a number of the meetings where this controversial subject has come up, and the best thing that we came up with was that we would try to have a kitchen that is simplified, with a very across-the-board food menu to everyone.

Our service deals with a general human need. That goes for occupiers, plus newcomers, and the homeless, and the public. We're doing the city a service in a lot of ways. But we also have, like, a soup kitchen where people can hang out all day and be able to score drugs at the same time. People can be able to get fed, hang out, also have drug dealers show up.

As opposed to an actual soup kitchen.

Yeah, they're open and closed for certain hours. And so we have kind of a difficult situation. There's a certain amount of overcrowding that's happening, and that has a tendency to cause negative situations to proliferate. So the kitchen is trying to help out with security issues. Some of the women who help in the kitchen—and other women in other parts of the camp—don't feel safe. Food is a basic right that everyone deserves, but safety also is a basic right. At this point, a lot of us in the kitchen feel that the safety of individuals in the kitchen or in the camp trumps some of the other issues.

It's not a prison, as far as trying to modify behavior through food rationing. People aren't trapped there, you know? For those people who really need help, I don't think we are ever going to be the best alternative for them. There are other people who specialize in helping them, whether psychologically or just satisfying their material needs. I mean, this is people camping out in a park! People went there by choice! Nobody's forced to stay there. All we're doing is trying to offer a basic service to help the people who want to stay there. Anybody who wants to disrupt that on a group of volunteers . . . they have issues.

I mean, the park's open. It's a public park, but the people in the park are people who went there for a reason. People could have gone there and dealt drugs before we ever went there. People could have lived there before, but nobody did. My impression is that Zuccotti Park just wasn't a major drug hub, you know? It was not a park the homeless like to stay at a lot. That park's actually not very conducive . . .

It's sort of a fishbowl.

It's not that comfortable.

How do you think this is going to get worked out?

Well, it's a bigger discussion. A lot of the cultural problems that the city has to deal with are also moving in here. I want to be cautious in slandering the police department, but we've heard reports of people who basically have been dropped off here from Rikers.

From Rikers! Really?

That's the report I heard. We would like to confirm that with our own surveillance and stuff, but there are definitely people who would like to see this stop. A lot of people would like to see this end.

◆

I've worked with different organizations that are involved in activism. One that's involved in environmental activist work is called Time's Up! There's also Inner Hands; we've been doing community dinners for a long time. We get dumpster food or donated food, and we offer a space where we can get together. We cook dinner together, support one another, work on community-building, and work on the Free Store.

Was that the one that was outside?

Yeah, it was outside, in Bed-Stuy. It got burned down, so when Occupy Wall Street happened, I was able to coalesce with the action. I came here on the first day. It was put on by *Adbusters*, or it was promoted by *Adbusters*. The very first day, we were serving peanut butter and jelly sandwiches and hot fruit, and it just organically came together. ❖

October 28

Andrew

Maybe some background?

Oh, boy . . .

If you want.

I've got a lot of background, so you may have to help. I'm from Kent, Washington.

Washington State?

Yeah, State. Work experience: I worked a year at a corrections facility, two and a half years as an army medic.

Where did you serve?

A few different units. That's a whole other thing in itself.

Last year or so, I was working E.M.S. out in Washington, and working at a free clinic as well, on the side. Right now I'm independently employed just running auctions.

Are you sleeping in this area?

I am, actually. My tent is usually here. I share it with a dude from Australia; he's a friend of mine. We're packed up for cleaning right now. Normally, this is, like, a neighborhood of tents going on here.

How would you describe your neighborhood?

My neighborhood? Most of us work at the Empathy table or for N.V.C., the Nonviolent Communications. Also, a lot of us are in the Community Watch at night. Community Watch—we take volunteers from the community who want to stay up and make sure it's a safe, livable area for everyone. But some of us are more dedicated to the Community Watch, like myself.

So what do you do in the Community Watch? You walk around?

Stay up, walk around, do a little outreach. If we see someone is cold, we'll run over to Comfort and grab them a blanket, you know? Try and keep noise down for people who are sleeping. Just try and make it a generally nice, safe community, and enjoyable for everybody.

I also work for Nonviolent Communications.

You're mediating?

Yes, mediation. Also, because of my past medical experience—a lot of it is trauma experience—while I'm not one of the medics for the Medical tent, if there's any serious trauma issues or any overflow, I run over there to help out.

Are you seeing a lot of trauma?

Oh, no, no, no. There's really not that much trauma here. Mostly it's just regular sickness and stuff like that. There hasn't been anything serious. Not like the Oakland incident,[1] thankfully.

◆

Most of the people who live in this area communicate with each other very well. We've become friends. It's like our own little family here. We agreed to face our area towards each other. When the weather was nicer, we were actually sleeping out in the open air, sleeping bag-by-sleeping bag, in rows. This tiny space—we fit eighteen to twenty-five people here, on certain nights.

That's awesome. Do you guys know each other from before?

No, not really. Some do, but I don't know any of these people from before I got here, and . . . let's see, I found out about Occupy . . . I live out in the mountains, so I don't get much media. When I did hear about it, I spent a little while researching it, and within six hours of finding out,

---

[1]Former Marine and Occupy Oakland protester Scott Olsen suffered a serious head injury at a protest in Oakland on October 25.

I was actually out my front door. On my way here, I spent a week and a half stopping at many of the different Occupy movements in the major cities in the northern U.S. states: Seattle, Portland, Chicago, Denver, Detroit, Cleveland, Grand Rapids, Philadelphia and Pittsburgh.

How would you describe the differences between them?

Well, the different movements have their own little areas and their own tactics. Most of them are concerned about topics and situations that are going on in that area. While each one has it's own personality, this one . . . because it's considered the heartbeat, it's such a huge mess. You're seeing all of them here at the same time! You've got Republicans, Democrats, people who are liberal, conservative. You even have the anarchists and the communists, but they're their own thing. [Laughs.] And of course, other people stop by. This is the heartbeat. You're going to see everything out here. But overall, the whole purpose is to spread awareness of the social and economic injustices out there. We're all bound under that unifying goal, more or less.

I asked you about where you sleep because this area seems to be the good-vibe area.

Well, it's the Empathy table and Nonviolent Communication, so a lot of us who work here, yeah, we're already good at talking to each other, and it is a pretty good-vibe area. We try to keep happy and, you know, keep each other entertained, because if you don't have an outlet for stress, you're just going to go nuts.

Especially because you've taken on a certain amount of responsibility for the collective good vibes.

Oh, yeah. Definitely.

So what kinds of things are you mediating?

Personal issues, general concerns. You know, just people who are having a bad day and want to talk. I know Claire, who sleeps here—she's actually a schoolteacher who occupies here—she was talking to someone the other day, and yesterday he actually came up to her to say that he'd started reconnecting with his parents and talking to them, after not talking to them for, like, three years!

My God!

And now they're back together again.

That's one hell of a mediation!

It's stuff like that: from being severed away from your family, to just being a little upset about a problem and wanting to vent. Whenever somebody wants to vent, I usually take it because I don't get mad when people yell. Yeah, it's a whole lot of different things. People who, we think, need more support and help than others, we'll send them to Outreach. Or we have a couple of the Protest Chaplains who like to sleep here at night. They're really close to us.

Religious folks?

Yeah, who'll talk to them about religious matters. We also have people with a mental health background who help out with the support group over at the Medical tent, if we need to refer people to them sometimes. So that's pretty much what goes on around here.

Some people are talking about going on strike against those who aren't pulling their weight. So far, the mediators have been like, "Fuck that! That's horrible!" Are you with the—?

No. I'm not with that at all. Just like you said, we shouldn't be turning against each other. We should be building a stronger community. No, I'm against ostracizing anybody, except for the ones who are being violent, of course, and definitely detrimental to the overall cause.

So what do you think needs to happen to improve that dynamic?

That's definitely, definitely difficult to answer. You take into account such a huge, diverse group that we have here, and of course, a lot of people without means or support tend to flock to here because of what we can provide. We're here for them, too, and we should definitely be supporting them, not turning them away. The problems you see here—it's kind of to the point where it's become a microcosm of the issues we're trying to address in the outside world. So we definitely should not be shunning the people who may have a bad lifestyle or don't help out, unless they're being violent or aggressive towards other people, you know what I mean?

So far, have you seen any problems that you couldn't talk through, or is it, mostly, you get somewhere?

For the most part, we do our best to get somewhere, but every once in a while, you'll come across somebody who's actually got a severe mental issue, or people are intentionally out here trying to instigate altercations between other people. We usually try to calm down the other people and get them away from the instigators. There are situations we can't handle, but we do our best to when we can. For the most part, we're more conflict de-escalation and prevention, not stopping. There are other people for that. Like, if somebody's out here fighting people, me personally, I'm going to get a cop to come in here. I support law. We try to handle situations to the best we can, but when we can't, we refer them to people who know what they're doing.

I was up this morning when the fire marshals were coming through. It was actually pretty funny because there were some people going around, "We're getting raided! We're getting raided!" It wasn't a raid; it was a safety patrol. But I'm a volunteer fire marshal back home, and I can understand their concerns with the generators. They weren't exactly set up according to fire safety regulations, and we didn't have an emergency spill cleanup thing set up. There's a lot of flammable materials near them, so what they did . . . I was speaking to one of the chief fire marshals—I can't remember his name; you know, it's hundreds of faces—but they confiscated them, then got names of people who could go and get them back once we provide a safe, designated area for the generators that sticks to fire safety regulations.

How would you do that in this situation?

I don't know the fire safety regs for New York City. I only know back home, but I'm very sure it's possible. Get a container for the generators. Get a bag of sawdust—even kitty litter—to dry-sweep any spills. Keep them away from any nylon fabric or any other flammable materials. Those are basics. It's just designating a safe area that sticks to fire safety regs. Once we can have that set up and have one of the Fire Department fire marshals check it out, we can get our generators back. Of course, again, you come into that issue where it's lack of communication, or people who are actually so against the Man, if you will, who don't really want to work with that, but it is possible for us to get our generators back. We just need to work towards that.

Well, that's good, because you're going to need them for winter.

Oh, yeah, definitely. ❖

Michael

Could you tell me a little bit about what your job is, besides just holding it all together?

Mom, dad, doctor . . . director, sometimes. I wear lots of hats. I'm in Comfort wearing lots of hats . . . and coats and shoes and bags. And I'm having fun. I'm absolutely having fun wearing all those hats.

Tell me about your day. What are you actually up to?

Well, I get up when everybody else gets up, which is, like, seven o'clock in the morning.

[Michael takes a donation of clothing.]

See, there's one perfect example, you know? You're given these dona-tions, and you just, like . . . you put it on, and you don't know. [Dons a hat.] Sometimes it makes you work fast . . .

Oh, I love it! That looks really good.

And then sometimes it just makes you work very slow.

[Laughs.]

Let me look at the label . . . three ninety-nine . . . oh, from the Salvation Army! I've stolen things from them!

◆

You get to use all your skills. I said something earlier today—I was talking to myself . . . talking to God, really—going over to Trinity to use the restroom, and really to smoke a little pot, which I do regularly.

Okay, sure. You don't mind that going in?

No, I don't care. Please, please put this in! Put this in the book, put this in the media, put this everywhere! Listen, it's kept me sane. It's helped me deal with my shit because it forces me to face my fears head-on. I could lie to you or I could tell you the truth, and it makes me answer that question within sixty seconds. I have to, I have to, I have to. If I don't, I feel like I'll die! That's what guilt does. It's Jewish. It's crazy.

I hear that.

Anyway, I was saying to myself, "You see, this is how you learn." See, the kids that are graduating today—getting M.B.A.'s and doctorates and all that—even they can't find a job. This is where you learn. You get to use every single skill you've ever learned in your life, from every person in your life—good, bad, and indifferent—in this place. Honestly!

In the place at large, not just the Comfort station.

In the place at large.

So you wake up when everybody wakes up . . .

I wake up when everybody wakes up. I try to start my day by cleaning because that centers me. That puts me where stuff is supposed to get done, you know what I mean? Just . . . it's basic. Everybody cleans up their own stuff—mentally, spiritually, emotionally, economically. Clean up your own junk, okay? So I like to do that. I go around spot-sweeping. I like to do that. I listen when the media comes up. I like to listen, and see what the kids are saying.

What are they saying?

Well, they can say whatever they want to, but they've got to be intelligent. They've got to be articulate. And when I say intelligent, I mean: Know what's going on in the park. Don't be talking about stuff like, "That's what happened at the baseball game." Say what's happening in the park. You can say whatever you want, but it has to pertain to the park, and this occupation, and what's going on.

Secondly, that they're articulate. Pronounce your T's and your duhs and your plosives and all that. That's important. I mean, listen: You should have learned those things in grammar school. Unfortunately, you didn't, but there are people out here who you can learn from. Open up your mind, you know? And that's it.

Somebody taught me that, a long time ago. But he had AIDS, and I wouldn't listen to him because he had AIDS. He was gay, like me. He was artistic, like me. He was fantastic, like me. But because he told me that he had A-I-D-S—not H-I-V, but A-I-D-S—and he was D-Y-I-N-G-ing, that scared the hell out of me.

But you know what? I fucked him. I mean, I took him for everything. His heart, his soul, his kindness, his grace, everything.

So this is the kind of guilt you're talking about working through.

This is the kind of guilt I'm talking about. When I say, "I'm channeling my ex-husband right now," he's sending me messages, and he's telling me, "Listen, don't get cunty just because I left you a little bit of money." That's my therapy. That's what happens when I sweep and smoke and sweep and smoke and sweep and smoke, yeah.

Well, that seems like a good way to address that. You've got to find a way. Guilt is really hard to deal with.

Guilt and grief. I was talking to one of the kids earlier today. I was saying, "Have you ever seen those Muslim women when somebody dies? How they grieve!" They roll around in the sand and they slap themselves. We don't do that. I mean, what did the mayor say after these towers fell? He said, "Go shopping." We never took that time to grieve. We never took that time to grieve, because when you grieve, you learn about yourself. You learn what's going on inside, and why these things would happen. Not just slap a label on it and say, "Muslim. That's why it happened." No! So much more, so much more was behind that, as with everything in life. Peeling back those layers, you know what I mean? "We're Americans! We're Americans!" is what he said. No, no, he didn't say that. He said, "We're New Yorkers." He said, "We're New Yorkers. Go to Broadway. Go see a show."

Well, there hasn't been a good show on Broadway since fucking 1970! Since *Company!*[2] And for a hundred dollars . . . ! I know I'm getting off-topic, but—actually, no! This is not off-topic! A hundred dollars to see a shitty show! Honestly! It's all homogenized. There's no original scripts. ❖

---

[2]*Company*, by George Furth and Stephen Sondheim, directed by Harold Prince, Alvin Theatre, April 26, 1970.

October 30

Sean

How was yesterday for you guys in the library?

Wet and cold.

Were you able to keep everything pretty much dry?

I'm not sure yet. I'm still opening up boxes. I'm finding lots of wet books, so I think we're going to lose a lot.

The Tupperware's not working that well?

Most of them do. Some of them are of superior quality, and some of them are not. We're going to find out.

Is that something you guys would need, better Tupperware?

I think that we're actually concentrating more on the solid infrastructure. It's going to be a canopied tent—it's ordered and on the way—so that we can remain open during the winter. If we use this Tupperware open-air system that we've been using, we'll have to shut down. That's not very conducive to what we're all about. We need to protect the library from the elements, and we need to continue to be open.

Are these all donations?

Yes. They're all donations from individuals, publishers and celebrities.

What kinds of things have you gotten?

Anything that you would normally find in a library. It's the People's Library. It's for the people. We don't discriminate books. I'm a book snob myself, but we take everything.

What does that mean? You like what you like?

I like the good stuff.

Me too.

We have a plethora of fiction because people donate a lot of fiction, but it's not necessarily being taken. This is a political space. People are looking for things on politics, economics, social struggle, labor, things like that. We have a lot of fiction, so we kind of recommend that if you are going to donate books: please, no fiction.

No fiction.

Bring it down. We'll have a look. We can't refuse anything, but . . .

What are the books that are really flying out of here?

Well, you know, we have a small reference section, and we mark it "Do Not Remove." We have a little seating area where we want to keep certain types of books in-house, the ones that would be flying out of here if we didn't mark them "Do Not Remove." People are taking them anyway, so lots of Chomsky, lots of David Graeber. Slavoj Žižek, of course. Chris Hedges, Naomi Wolf, Naomi Klein. You know, Karl Marx.

In your outside life, are you also a librarian?

I'm not, no. I'm a writer and a traveler and a man of the road, I guess, and I'm fortunate that I'm very comfortable living outside and with the elements, and that I'm a very able-bodied person to occupy. And I just love libraries and I love books so much, so I help out here. We do have several actual librarians on staff here, though, with master's degrees in library science and whatnot.

What's your system of withdrawal? Are you just . . . they go out and they don't come back?

Complete honor system. It's up to you. Like, we encourage you to bring the books back. I mean, it's all about sharing and having an abundance of literature that's available for free. And so if you feel like you should bring this book back so someone else can read it, awesome. If you feel like you should give it to your friend, great. If you feel it has to remain on your shelf for the rest of your life, okay. That's kind of the policy.

What drew you down here?

Well, I was kind of off the grid for a while, and when I opened up the Internet again, I saw that the occupation had happened and that things were taking place. I wanted to come to New York anyway, but I thought that it was just a beautiful thing, with such momentum and magnetism. I thought that, finally, it was time to get involved, and so I came down here to occupy. I saw that the library existed, and just sort of made myself at home.

Do you sleep in the library? Is that your spot?

I just took my tent down.

What's your winter plan?

You know, there's no such thing as bad weather, just bad clothing. That's a Swedish saying, I believe. I'm fortunate. I'm an able-bodied person who knows how to take care of myself. It's about layers. It's about goose-down sleeping bags. It's about having the proper equipment to maintain your space. There's lots of people who don't know how to do that, so we try to help them. But it's really just a matter of dressing for the weather.

I'm from Canada. An average wintertime temperature of minus four degrees Celsius doesn't really trouble me. I'm used to minus twenty-five degrees Celsius. I'm from Winnipeg. It's, like, the coldest place in the world. It's not really an issue for me.

Xìnbù: Hànwèi rénlèi hépíng zìyóu mínzhǔ!

Sean: Peace, and a few other things.

Do you speak Chinese?

I speak Chinese, yeah.

You've spent time in China?

I've spent a lot of time in Taiwan, studying Chinese poetry, writing. Autodidactic pursuits in culture and language and things like that.

So you're a man of the world. New York is not too—

New York is amazing. It's great. I wish I had time to go and see it, but I'm too busy. But you know, soon. I need to take a break soon.

How long have you been here?

Two weeks.

You've been outside the whole time?

I have, yeah.

You should take a break.

I actually am. I'm going to go home and see my family. My sister's having another baby, so I'm going to go play uncle.

That's fun.

Yeah, it's good. And then I'm going to come back with all my winter gear extraordinaire.

Any specific books you'd like to see people bring down?

More David Graeber; people steal them. I haven't had a chance to read it. I say steal . . . that's an incorrect word to use, but I'm like, "Please do not remove them from the library!" It's a hot commodity.

What are the titles?

Debt.[1] We need everything. We need more Zinn, things like that. We need everything. I can't specifically say because it's a library. We accept all books.

I was thinking about what to bring. I have an absolute surfeit of books, but it's mostly fiction.

That's my baby. I love fiction, but I'm trying to educate myself here.

Do you like old writers or new?

Oh, old. You want to be a writer? Then you have to read the best stuff. You should never read a bad book.

So who do you like?

The Russians. I like Tolstoy.

Tolstoy more than Dostoevsky?

No.

I like Dostoevsky more than Tolstoy.

---

[1]David Graeber, *Debt: The First 5,000 Years* (Brooklyn: Melville House, 2011).

Yeah, I started to like Dostoevsky more when I read Coetzee's *Master of Petersburg.*[2] That was just brilliant. I love that. And I like Tolstoy because of how he revamped Christianity for cool people, which was interesting and a brilliant move.

I love American literature. I love John Steinbeck. The Beats got me into poetry and reading. Before I was here, I was in Lowell for the Jack Kerouac festival. So I was doing readings with David Amram and Steve Dalachinsky—great New York jazz poet—and rubbing elbows with all these guys who are the last living Beats, and I was like, "Wow!" Yeah, it was beautiful stuff.

I just read this Allen Ginsberg biography—what the fuck was it called? It's a quote from Walt Whitman.[3]

We have an Allen Ginsberg section here. The Allen Ginsberg Society came down here and gave us a big donation, so I made an Allen Ginsberg section, because he would have . . .

He would have loved this.

He would have been here.

Yeah. He would have just been here.

Anne Waldman was here last week. She submitted to our Poetry Anthology, and she dedicated her poem to Allen Ginsberg. He would so be here. His spirit is here, without question. ❖

Josh I

Do you want to tell me a little bit about how yesterday went?

Yesterday? Well, it was snowing. It was cold and wet. I stayed in my tent most of the day. That's pretty much what I did yesterday.

Were you able to keep dry?

---

[2]J. M. Coetzee, *The Master of Petersburg* (London: Secker & Warburg, 1994).

[3]Bill Morgan, *I Celebrate Myself: The Somewhat Private Life of Allen Ginsberg* (New York: Viking, 2006).

To a certain point, yes. My sleeping bag got wet. A lot of other stuff got wet. I stayed pretty warm; it wasn't too bad. Everybody just kind of stayed in their tents.

That's what it looked like on the feed. We saw somebody coming by with bananas and fruit.

Yeah, there was people giving out hand warmers.

Do you want to tell me a little bit about yourself and what led you to come down here?

Yeah, well, I'm from Arkansas, and I had a job working at a company called Whirlpool. I worked there for five years, and then they laid off almost a thousand people. They outsourced our jobs to Mexico for cheaper wages. So I guess I came up here to try to change that. Bring our jobs back to America.

How long have you been here?

I've only been here about a week.

How are you finding the experience?

The people are nice. It's kind of, you know . . . it's a love community, I guess you could say. Some people have their own agenda and they don't want to help out the community, which is fine. But mostly, everybody is caring. They'll help you out if you ask them for something.

Are you connected with a working group here?

Not really. I just kind of help out wherever I'm needed. I volunteer when people do the mic checks and stuff. If they need somebody to clean up, I'll do that.

What's your game plan for the winter?

I'm here for about a month. After that, I plan on occupying another place.

Where are you thinking of going?

Probably south somewhere.

Somewhere warmer.

Yeah. ❖

Adam

You guys got here the same night?

That is correct.

But not from the same place.

No, he came from Arkansas, and I flew up here from San Antonio. We got here Saturday evening. We were checking out the place, and we just happened to sleep in the same area. Back then they didn't really have a lot of tents up yet. We were just sleeping next to each other in a pile of people, shoulder-to-shoulder, pretty much.

As it progressed and more tents moved in, we had our little tarp area set up. We constantly had to take it down. It was either for cleaning, or other tents were moving in, or it was raining and it didn't really work out right. So now we finally got a tent.

How's that going? The tent works pretty well for you?

Pretty well. It's just getting a little damp because of that hurricane-like storm last night, but overall, it's a lot nicer than a tarp.

What was the thing that drew you here?

I saw a lot of angry people—angry at the same things I've been thinking about this whole time. I was in college before this happened. We were hearing about, oh, corruption in the ballot machines, and the way people value the dollar over humanity, over helping each other out. So that's what drew me here.

They're not judgmental. They take in homeless. People from *America's Most Wanted* apparently also sleep here, and there's regular people, so . . . it's a unique atmosphere that I haven't been in before, so that's one of the things that attracted me. Also, the message of "corporate money out of Washington." That I agree with.

Can you tell me about your experience of the occupation itself.

Let's talk about the structure of the organization: There's not really a structure. As far as it's organized, it's just a bunch of different working groups. We have the drum circle, Pulse; Security or Community Watch; the kitchen; Media; and—what's that?—Sanitation department;

and they all form consensus within their groups. I guess they have a delegate or something, who comes in and presents what they need, or what they want to have happen.

As far as cleaning goes, it's a little bit disorganized. Yesterday or the day before, everyone was trying to clean up their tents or clean up around their area after the rain, but they weren't exactly sure how to do it. I guess some guy came up and announced, "Hey, we're going to clean up! Take everyone's tents down! Wipe up around them! We're going to have hoses come and spray the place down!"

This was before the storm?

Yeah, before the storm, the night after that rain. They wanted to bag up everyone's wet stuff, like, and don't even care whose it is. Just bag it up if it's wet, put it down at the laundromat pick-up area. Just have it washed. And stuff usually gets lost there, so a lot of people wouldn't want to do that.

How are they doing the laundry?

I just know that every Friday, they have a truck come that picks up all these clothes—we bag them there at the front of the steps—and they take it off to some mysterious laundromat that no one seems to know where it is or what the name of it is.

Are they paying for it, or is someone donating that?

I'm not sure.

Have you joined any committees?

I tried to join Security, but they didn't get back to me. I'm thinking about trying to talk to some of these organizers—some of the main people who have been around for a while, kind of know how things work—and see if we can't get some more fluidity in the camp. You know, better communication, because it seems like messages that go out here about cleanup don't always reach down to the lower end of the camp. People get antsy when you take their stuff down and they don't know what you're doing. They get antsy about taking their tarps down that they took so long to set up, or about bagging up their stuff.

Me and Josh feel their pain because that's what they were doing the first couple of days. We had our tarp set up all nice. They wanted us to take it down and put our tarps back in a pile. So people had their perfect setup and had to take it down, and then some random person just took their tarp from the pile. You've got to start over from scratch, pretty much.

Our idea was to go around and ask people if they wanted help cleaning up. We weren't going to bag up their personal items unless they wanted us to; we just let them do it themselves. But if they had better warning beforehand instead of right then and there, people might have agreed with it more.

[Olivia offers Adam a cigarette.]

What is it?

It's Merit Ultra Light—the especially long ones, the one hundreds. It's the same price, but it's more cigarette.

How much is it?

It's, like, over ten dollars here.

That's ridiculous.

I know, it's insane. They're taxing, like, eight bucks on it, something like that.

Where do those taxes go? Not to the people.

Not to the people. I don't know, that's a good question.

◆

What has been your best experience so far?

The best experience is when people come down here who don't stay overnight, and they say, "Here, take this! We really believe in what you're doing! Keep it up, guys! This is the right way to go! We agree with you! We're here for you!" Having the support of the people is the best part. There's times when you can lose faith in it, and just be like, "Is this really going anywhere?" We don't have Internet or anything; we can't really tell what's going on outside this camp. So to have people come down here and give their support really means a lot.

Would you say it's all different types of people, or is there a specific group who's coming down?

It's very mixed. People come down who have jobs, a family to look after. If they weren't tied down, they'd probably be here with us, but they have the family, have the job, and just come to donate supplies, whatever they can find for us.

The people staying overnight here are of all different kinds. They don't have anything to tie them down, so they're here.

Did you drop out of college to come here?

I did not drop out of college. I withdrew from the classes, but I'm still enrolled there for three semesters, not including this one. Depending on what goes on here, I could just go back to school in about a year and everything would be the same. I don't have to re-apply or anything.

But I withdrew from my classes to come here. I was in the middle of college, but then I saw Occupy Wall Street going on. I always had this feeling of: I could be doing something more than this.

Do you have anything that you want to add to the record, or anything specific you want to say?

I think if this group is going to work, everybody's got to be behind it, because it's not just the system that we've got to change, it's people's minds and what they value. It's not going to be a paper, at the end of the day, that's going to keep you warm and safe. It's going to be people that you can rely on. That's my own take.

What do you think is the way to change people's minds?

If Occupy Wall Street keeps going on—and the other Occupys around the country and the world—then people will start to get the message that we're here to stay. People will start to realize that they need to change—that something's really wrong here. I don't think there's an exact way to do it. Just got to see what happens.

You're in it for the long haul here?

I wish. I've got to go back to Texas to take care of the animals.

What kind of animals?

I've got two dogs and a cat. My mom is going to go off to D.C. to visit family, so I'm going to go back to take care of the animals.

What does she think of this?

She loves it. She didn't love the fact of me coming down here. She said, "I don't know if I should be more worried or supportive of what you're doing," but Occupy Wall Street she supports.

Now that I'm here, she's happy about it, but she's just like, "You call me almost every day. Tell me what happens, so I can make sure you're safe," like, after the storm and everything. "Okay, mom." Yeah, she's a big activist. My dad's not so much.

Is he in favor of the movement?

Not really. He's one of the guys. He makes a six-figure income, and he didn't really think Occupy Wall Street had any momentum to it. ❖

Daniel

Tell me about the jobs you're doing.

All right. I am working for Community Relations, trying to continue the relationship we have with the outside community. Putting out fires, basically. I'm a firefighter. I go from group to group and look at the bigger picture about what the hell this occupation is doing and what brick walls we're going to run up against. See them off in the future, and try to stave them off—stave this car off from hitting that wall in the future by doing things now. That's what I do.

What are some of the fires?

Security, hygiene, community relations, and public safety. Those are all huge issues. There's so many people here. A few of them are putting in ridiculous amounts of energy, but there's a lot of people here that aren't doing a lot.

The few people that are thinking about this stuff are run off their feet. All they can do is look at what they're doing right now, at this moment, and there's no planning. I shouldn't say "no." There's very little planning. No one has the time for it because we're so busy. So I'm trying to be the hover-guy that overlooks the entire thing, and then says, "What do we need to do?" Start alerting people: "If we don't do this, here's what's going to happen!" That's my job. ❖

Paul I

This movement, O.W.S., is evolving. What many wished to portray as a radical kids' movement—that was a far stretch, and certainly not the truth that is evolving. What the mayor, the people in the city, the people in the nation, and our own president are seeing is a broad tapestry of faces, ideas and ideologies—the true essence of what this country is and was founded on.

All that we could ever hope for is to make a valid contribution to the existing structure of the nation and the world. The world structure is changing, but we have the ability, based on our constitutional rights, to peacefully assemble, to come up with ideas and grievances, and to present them. And I'm sure, at the appropriate time, that will be done.

For now, all we can do is remind people that we are gathering here for a reason. We have people in the unions—international, national and local unions—who have completely thrown their hats into the ring here. They have their reasons to be here. We did not invite them, initially. They started filtering in on their own. And then we said, "If your heart's in it, please come out in full support of Occupy Wall Street." That's ten to twenty million families, with their children. That's a lot of people. They are the electorate.

We had a family night: a hundred fifty families with their children. That is the face of this movement. So the mainstream media or any politician who wants to go up and paint negative pictures of these kinds of happenings and events is not taking an honest look at what is actually happening here. If they do take an honest look, and they're being honest with themselves, as individuals or corporations, then they will certainly come to terms with it and be supportive.

The intent of this movement is simply to help—to assist in steering the ship of state back onto its appointed course, which is our obligation based on the Declaration of Independence. We were instructed by the founders to be here should the government fail to govern to the common benefit of all of us. So we are simply fulfilling a promise, okay? And that is why we're here.

When they founded the country, they didn't have any clear set of principles. The concepts and the ideas that eventually founded the nation were scrutinized and debated, back and forth, and there were open, heavy dialogues about: What's right? What's wrong? Should we limit freedom? Should we have no limitations on freedom? And they came up with a constitution. They came up with our founding documents, in essence. It took them years to do that.

So all we're trying to do here is pool our ideas, gather our thoughts, with probably one of the greatest reasons that one could ever gather for, and that's to ask the people that wish to be tyrants to pull back. If they refuse to do that, then compel them to pull back. Allow the system to function. Allow Congress to once again represent the people who elected them there. And perhaps one of the real reasons they have not come into this park is because the mainstream of this nation is very vocally, vociferously saying, "This is our obligation! We are your electorate! Don't go up against us or we will vote you out!"

So coming into the winter—and it will be a difficult winter, coming into the election of 2012—our hope and our dream is to make a valid contribution. No matter what Fox News or Murdoch or any twisted logic tries to say—no matter what they try to do—I believe wholeheartedly that the voice of the American people is far stronger than theirs. And I believe that our nonviolent approach—our inclusive approach in trying to speak to them, to communicate to them our good intentions—will take root, and perhaps already has.

All we can do is hope that the people out there who wish to provoke violence—to pick at us, and to challenge these movements in other cities—begin to understand that they're doing harm to this country when they do not allow the people of the country to gather and peacefully assemble. It is our obligation and right to do so. ❖

Joe

This is what they tell me to hand out, so this is what I hand out.

It's not coming out every day now, is it?

Oh, no. This is issue three. Every week and a half, two weeks there's an issue.

**Okay, I must've gotten number two yesterday.
So are you occupying?**

Yeah, I'm an occupier.

How long have you been here?

I've been here four weeks.

Where are you sleeping?

I sleep in a tent up front.

Do you have a specific area you sleep in?

No, no. I move around sometimes. Yeah, sometimes you have to move, you know?

What originally got you involved?

Day three I was here, and I stayed. I lost my apartment and job in one day by Hurricane Irene, and I haven't seen a single cent from Uncle Sam. I had flood insurance and the whole nine yards. I lost eighteen thousand dollars in cash. I lost a lot of stuff. Uncle Sam ain't helping nobody now, man. I didn't think the government was that bad until this happened to me.

I've never asked for a single thing from the government. I've never asked for disability. I've never asked for unemployment. I've never asked for anything whatsoever. Now I need help, and they're not helping. I graduated college, can't even find a fucking job, you know?

What's your field?

Radio and T.V. production. There's nothing. I almost got into Fox News, and then the day I go in for my interview, they start their cutbacks. I was freaking sure about that one . . .

How's your experience of Occupy Wall Street been?

Other than the weather, you know, that's pretty much it.

You had some weather yesterday . . .

Oh, it sucked! Luckily, I stayed dry—my tent stayed dry because I had tarps over it. It's still a little wet. It's damp inside and stuff, but that's what happens when you're outside, you know?

Do you feel like you're ready for the winter?

Well, I live right in Jersey, so I think I'm going to transfer. After this gets a little colder—once it gets, like, snow—I'll probably be in my house, you know? Occupying Jersey City because it's closer to my house.

It was really cool here in the beginning. Now it's . . . different.

What's the difference?

The difference is the people. We're feeding the homeless now, and I can't even get food. I mean, I didn't eat breakfast for, like, four days. I get in the line and it's too long. I'm supposed to be doing my job, and I have other things—personal things—to do, too. This isn't just my whole life, you know. I have other things I have to do, too.

I have two grandparents in the hospital, you know what I mean? So I'm bouncing everything back and forth. My parents are there today, so I'll be there tomorrow. My grandma's in New York City. She got switched from Morristown Memorial in New Jersey, and I'm the only one in New York City; I go there as much as I can. My dad works during the week. I'm usually there Monday, Tuesday, Wednesday, and then my mom takes Thursday and Friday, and my dad does the weekends.

I feel for you. It's really hard when you have family in the hospital.

Yeah, it's ridiculous!

So it's changing a lot here. What was it like in the very beginning?

In the beginning it was peaceful. Everybody was giving. Everybody was helping everybody out. Now it's just, like, New York.

Some people are saying that they would like to strike against the people who aren't working. Are you with that contingent?

I don't think it's at that point yet, but there should be something done. We do have a new security team, so . . .

What's the game plan? More patrols?

I don't know; he's only been here for two days. I guess we'll find out.

Your job is distributing the paper?

I do donations and I help with Comfort. I do the blankets and the sleeping bags at night—to make sure everybody gets one.

Have you had enough blankets to go around?

So far we've had a decent amount. If not, we have emergency. ❖

Garth

I dropped out of society a couple years ago. I didn't feel comfortable being a part of it for a lot of reasons I won't go into. My girlfriend felt the same way; that's how we met. We were just waiting for something like this to happen, and we were surprised it didn't happen sooner. So as soon as we could get here to the head of this thing, Manhattan, we came to this particular spot. We plan on staying as long as they're here.

Since we got here, there's been bad weather twice and we've only been here for a few days now. Every time the bad weather strikes, there's lots of donations coming in, but there's not enough volunteers here that are willing to brave the weather, so we end up with lots of waste. That's really what we need is more people. We have the right amount of donations, but we need help distributing it.

You need people to help in the kitchen?

All over. That's why you see there's a lot of chaos right now, because yesterday was one of those terrible-weather days, and now we're picking up the mess.

How'd it go for you yesterday?

For me, I had a good tent. I had good gear. In the morning, I worked for a while until I got cold, and then I went in my tent for the rest of the day and stayed warm.

You're dry and everything?

Yeah. Condensation, but no soaking wet.

Are you somebody who camps and stuff?

Since we dropped out of society, we just travel with backpacks. We try to write about our experiences of that lifestyle. We try to provoke other people to do that, because that's a form of protest. If you're not buying into the system, then the system can't perpetuate itself.

Do you work primarily in the food tent?

Wherever people are needed the most at any time. No committees.

How's the consensus going?

I don't think there is. Maybe in the wintertime when the bad weather drives out a lot of the chaos. Right now, there are a lot of people just living here. We want to help everybody, but it's really hard to organize. As people move into homeless shelters this winter, that will leave the core group here, and hopefully we can get a consensus.

Where are you from originally?

Illinois. Southern Illinois.

What's the winter like there?

Well, hit or miss. It can get twenty below, or it can never snow. It just depends. Lately it has been pretty chaotic, though, for everybody.

But the Comfort station always has plenty of gear coming in, not just clothing, but tents. A lot of it's brand-new, high-quality gear. It's just a matter of having enough volunteers to keep it organized, because when it falls into chaos, people take off with it in bulk.

Oh, really? Has that been happening a lot?

Watch the piles. If someone walks away, yeah. People drag off a bunch of stuff. Not the people that are Occupy Wall Street, of course, but we're in the middle of Manhattan. Considering everything, I think it's going great. It hasn't fallen apart, and that shows that the core here is strong. They're not going to let the situation destroy it.

Can I give you a card and communicate by email? I'll feel bad if I stay away too long. Yeah, this is a chaotic day, or I'd talk to you longer.

I totally understand. I'm surprised you wanted to talk at all.

Yeah, I was back there but it got too crazy, so I decided to work the perimeter for a while. ❖

Yvette

I'm here for the teachers. Stop laying off our teachers. This is for our children, our grandchildren, and the ones who are going to be coming up in the near future. That's what I'm here for.

I got laid off three years ago when they decided to combine special ed with the regular ed. It was a big mess.

Education is so important, and they don't seem to realize that. The first thing they want to cut is education. Why? That's what built America. You continue to cut it and cut it, and make the students pay so much of a loan that it takes them years to pay back. I don't think that's fair at all, cutting off education. I believe that every child, regardless of special ed or regular ed, should have an equal right to learning.

How did you decide to throw in with the movement?

It was my husband's idea. He just one day talked about, "Let's go to the park." Like everybody else listening to the media, I was like, "Are you out of your mind? Did you hear what they're doing in there?"

The first night, I was scared. I'm not going to lie. Yes, I was scared. But when I woke up the next morning, I saw how many people were here for whatever different agendas they have. I saw that they're fighting for what they believe in. I turned around and looked my husband in the eye, and I told my husband, "I can do this."

I fought the Board of Ed for years. Since they didn't want to hear me face-to-face, maybe they'll hear us now. You cannot continue to cut education. What's going to happen to my four-month-old grandson? Is he going to be able to become what he wants to become?

Whatever the American dream is, what happened to that? What happened to the people that we voted for? The promises that they made to get into office, and then they did a whole one-eighty. I wasn't born with a silver spoon in my mouth, but why can't I get the same thing that everybody else is getting? You're raising the M.T.A. You're raising the health insurance. You're raising student loans. You're raising everything but the pay checks! Instead of raising the pay checks, you're laying people off, and it gets to a point that the ones who are laid off—we can become homeless. That's not fair.

Me, okay, I'm glad I'm here fighting for a cause, but I have nowhere to go. I'm sleeping in the park. It's not cool—it really isn't—but I've got to do what I've got to do for somebody to hear us.

Since your initial feelings of worry, how has the experience been?

I haven't had any problems. I'm very careful who I talk to, and who I'm going to allow into my life. I'm not trying to get into anybody's life. And I'm careful of who sleeps around me and my husband.

Who's around you guys?

We have a couple here who came from Miami. We have a gentleman who . . . I haven't gotten to introduce myself to him, so I don't know where he's from. We have another young man who plays the guitar. I don't know what his agenda is, but it's all the same thing. We all had jobs, and we all either got laid off or fired or quit or whatever, and we're all homeless. In this area here—I don't know about the rest of the park, but in this little area here—we're homeless.

But you feel good about who's around you?

Yeah. As long as they stay in their tent, and whatever problems they have, they deal with it in there.

What are your plans for the winter? Are you planning on staying?

Um, to answer that question as honestly as I could, if they're here and they do whatever they have to do within twenty-four hours, I'd be glad to go someplace else. But if it doesn't happen that way, yeah, I'm going to stick it out to the end.

Do you guys feel like you have the gear? You're going to be comfortable?

Yeah, well, my husband is a wanderer, so . . . [Laughs.]

So he's ready.

Yeah, he's getting prepared for whatever needs to be done, so I have to support him.

How did you find yesterday? Did you get really wet?

I was cold, and being inside, especially in a small tent . . . after a while, it gets frustrating, you know what I'm saying? Like, "Aagh! Got to get out!" I became more or less claustrophobic at three in the morning, and I had to get out.

Was it still snowing then?

No, it had stopped snowing. The wind had died down and whatnot. They were giving us these little heating pads. I took about twenty of them, opened them up, put them together, and threw them in our tent.

And that worked.

Yeah. ❖

October 31

William

My name is William, and I live in Pittsburgh, Pennsylvania. I'm a professor in the English Department there. I have been teaching there for six years, and I have a sabbatical this semester—a research sabbatical—and that's the reason why I was able to come down. So I do have a stable job, and the luxury of having some free time to be here.

It would be impossible to identify one reason why I'm here. All the things that people are talking about—that they're upset about and that they're speaking out against—are things that hit me on some level, directly or indirectly. I have a lot of loans that I'm still paying off. I can't even think about buying a house because I don't have any savings. I've been working now for eight years, have nothing really to show for it because of debt, you know? Credit card debt, student loan debt.

So there's that, but more broadly, the things that I'm deeply and profoundly concerned about are the influence of corporate interests in Washington which is making our democracy, essentially, a sham; the sway of financial investment banks on Wall Street; and the sort of shenanigans of derivatives traders and derivatives investors which led directly to the crisis we had in 2008, and have not been regulated since then. There are no signs on the horizon that there will be more regulation in that area, and that market has, really, the potential to destroy the world that we live in.

So those are the biggest kind of mega issues, and then there are a whole range of local things. There's a lot of fracking for natural gas going on in Pennsylvania, destroying our environment there. Budget cuts to education, widespread throughout the country. That's one particular reason why I like working in the People's Library, because the library, for us, represents the values that we all share of equal access to information, equal access to literacy.

That's part of the reason for making a book, for people who are maybe a little bit outside of the Internet world.

Absolutely. You know, there have been some people who've visited the library and said, "Well, wouldn't it be easier just to have e-books?" But the problem with e-books is: You can't walk into a space and pick up an e-book and walk out with it. You have to have a gadget of some kind. You have to have access to the technology, in spite of what a lot of pundits and cheerleaders of technology insist on—that technology is liberating us all and leveling the playing field. There's a lot of folks living in the park who don't have the resources to purchase that stuff.

On an even more practical level, we here working in the library—we sleep here. We don't have access to the Internet. Actually, when we had our power generators, we had Wi-Fi going. We had some donated laptops, and so we were able to see a little bit of stuff, but for the most part, I haven't been able to do email or stuff like that for a long time. So there's a lot to be said for physical books. Also, I don't know if you know about our Poetry Anthology?

I haven't seen it.

Well, this is it right here. And you know, it's impossible to put this all up online right now. These are printouts of submissions that people have given to our editor, who's another librarian here, Stephen. He accepts everything that's submitted. There are submissions in here from little children, from prominent poets like Adrienne Rich, and everything in between, you know? So this is the Occupy Wall Street Poetry Anthology. We ask that people keep it in the library. Don't walk out with it. But you know, this kind of thing right here has to be held in your hand. You have to be able to browse through it.

We also have a Poetry Assembly every Friday night, here on the steps at nine thirty. Local poets and anyone who wants to participate in that is welcome to come down.

But on that subject of real books, I'm a big fan of real books, and my first book is going to be coming out, actually. It should be out, like, literally today or tomorrow. I've ordered three copies to donate to the library. I haven't actually held it in my hand. I haven't seen it yet, so when it arrives, I'm really excited to be able to put our stamps on it, and to stick it out into the bins here. And that's something that, like, if I got the Kindle edition of it, it wouldn't be nearly as exciting. I mean, I already corrected the proofs—P.D.F.'s—and then there's nothing to hold in your hand. That's what I'm really looking forward to.

That's so exciting! What's the book?

It's called *Troublemakers*,[1] and Rutgers University Press is publishing it. I teach literature, and so it's a critical study of novels about mass-worker movements.

Like *Germinal*?

Uh, not—

English.

Yeah, English. I mean, I studied comparative literature, and I'm a huge Zola fan, and I studied *Germinal* as well, but . . . no, I teach English. I teach twentieth century American literature.

So what are the books?

The books are, basically, not very well-known titles. Many of them were well-known in the time that they were originally published, but they're novels from around 1900 to about 1945. The most well-known novels I talk about are *The Jungle*, by Upton Sinclair; a book by Thomas Bell called *Out of This Furnace*, which is about Western Pennsylvania steel workers—terrific book; I had a little bit to say about *Johnny Got His Gun*, by Dalton Trumbo, the antiwar novel; and Jack London's novel *The Iron Heel*. I'm sorry to say that these are the most well-known titles today, but again, a bunch of the books I write about, like *The Harbor*, by Ernest Poole—he was a bestseller. It came out in 1914 or 1915. *Comrade Yetta*, by Arthur Bullard, another bestseller from 1912–1913.

These were I.W.W.-era novels. I talk about a bunch of books from the thirties—from the Depression. The novels are all about mass-industrial workers—assembly-line workers—like auto workers, people working in mechanized industries like rubber, steel, that kind of stuff. I focus on

---

[1]William Scott, *Troublemakers: Power, Representation, and the Fiction of the Mass Worker* (Piscataway, NJ: Rutgers University Press, 2011).

those types of workers for particular reasons that have to do with the argument. The book's also about how representation works—representation of the working class—and how power works in the working class, and that kind of thing.

The idea that we need to hold books in our hands—you know, getting back to that—is, I think, something that will be ... I don't think we're ever going to make the transition to a book-less kind of society, in spite of what all these people are speculating about.

I sincerely hope not, personally.

I really hope not, either. There's so many people living in the park here who use the library every day. They're coming over and getting books, and then bringing them back and taking out more books. Also, what's really special about the library—you've seen how crazy and chaotic and packed it gets [in the park]—well, the library is one of the few places in this whole square where it's relatively peaceful and quiet, where we actually do still maintain a kind of a clear little space. People can come and read, and just sit down in a chair, and in the middle of all this energy and stimulation, just be able to get out from that in a minor way. I think that's a really important thing.

◆

I didn't realize the librarians sleep in the library.

Not all of us, but about four of us do every night, really to watch the books, to protect them, to make sure that people don't come in and steal them, or that the weather doesn't destroy them.

How long have you been here?

A little bit less than a month. I came here on October the sixth.

What was the first thing that you had heard in the media?

For the first week of it, I was living in a cabin, actually. I was in Europe over the summer, living in a cabin—in August and for much of September—because I was doing research and writing. And I thought I was going to stay in this cabin for the whole fall, so I didn't hear the original calls to come to Wall Street. I wasn't sort of tapped into that.

And then for the first week of the occupation, there was no media coverage, really, at all. After the Union Square police brutality stuff, the pepper spray incidents, and all the people being beat up and arrested, the media finally picked up on it. This was the week before the Brooklyn Bridge arrests. The initial stories I heard were almost uniformly ridiculing the occupation, saying that they didn't have a clear focus, a list of demands, concrete goals, and those kinds of things.

I'll say honestly, I was a little swayed by that. I thought, "Oh, well. Maybe there's something to that. Maybe these are just a bunch of sort of aimless, angry people who don't know really what they're even saying. I'll wait and see," and all that.

I went online, and I looked at the minutes from the General Assembly meetings. I saw some videos of speakers, I read updates of what kinds of activities people were doing, and I learned about how the working groups work. Then I read something by Naomi Wolf, who said that this amorphous, organic kind of mass movement was challenging the power of corporate capitalism, and even if it doesn't have goals, you still ought to support it. That completely sold me.

So I realized, "I've got to go down there immediately and check it out." I got a bus ticket for the next day. I left Pittsburgh on the sixth and got down here, and within five minutes of being in the park, I understood why there was not a clear list of demands or a limited agenda of concrete and realizable goals. This is way too big for that kind of stuff. There's too much frustration and anger at the way our government works, at the wars in Iraq and Afghanistan, and the list goes on, you know? You could not reduce that to a clear set of goals.

Were you an activist before Occupy Wall Street?

At school, I was involved in a Student Labor Action Coalition. We did consciousness-raising things about sweatshop-produced college gear. We also did a major campaign that was drawn out for several years.

I went to Johns Hopkins University, and we wanted the administration to pay their workers a living wage. This is back in the nineties; I don't know if you're aware of the living wage campaigns. Years of talking—being stalled and not making any progress—culminated in an occupation of our administration building. We locked ourselves in, and we lived there for three weeks. That was about ten, eleven years ago, and that was a very important, life-changing event for me, personally.

I had done activist stuff since I was thirteen. I had gone to the Mall in Washington, D.C., for the antiwar rallies and all that kind of stuff where you used to spray-paint body silhouettes on the sidewalk. I've been doing stuff like that all my life, but I had never done anything like occupying a space before. The way that that draws attention to a movement or to an issue is extraordinary. I mean, much more powerful than walking around with picket signs, or just convening on a field somewhere. My research—my book—is actually about the particular kind of power that occupations have, as opposed to, like, walkouts or strikes or picket kind of things.

So I've been studying this since that occupation in graduate school. I've been working in that area for a while now, and have become thoroughly convinced that occupation in general is the way to go to get your message heard. So when this finally broke out . . .

And then on October fifteenth, it really blossomed and turned into this worldwide movement. To see all these things going on around the country confirms for me that people have finally sort of realized, "Oh, yeah! This is the way to do it!"

Who knows where it's going? Part of what makes it exciting is that it doesn't have a clear trajectory or a predictable path, but it has the momentum. It has the popular support, genuinely popular. I've never seen this kind of assortment of people in one place, all saying the same thing. That is so inspiring to see that it kind of leaves me speechless.

I mean, you have college students, college dropouts, homeless people. You have unemployed. You have grandmothers. You have people who look like every part of America here, and they're all on the same page, all singing versions of the same song. And organized labor working with protesters like this—a first in American history.

What do you think was the turning point for them?

They've been supporting it from the beginning, and they've been coming on marches. The day before I arrived here, on October fifth, there was a gigantic march to Foley Square with labor unions, and leaders of different unions gave speeches at that. We have a table—this table here with the flags and the hard hats set up—where we usually have representatives from unions talking to people. So their presence has kind of ebbed and flowed, but they have donated a lot of materials, space, and resources to us, and have supported us across the board.

This is a tremendously significant coalition. As far as I am aware, this has never occurred in American history. The analogy is Paris in May of 1968, where a very powerful coalition was created between labor unions and the student movement. If you look at the sixties in this country, though, the antiwar movement that was spearheaded by students had very little support from organized labor. They were actually at odds with each other.

And so to see this kind of coalition is incredibly exciting. It means that we might actually have another labor movement in this country, which has been, you know, killed, right? We may actually see unions gain strength again. They have been decimated, and now public-sector unions . . . I didn't even mention Wisconsin, as far as my reasons for being down here. When that happened, I just was . . . you know, I cried for weeks after they were kicked out of the Capitol. I thought that that was actually going to be the spark of the Occupy movement.

Fukushima happened. Japan. Unfortunately, I think, people forgot about Wisconsin pretty quickly, but . . .

Sort of a slow burn?

Yeah.

I was a teacher, so I used to be a member of the U.F.T. For a certain huge group of people, that lends it validity. They won't sign on if it's too inchoate.

U.F.T. has donated a lot of space and resources to us. Were you aware that we did an Occupy the Department of Education Board Meeting? Walcott—what's his name?—He was giving their weekly, open-to-the-public, sort of . . .

Bullshit session?

Yeah, policy. A whole group of Occupy Wall Street people—families with kids—did a People's Microphone series of speeches. They could not have their meeting. The D.O.E. could not continue to meet because it was just too loud and cacophonous in the space. But they had a right to be there. It was open to the public. Then they had testimonies from little kids, standing up and talking about how they want to have good teachers and good schools, and they've been getting cuts and cuts and cuts to all their programs.

When was that?

Last week. If you go to the Occupy Wall Street Web site—there's actually two Web sites: There's the General Assembly Web site, and then there's the regular Occupy Wall Street Web site. Go to that. It's Occupy Wall S-T dot org. They list the most recent events. If you keep scrolling down, they'll have videos and stories about prior events going all the way back, you know, how long. And it just happened last week. I saw it on Thursday night, and it had just happened Thursday day, or maybe Wednesday day, so . . .

It's a great video, too. The Media people here who were filming it did a great job editing it and putting it together. They just turned it into, like, a five-minute kind of thing. You can also just probably go to YouTube. The title of the video is "Occupy D.O.E." If you type that in, you might be able to just get it on YouTube. ❖

Betsy

You've already talked to them, so you have the details.

Well, they said that you set it up, you started it.

I showed up today, and I'm just off one interview and on to the next!

I'm sorry.

No, it's fine. It's an important part of being here.

I was here in the second week. Originally, I was aware of it, and I'd been following online from Brooklyn, where I live. I'd been watching the LiveStream of the meetings, but I lost my Internet connection over the weekend. I think it was the twenty-third or twenty-fourth of September that I came down.

When I got here, there was already a stack about this high of a half a dozen books—law books—on a plastic sheet, and someone had made a sign on some cardboard with paint that said "Library," and it was taped up on the wall. And there was a list of needs. It said, "The library needs books, people," you know, "volunteers," all these things.

So either that day or the next day, I went to a G.A., a General Assembly, and I said, "I've noticed there's a library but I haven't noticed anyone taking responsibility for it, and I would be happy to do that. I would like to establish the working group for the library, if everybody's okay with that." And everyone did the up-sparkle, and that's how it got officially established as a working group. The books were here from the beginning, so I don't want to at all claim that I built it, but I did step up to take responsibility.

You are a librarian by trade?

Yes, I have a degree in library science. My last paid job was as an art librarian at the National Art Library in London. I'm a mom and I have a small child, so I've been home with him.

How old?

He's five. He just started kindergarten. He literally had just started kindergarten, and then I heard about this and came down. He'd been in school for a week, and then suddenly, I stopped doing lunch at school and everything, and started coming here instead.

How's he taking it?

He takes it really well. It's his protest as well because I bring him here, and he was the first children's librarian. He put together a bag of some of his books that he didn't need anymore—for little babies—and brought them down, and he set up a little area for kids. He has a sense of ownership about it as well, and he always checks on the flowers. At the beginning, it wasn't as crowded as it is now. He could draw his train tracks of chalk around all the flowers, and make mazes for himself. He was the only kid running around, so it was . . . it really was his thing. Now it's a lot more crowded, but he enjoys it. In the mornings, he's like, "Have a good day at the protest, Mama."

How's the library coming along?

It evolves every day. Everything changes. We've got about twenty people in the working group now, and I think maybe a quarter of us are trained librarians.

It snowed on Saturday.

Yeah. How did the books fare?

I don't know. I think things did fairly well. At this point, everything is pretty much in a plastic box, and we've got all our tarps, and we've done it with the rain enough times. But every time there's bad weather, we lose a lot of stuff. So we do lose things, but it's expected.

Sean: Library mic check, if anyone cares. Jean-Louis Bourgeois, who is the son of some famous sculptor Madame Bourgeois, is donating shelves and bookends.

Oh, that's nice.

Betsy: That's great. When?

Sean: Posthaste, so within the next week. I'm in touch with him. So we don't need to spend money on shelves and bookends. As an *artiste*, I'll probably assume that they'll be rather æsthetically pleasing.

It seems like the library is attracting a lot of the sort of name—

Betsy: It's a destination.

◆

I was talking about how the library is different from the other working groups in that it's a welcoming place. It's an inviting place for people who are walking on the street—people who are not sure what to make of this, and who may not feel comfortable just wandering around the tents. The library is open and engaging. People come in, and they chat with each other and engage with everything that we have here. I feel like it's a nexus for dialogue within the park. I mean, the meetings are that, obviously, but it's more of an intimate connection . . . a center.

It's not just that we're giving out information, although that is part of it. I feel like it's really about people coming together. The whole park is about that, but this is, like, the place where it can happen. People who don't know what we are about and what we are protesting can find answers here for themselves about all the topics. They can find people to talk to here, whereas in other parts, there might not be as much engagement. We're not here to convert anyone to anything or to convince them of anything, but we're open to discussions.

What's your dream for the library, other than getting a good tent?

That's my dream. My dream right now is just to keep my librarians warm and dry. I'm not sleeping out here, but a bunch of folks are, and it's stressful. Part of the challenge right now is to get out of crisis mode.

[A commotion erupts nearby.]

I'm not sure what's happening.

Strange reorganization of the library.

I don't think that's good. They're taking over the library.

◆

The challenge is to get out of crisis mode, and get to a place where we can think about where it's going, because every day is ... Saturday it was snow and rain, and then yesterday it was something else. Today, Bloomberg is supposed to come down here.

Oh, is he really?

That's the rumor. And the other day it was N.Y.P.D. and the firemen coming through and taking all the [generators]. Every day something. So it's hard to get to a place where we can project forward because we're just getting through each day.

I've been hearing that from a lot of people.

That's the big challenge, but I feel like the Spokes Council might help.

What is that?

Structure. The G.A. has gotten to be very unwieldy. The meetings go on for hours and hours. It's hard to get proposals through because people come to the G.A. who don't know what's going on. They'll block a proposal without having the background, and you know, it's just been really hard to reach consensus on anything. So the Spokes Council is an attempt to make things run more smoothly. All the working groups are going to meet in the Spokes Council. It's an operational meeting. The G.A. will be sort of movement-wide issues, and the Spokes Council will be concerns of the park, the operations in the park. I think it works.

When are they starting that?

Starting tomorrow.

So they're going to meet every day for that?

I think it's going to be every other day, but I'm not sure. I didn't make it all the way through the meeting because it was a three-hour meeting.

We try to be in touch with other occupations, and I've heard from Boston and Chicago and San Francisco and Oakland that everybody's got the same challenges in terms of looking forward. I mean, Oakland, [laughs], they're just trying to be there in the space. I've heard that we're actually a little farther along in terms of being able to do planning and strategy, so we'll see what we can get done.

With the winter upon people, I guess that's the other—

It's a challenge, but it's not impossible. You know, I was getting really depressed about the cold weather, and then I talked to a guy who was stationed in the mountains in Afghanistan. He was like, "Are you kidding me? This is New York. There's nothing about this winter that's going to be harder than sleeping under a tent in the mountains in Afghanistan." And I was like, "Okay, I believe you." [Laughs.] And Sean was in the Arctic. He was in the Canadian military, stationed in the Arctic, and he was like, "You know, get some wool socks."

What did he say to me? "There's no such thing as bad weather, only bad clothes."

Yeah, I think that's true. I mean, the will is here. There are a lot of people who mean to stay, so I don't think that the weather is as much of a challenge as people think it is.

I've also heard people say that it's going to help the movement coalesce.

That's been true throughout. Every time there's an obstacle, it redoubles the will to make it happen. Zach was just saying he was sort of off-and-on about being here until he was arrested on the bridge, and then he's been here almost every day since. Anybody who gets arrested, anyone who has any kind of brutality experience, anybody who just hears enough times how it's nothing and you're going to disappear . . .

Do you have any previous activist experience?

Previous activist experience? I was just talking to someone else who asked the same question. My background is that if there hadn't been a civil rights movement, I wouldn't exist. My parents got together because of the civil rights movement. My father's black, my mother's white. So I've been to protests and marches my whole life, but it's not so much a thing that I do; it's just who I am, you know? I'm not an organizer. I'm not an activist in that sense, but people ask me, "What are you? Where are you from?" Well, let's talk about this whole reality that I embody that you don't understand! [Laughs.]

That's difficult to have to come up with.

But that's my activism. I went to marches and I volunteered when I was a kid, but that's not really . . . I don't think that answers the question.

No, it does answer the question: The personal is political.

Do you know what I mean?

Of course!

It's a trope, but it's true.

It's true, it's true.

I'm a lesbian mother of a small child. That's politics. I'm here and I'm a librarian. That's politics. My politics—they're reflected in my actions. I'm not much of a flag-waving, banner-carrying person, but . . . ❖

Russell

[Russell is busy rolling cigarettes for people in his neighborhood.]

What was the question again?

The question is: How's your occupation been going?

As far as how it's been going, it's been pretty smooth sailing, I guess, except for just the weather. But all the people here, specifically in this area, they're all . . . they're all almost like a family, really. I mean, we all help each other out when we need to, and it's been going—
    Yo, Mohammad!

[Russell gives Mohammad a cigarette.]

It's been pretty smooth sailing staying here. Me and him [Phil]—we're kind of like the founders because we've been here longer than a lot of the people. But all these people come in and they're absolutely great people. They're very nice. If they need help, I give it to them.

Did you know Phil from before, or did you guys meet here?

We met here. Everyone I know here, I met here.

How did you guys find each other?

I came here after a week of being homeless, and I was staying over near the flower bed. I was just sleeping there, and then I met this guy named Landon, and he met Phil. Landon was only staying here until he went to his New York farm upstate, but I met Phil through Landon, and we've become good friends.

Are you involved in doing mediation?

I try, when I can. I have work pretty much five days a week, from three thirty to, like, two in the morning, so sometimes I don't get to. When I can, I do some Community Watch and everything. I do sanitation sometimes. I do what I can.

Did you want ice cream and I'm getting in the way of that?

No, no, no. I don't want ice cream. I'm good.

How'd you get involved? What was your path here?

I came to New York to study acting. I came here not knowing a single person, and I only had a hundred bucks, so that first week was ridiculous. I mean, I found a job as a dishwasher. [Laughs.] I only worked for a day, but those guys are ridiculous. They make, like, sixty bucks, and they do everything.

Sixty bucks under the table?

Under the table. After I quit that one, I got a job as a bus boy. My manager told me—because I still didn't have a place to stay—she told me to come here. I had not heard of it. I came at, like, four, and passed out, just slept, because I needed sleep for that while. It's not just a place to stay for me. I mean, I've been thinking about this for a while, but these things never happen in California, or at least not where I live.

Where are you from in California?

Santa Clarita. It's Southern California. It's always warm.

So how are you doing with the cold?

I actually really like it. Yeah, I hate how hot it is [in Southern California]. I just hate the heat.

What has been your best experience here?

I've been here awhile—almost more than a month—so I've experienced a lot, but I think my best experience was when they tried to evict us at seven in the morning. None of us really got any sleep because it was raining and we didn't have any tents, and it was just really tense that whole night. All of a sudden, at four in the morning, people started showing up, showing up. There were thousands of people—over here, everywhere. And then at seven, they came here and they said, "We can't do it," and they left. I was just elated. That was incredible. The show of support from other people to keep us here is just . . . I don't know. That was the best experience that I've had. There were countless many, but . . . I mean, that was really good. ❖

Claire

When I first got down here, I was totally disoriented. I just saw this big crowd of people, and I was like, "What do I do? Do I become the crowd?" So I came here [to this neighborhood] because it said "Tree Empathy," and I was like, "I bet these people are nice." I don't know if you know Stacy, but she started talking to me. Then she just gave me a hug, because she was like, "You look so lost right now!" [Laughs.]

When was that?

Two weeks ago. I stayed here one night, and then I left and kind of freaked out, and then came back.

Freaked out from the experience?

I'm not used to there being so many people, and sleeping out in the open. It's all very . . . I don't know. I'm sort of a private person, so this is very unusual for me.

I'm the same way.

But after that, I rapidly became more comfortable. You know, we had rainy nights, and everybody helped make a shelter and crowded under it. That was nice, even though it actually went wrong that first night. It was kind of a miserable night, actually, but setting up the shelter was fun. I was also sick.

Have you been doing mediation?

Yeah. I try to spend some time staffing the table, which is kind of . . . like, you have to talk to passers-by. The longer you talk to them, the more they open up sometimes. It definitely helps if there's a chair for them to sit in. And sometimes they call for someone from mediation, which . . . have I done that yet? I don't think I've answered a call yet, but I'm ready to!

Have you been doing training?

Yeah. I already consider myself fairly experienced in this area. I was part of an organization at my Quaker school that was run by consensus, and I was the person who, like, ran the consensus.

Like, a Friends school?

Yeah, a Friends school. And then I taught last year.

At a Quaker school, also?

No, at a city school.

Are you from New York?

No, I'm from Philadelphia.

We have a lot of Quaker schools here, too. My mom and my sister both went to Quaker schools.

I feel very lucky to have gone to that school.

What made you originally want to come down here?

I feel like I sort of gave up on activism long ago, maybe high school. We were addressing it issue by issue, but I saw it as a deep systemic problem. It didn't seem worth my time to try to fight for each individual issue when I know that there's just going to be another one tomorrow.

But this . . . I was skeptical at first, but they had already stood the test of time when I got here. People were actually noticing them, and the movement was actually spreading. I was like, "Maybe this is my chance," you know? Maybe we can have democracy back in this country. That's what I would like. ❖

November 1

Josh II

What you do here in Comfort?

What I do kind of shifts every day. That's not enough of a prompt.

Well, how does the Comfort station work?

How does it work? I mean, we hand people things. Internally, it's fairly amorphous. The personnel change a lot.

Actually, there's been this strange evolution. We started a good ten feet that way as our front wall, and then we started moving out this way more and more and more. I am ashamed to say that I pushed for the first step out—I mean, storing stuff in front of this wall—and since then, we've been moving a little bit in front of that. We've just been inching out and reorganizing. I feel that now there's some wasted space back there. We were just having a conversation about this.

You need to move back that way?

That's what I want, but different people want different things. Back there, the space that used to be the center of Comfort is now tents.

So how long have you been occupying?

I started on, like, the second or third of October, but it hasn't been a full month. I took a little bit more than a week off, occupied D.C. a little bit. I went down and saw some friends in Pennsylvania. D.C. is nothing, in my opinion, compared to Wall Street. I love it here.

What's the difference?

It's cultural. And, well, the energy and the population are different. I was only there for four days, but a big difference in the culture is that defusing is an important thing here. You could say metaphorically that this exercise on a larger scale and a smaller scale is a big practice study of defusing and calming and slowing.

Something that I often do when somebody comes up with a great idea that's really . . . I don't think it's a great idea, but they love it. They pursue it loudly and talk about it for a while. I'm often not interested, and so the way that I don't take responsibility for it? I say, "I don't really understand, but I support you in pursuing that."

That works plenty well in New York, and I do that all the time when it comes up. But in D.C., there was this one guy—I said that to him and he was really upset about it, that I wasn't accepting the responsibility from him. He was trying to give me responsibility, and rejecting it was something I shouldn't have done. He was upset about that, and he said I was rude and my parents had raised me wrong or something. He was fairly vocal in that regard, which I thought was pretty silly. I didn't think I did anything all that rude, although maybe there was a little spark at some point that I didn't notice. Whatever, that kind of thing seemed more common there.

I was working in the kitchen over there and there was this one guy who . . . am I talking too fast?

No, not at all.

There was this one guy who . . . when it's difficult to get food out, we invite people in. I always say, "If you want food faster, come back here." But he was, instead, protesting. There were a bunch more crazies in D.C. than there are here. I don't like that term, but if you're going to reduce it in that way, he was protesting, saying, "We want food and we want it now!" It wasn't a pragmatic approach. It was clear that this was a city where Congress took place.

You mean how they can't get along that well?

I mean there's not a whole lot of honesty. Not that people lie; people don't go all the way. They don't allow themselves to be persuaded. They remain distant and sturdy in their flimsy beliefs.

How would you characterize the New York occupation?

It is not that way here. That is all distinguished from New York. I like people, and getting to know people here is different than getting to know them elsewhere. It's a fairly intense lifestyle. Something about it brings out the multiplicity of roles that everyone has to be, has to em-person. People seem a little more human and complicated.

How'd you hear about it?

I was a rambling man. I went to a college last year. It was not the place for me, Juniata College in Pennsylvania. I didn't like it, and I decided I would take a year off, hitchhike across the country looking at colleges, then return to an academic life, which I'm very interested in. Once I got started, I loved it. After a month, Rosh Hashanah fell upon the land. I came down to New York City for family, and my sister was interested in Occupy Wall Street. I dropped by, and having a significantly more free life than her, I stayed.

Your sister didn't come with you?

She had a chance to visit. She's up in North Hampton. She wants to be here, but she's got other obligations there.

What does your family think about your occupying?

My immediate family loves it.

They're politically-minded.

Yeah.

Is there a red diaper story in the family?

Diaper?

Red diaper babies. When you come from socialists, that's what they call it. Has your family been politically active?

Uh . . . politically-minded. They're very proud of my presence here.

Have they been down, other than your sister?

They came down. We were all here together, but they just dropped by. One of these weekends they're going to show up and stay awhile.

Here in Comfort, do people requisition stuff? Or they just show up and they're like, "I need boots," or whatever?

That's actually switching right now. We're switching to a program for, I hope, only the more valuable items and less specific items. We have a storage unit, and when somebody wants something, they say, "Can I have this?" Then we say, "Come back in an hour." We get the stock—a specific list of what we have, what they want—every hour.

Oh, you have storage off-site? If you don't mind me asking, is that because people were walking away with stuff?

I mean, that's one of the reasons. Also, we have way too much stuff to store here. We're switching to that other program because people were walking off-site with stuff, and people who weren't staying here were getting things that—I don't want to say they were getting things that we need, but . . . I want to motivate those who have commitment. An hour of commitment is good. That means they're here for an hour, they're coming back, and they're organized. I don't want to say no to anybody, but there are certain people who I also don't want to say yes to. This is a way where it's okay. We don't have to say either.

What's your dream for Comfort? What direction—

Move that way. [Points.] That's the direction we need to go in. That way, because this path gets so crowded. ❖

Priscilla

Are you sleeping over?

Yes. I go to work on Long Island, and then I come here. It's, like, an hour and a half travel. I come here and I work in Comfort as long as I can. I'm really trying hard not to exhaust myself, because for the first couple weeks, I definitely was. But to me it's a beautiful place. I feel really good and empowered here.

How long have you been here?

I've been here since . . . October first? I think October first is the day of the Brooklyn Bridge thing. I'd gotten arrested, and it empowered me more to come here.

You weren't staying here when you were arrested?

No, no, I was not staying here yet. That's true. I stopped by once or twice. I'm here alone. Not alone—I don't want to say alone because I've met so many people here, but at first I was scared of coming here alone. I didn't know what the situation was. I didn't know what was up with here, but as time progressed . . . you meet so many beautiful people here that are truly looking out for each other.

Do you sleep in the Comfort area?

I don't have my own setup. We give our own things away. Often I don't have a sleeping bag or anything like that. I have some friends; sometimes I stay in their camp. I don't have my own spot. I've even slept in the tents back there. We just put them up.

Is this your first stint in activism?

Yeah, actually, it's my first full-fledged. I'm out, I'm doing things, I'm alone. Yeah, I'm really doing this.

What brought you on board?

Just the whole life of being comfortable with being uncomfortable. You know, people always come here and they're like, "How are you protesting? You're so young. Blah, blah, blah." Yeah, I don't have parents that are paying for my school and my necessities. When rent comes before food, you know that there's a problem. It just took a lot of time for me to figure out how to do something about it. I think that this was just the best opportunity to. So yeah, that's why I'm here.

Are you in school?

No. I can't afford school, and I'm extremely afraid of loans. I don't have the money to pay for it, so I don't want to apply for it.

Is that something you would like to do if you could figure it out financially?

Of course. Yeah, I would love to go to school. I think it's a really great thing, you know what I mean? A lot of people here would love to.

But don't have the resources.

It's difficult for a lot of young people.

Any great moments you've had so far at the occupation?

It's a really great community, and everyone's really truly watching out for each other. It's great when people come here to donate things. They experience it, and they're like, "Wow! This is so much different than trying to figure out what's going on by watching T.V." So for me, the best part is teaching people by showing them what's going on.

Here at Comfort, we do so much. People are very surprised that all of this is working, and that we are able to support people here and beyond. A lot of things here are really astounding to people.

Can you tell me a little bit about the evolution of Comfort?

Comfort is in a constant state of construction. We're constantly trying to minimize, and get things to where they should be going. We do have issues where people come here with bags and stuff them all day long. We're asking people for sizes now. I don't know what Josh told you . . .

Not about sizes.

We're trying to implement a system where people request things that they need. We're going to have necessities here like socks, hats, gloves, things like that to keep warm, but we're really trying to get people to hold more responsibility for the things that they're taking, and be more accountable for them.

When it rains, a lot of people ditch their things. It's sad to see a really large pile under that tarp when it rains. Now that there are tents here the past couple weeks, there's plenty of space for people to, you know, actually take care of their things.

Not just giving things out at random.

Yeah, we know who's taking it. We don't want control of anyone, but it makes our job easier to get the right kind of clothing on people.

That makes a lot of sense.
I like those boots.

[Laughs.] A lot of people donate great things here, things you wouldn't even imagine. Things like, "What is this silk shirt doing here?" or, like, really big name brands or whatever. And all these fur coats. They come in, and I don't know where they go, but I see people wearing them, so, it's good. People are wearing all kinds of things here. It's interesting.

So it's, like, fancy ladies coming with fur coats?

I mean, some people. I guess they just had it sitting there. Yeah, not exactly all fancy ladies . . .

Just people with old furs. Well, I have old furs, so. . . .

Yeah, in the beginning of me coming here, there were a lot of fur coats, and I was like, "What's going on?"

There are a lot of vegans here, I would imagine.

I don't even think this is fur. I'm hoping it's not. [Laughs.] Someone gave it to me personally yesterday, and it's keeping me really warm.

That's a really nice coat.

Yeah. All I had was the jean jacket, so I was just like, "Aagh!"

That's terrible.

It's okay. I layer like crazy to be here.

Do you have winter plans?

We're trying to get more wool things and less cotton so we can actually stay warm. When it rains, the absorption is totally different, so we're working on getting less cotton, more fleece, things like that. I don't know what's going to happen with the tents and things. We're trying to get porta-potties off-site. We're actively working on that.

Comfort specifically is working on that?

Yeah, because it's a Comfort thing. But we need a permit. That was put on the back burner; there's a lot of things going on.

Where would you put them?

We're hoping not to put them on-site. That would be a really terrible thing, if they were. The thing is that we do have sanitation crews. We have sanitation crews going to McDonald's and the areas where we are going to the bathroom, and cleaning up as much as they can. We have a lot of things going on.

It's like supper. As disheveled as it looks sometimes, it's so beautiful. Yeah, I can't describe it. It's something I've been waiting for, this community, and everybody realizing that things are messed up, and that they should stand up as opposed to, like I said, being comfortable with being uncomfortable.

I didn't realize Comfort was responsible for other stuff besides the physical comfort stuff.

Yeah, it's just general comfort. We try to take care of all aspects. There are a lot of parts of us. Right now, we're having a problem with laundry and things like that.

I had heard that they do a big collection on Fridays.

No. They did it a couple days ago, but there's so much. And when it rains and everything gets left out, someone's got to pick it up. That's a huge pile over there, and it was bigger. There's always a really large pile. It's unfortunate, but we don't have a working group for laundry, exactly. It's all volunteer right now . . . it's going to be a great thing in the winter when someone wants to escape from the cold.

To go to the laundromat?

Yeah, I think it'll be great. There weren't that many people this time. Josh went the other day, and it was, like, sixteen hours of doing laundry. They filled a whole truck, and they went to the Bronx or something.

Is there any way to pay for a service?

It's expensive. Comfort doesn't get help from Finance, as far as I know. It's pure donation, and we try to keep it separated so we can make sure that we are making decisions with the community.

Not many people here go to the G.A. I know I definitely don't, and a lot of people don't that are working damn hard here. There are people from the park, I'm sure, but a lot of us don't have the time for it because everyone's trying to do their job. You have to come up with proposals for things and stuff like that.

We've kept separate from that, and I personally think it's better that way. We have more say, as opposed to someone telling us what people need. We know what people need. I mean, it's hard for a group that's not exactly working here to know what people need.

Would you say that they're not exactly working here, the people who are more involved with the G.A.?

Everyone's got their different personal opinion.

What other groups are totally self-contained?

Actually, a lot of groups are. We have a tobacco-rolling station, and we have Nick @ Nite also. Nick @ Nite has been here for a while.

Do they charge? Someone told me they charge, Nick @ Nite.

No, it's pure donation, but I think they started getting some help from Finance, maybe through the G.A.

That's magical.

Yeah, I'm not sure what's going on with that. I was just talking to them briefly the other day.

It's very unclear where the—

Yeah, it's unclear where a lot of people stand here. A lot of people get frustrated with us, you know what I mean? They're like, "Don't you have all this money to do this and that?" Uh, no, we don't. When we get donations, we spend it on things that we need here, like, to keep more organized.

Like the racks.

Anything that we need. I'm going to go buy a bunch of deodorant because I can't find any in storage. There are things that need to be bought with donations.

What kind of things do you need, other than clothes? Toiletries?

We're fine with, you know, wipes. We're fine with things like that. I feel like we're good.

Fine in that you don't need any more, or fine in that you could use some?

I guess we could always use them, but there is a lot in storage at the moment. People are constantly donating simple things like toothbrushes and toothpaste in bulk, so I know that we definitely have lots of that.

Who's donating that stuff?

Oh, a lot of people. People from New Mexico and California came together in a small group to donate all these yoga mats and things. It was so good. There are a lot of congregations coming together. There are so many different groups—it's incredible—that support this, from small non-profit groups to large companies—even C.E.O.'s. They come in here: "Oh, hey, what do you guys need?"

That's a little weird.

Yeah, it's weird.

I guess there are all kinds of companies.

They're small. Not Wall Street companies. Not like J. P. Morgan Chase, no. I'm sure they don't want us here, no. Brookfield's not exactly sponsoring us. I mean, you *could* say that they're sponsoring us. We're here, so they *are* helping us.

By not kicking you out.

Well, not just yet. They tried, but we were like, "Uh-uh-uh, we know your deal." I mean, cleaning a third of the park at a time, whatever the deal was, and then implement all these new rules where we can't do anything but basically stand there without any of our belongings? Yeah, that really works! I don't know if they think we're mentally challenged here, or we're all deranged, whatever . . .

Were you here for that?

Yeah, I was here. I was here when they were rolling by. They came with a bunch of cops—I guess five cops—and they were passing out these flyers that I still have somewhere. It was, like, a two-page thing. The second page was warning of all these new rules, but the first one was all kind, like, "Oh, hey, we really need you to get this place clean, and we need you guys to be sanitary."

A cop was passing by. We do Copwatch, so I took a picture of him with my cell phone camera. He was like, "I'll see you later!" I think they were maybe afraid because there was supposed to be a lot of support coming in at six. Not many people were here, actually.

Really? I'm hearing different things about that.

There were a lot of people here, but there could have been more. It was supposed to be organized that people were coming.

You were a little disappointed.

There weren't that many people here, numbers-wise. It was kind of scary. I mean, there's a constant threat from the police. It's hard because my uncle's a cop. I feel for them. They have the same issues we do. Of course, there are some corrupt cops, but I'm totally not against them. I just want them to do their job and take care of us. They have no right coming in here or anything like that, and they don't.

They don't.

No, because we have our own security. Oh, yeah, and there's this security group—I have the card that they gave me last night when I was walking around—they come here on their own accord, but they don't have anything to do with the actual Security. There are a lot of great people that have come here.

[A crowd of people starts shouting nearby.]

Is that supportive or razzing?

I can't tell by their faces. Maybe it's not supportive. I can't tell. ❖

Christine

Christine sparked a joint as the interview got under way.

You've been working in Comfort for a while, haven't you?

Yes. Since, like, day five or day six. I have an apartment in Brooklyn, so I do what I can to work. I like to work.

So you're coming during the day?

No, it's actually my day off today. I work five days a week.

What field are you in?

Fine art paper retail. [Laughs.]

Are you a paper artist yourself?

I'm actually a painter. I like to paint on wood. I don't have the facilities to make canvases, so I'm trying to get into paper.

Are you sleeping in the park?

Sometimes, yeah. Like, when I'm here late.

How is that working?

It works. I have a weird sleeping schedule. When I was in school—I just graduated—I would sleep in studio all the time, sleep in my chair. So this is no new thing for me.

Let's talk about Comfort. I didn't know you guys had a shower schedule. How are you able to get showers?

Well, we used to have a shower guy who was here during the day, but he got kind of burned out, so he left. Anyway, he used to be in in the morning. People would come by and say, "We need a shower." And then at noon, we would make the calls, and give people the showers. We had a paper list going on.

Wait—you had a shower here?

No. People tried to install showers here, and I was like, "No, no, no." That was my vote, at least. But people in the area come in, and they're like, "You can use my shower. I really want to help. Here's my shower. This is what I can do." So we send occupants there.

What kinds of people are volunteering for that? I mean, who offers up their showers?

What I assume to be normal people! [Laughs.]

[Laughs.] With cameras in the bathroom?

I've only written down the list maybe four times, but there are these two girls from Staten Island that came by, and they're just like, "Hey, we want to be in the shower list. We came in earlier, but we never got the phone call, so we want to remind you that we have a shower in Staten Island." You can take a free ferry over there—thirty minutes, awesome ride—and then just walk to their place. It's a free ride to a free shower, and they were going to feed people also, which is awesome. Creating a sense of community is really integral to this occupation site and the movement, so I feel like they're really helping.

What other services do you have? I know there's laundry—

That's become a separate thing because it was too much for Comfort to handle. We can't hold both laundry and fresh clothes here; it gets kind of confusing. So we make a pile, and the laundry people just, like, take it. They do the laundry, and they bring it back here or to storage.

◆

How did you first get involved in the movement?

I have an anarchist friend who I follow on Facebook. A couple days before September seventeenth, it was just like, "Oh, Occupy Wall Street!" I was like, "Cool. I intuitively agree with this, but I want to go there and learn more about it, see what people have to say." Day one I got lost, so I didn't come. Day two I started coming here all the time.

Back then I would just hang around and make posters, but I wanted to have a place to help people. I tried Comfort, but they didn't need volunteers at the time because it was just, like, open bins on benches and "look under the tarp for whatever you need." People were more honest then, also, as far as strangers go. They really just took what they needed, which was pretty awesome. I mean, anyone who's been here since the beginning can tell you it was different back then.

And then Comfort became bigger. I would always come after work, and so I learned how to make a bed. I'm learning how to camp out for the winter. I'm learning how to survive outside, so I feel like my knowledge is really helpful.

What are some of the things you've learned?

Wool. [Laughs.] I mean, that's obvious, but I didn't know how much of a science wool clothing could be. And I've learned a little bit of physics on how to create the tarps. Like, this [tarp draped over Comfort] is bad because it would flood, so we need a way to get rid of the water. We need to think of where the water will drop.

Let's talk about organization. I heard you guys got a phone?

We do have a phone. I don't really want to talk about that phone because I have disagreements with that. They're giving out phones for working groups that stay here. That's the organization, but each group has their own internal organization, and there are other groups who just try to manage communication between groups.

Priscilla was telling me you guys are kind of autonomous here. Financially you are, at least.

Yeah, and that's become a problem.

Would you want to be more financially tied in?

I would. I understand it's weird to work with a financial committee, but from what I can reason logically, I think that it just makes sense. The money that Occupy Wall Street has gotten is for the occupants, and Comfort works with the occupants. It makes sense to tap into that money. We need to make sure it doesn't go anywhere else.

Autonomy is running away from the problem. This is my opinion. Why are we raising our own money? We should be taking that money because donators voted to support the movement. We need help! Why are we going outside when we can just directly take those votes?

And it's taking control of the money. You know, what if they want to do something crazy and absurd? We're doing what the money was meant to be used for; they can raise their own funds for that stuff. And then it's the right group of people doing that. That money, decisions are made through the Spokes Council or the G.A., so it's a community decision, but us? Our autonomy? I don't think it's really working for us. It's sketchy and uncontrollable. It's a wild animal. I prefer order, but I understand the moral issues.

My perspective is: We understand what money can do. Let's direct it to where it should go. This [clothing] is money. We need to make sure it goes to the right people. If it goes to the wrong people, they take it for themselves. But there are a lot of sincere people who donate things, and I feel like it's our responsibility to make sure it works out.

I work nine hours a day at a really shitty job. It's so shitty, I'm weary from how terrible it is. But I come here and do work, and that's part of my contribution to the movement. You know, other people need to find their place, and if it's giving the blanket to the right person, let's do that, man. Let's make sure each tent is warm, you know? We've got to think about the future. What's going to happen in the winter? "Oh, sorry, all our wool blankets were sold on Canal Street because they didn't feel like buying from China this week," or whatever.

Over by Nonviolent Communication, they've shored up their tents with pallets. They were talking about going around and making sure everybody's tent is good. Maybe you should form a coalition.

There are groups doing that. I would love to be a part of that.

So it's not just rogue people who care? There's actually someone doing that?

[Laughs.] Yeah.

But rogue people who care—that's how Comfort started.

Oh, really? Who started it?

It was a woman named Lizzy from San Francisco. She was like, "I have socks! I have a lot of socks! Come take socks!" And you know, people took socks. Or we just got blankets or carpet from the street, and used that to keep warm. I got bed bugs. [Laughs.]

Or, like, Shon, who started Medical? He was just around. He was a street medic for an organization, and he's political, so he just hung around. And then people came in. Doctors started getting interested, and the right people were doing what it took to organize and create that. It's amazing!

And Paulie, who's on this [shower] list—he's one of the main contacts—he's really one of the important people in Medical. He didn't really do anything. He was just a traveling guy. He just wanted to swing by here, and he ran into his old friends from doing medics in Haiti and Dominican Republic. He just used his skills here, and that's what's come out of it. I don't know everybody's story, but that's really, really, like, forty percent of it, at least. And there are about nine to fifteen people that work there. Yeah, they have applications for people to work there, which is understandable because you don't want chaos.

It's amazing how organic this whole thing is.

◆

Comfort people need to know how to keep people warm, not know how to pass out stuff. This should not be a retail job, you know? We run out of socks. Comfort runs out of socks. We can't keep people warm, so people are like, "Fuck it! I can take care of myself." They get hypothermia. Endless problem. Automatically, we've developed a relationship to the Medical tent.

Because of the sock thing.

Yeah, because of socks. They don't have warm socks because they're wet, or we run out of socks, or nobody teaches them to put plastic over their new socks. Or it's because their shoes are wet Converses. They keep getting wet, so they're just going to get sick. Their body isn't becoming warm; it's not insulating itself. So that's a really interesting relationship between weather, Comfort and what we do, and Medical. It all balances around. When I go to Storage, I make sure I drop off socks to Medical or fresh blankets, so that they can warm people up and give hypothermia patients a new bed.

Are you finding that a lot of people are getting hypothermia?

During the snowstorm there were twenty-four.

Oh, my God! Really?

Yeah. All day, all day.

Did they have to go to the hospital?

I think some of them did. This is what's happening around here. This is why I take really seriously what we do here. I don't know if you saw me yelling at the girl taking six sweaters. I don't care if you work in Media. If you work in Media, you're here all the time. When you're cold, you know, you come here. You don't have to store stuff.

She was hoarding sweaters.

Yeah.

And what did she say when you yelled at her?

I told her just to come back. And then she was speaking in Spanish to somebody, trying to get around what I was saying. "I've been here since the first day!" That's fine, you know? You should know this is communal property. Sometimes we slip and give it to the wrong people, but we've got to do what we can to make sure that everybody's warm. Serious problems can arise, and we have to be ready for it.

Like weather problems?

Weather problems or . . . like, we had so many socks the third or fourth week, we were just like, "You need socks? Here, take two." Then, during the snowstorm, we only had one bag of socks to give out to people.

We had to use those as gloves. We had an open bin of gloves, and we were like, "Yeah, take that." I don't know . . . we're not thinking as far ahead as we should be.

And the moral problem is that on a nice day like this, we get cold people here who don't have a place to stay. Last week, there was a mob that went to S.I.S., the storage facility, and they were like, "We heard you have sleeping bags here!" And it's true, because they are freezing-weather sleeping bags, so we have to store those. The money was allotted by the G.A. for winter, so that the movement can survive.

People have needs, yeah, but I feel like a sense of personal responsibility is lost in desperation. You can go to McDonald's if you have a problem. You don't have to give us a problem when we're just trying to think of the future, think ahead. It sucks! Isn't that, like, a Republican thought? I don't know. [Laughs.] But I just think it's important to keep things in reserve.

Do you have enough sleeping bags for everybody?

Yeah, we do.

So you're going to start rolling that out when it gets colder?

Dead winter? I don't know about that.

But you have a fair amount.

Yeah, and I'm sure some people here are going to buy their own stuff, whatever works for them.

So you're putting together a deep-winter Comfort plan?

People are trying to work on that. That's between a lot of different groups, yeah.

You don't have a specific working group that meets for that?

No, and I don't think there should be. A lot of different groups know what's going on in a lot of different areas. It should be a conversation. It would be Medical; Comfort; Safe Spaces; Sanitation, because they have to pick up the mess; Sustainability, so that they can handle the trash and, you know, keep up the green thing; and I think that's it.

What are they doing with the trash? Do you know?

We put it off to the side. I mean, I do what I can to recycle. I'm trying to get money for bins and metal blankets and all that shit, excuse me.

Is the city picking up garbage from you guys?

Mm-hmm, yeah. And we also have someone pick up cardboard, and they put it off to the side over there. They keep it clean for the media, since it's just on the sidewalk.

Do you have anything else that you'd like to add for the record?

I don't know . . . I really wish that it was easy to educate people on things. I only have wishes. I wish the world was this, that, I don't know. You could come back next week, and things would be different. ❖

Red

I'm a street medic. When I'm here, I man the clinic between two and eight in the morning. Also, I kind of just do whatever needs to get done. I've been here for a while, so I can give a certain level of direction to people who are new.

As the clinic and the street medics separate, I've been doing less on the clinical side, leaving that to the trained nurses and doctors. I just do street-medic-related things. You know, bandaging people up after actions, before actions, during actions, and small stuff when they're around the camp. Around here, it's a lot more general-well-being-type things. Like, during the storm the other night, I was running around knocking on tent doors, making sure no one was freezing to death inside their tent.

Christine told me twenty-four people had hypothermia.

Might be a little low. People weren't prepared. It was nasty out here. It would have been a lot worse if we hadn't been running around all night, because barely any of those people actually came here and said, "I need help." Most of them were shivering their asses off, or couldn't walk. They were just sitting there, wherever they were.

What do you do for that? Do they have to go to the hospital?

If it's really bad. We sent one or two people to the hospital. Most of them we just warmed up. We had space heaters in our tents, and we just nursed them back to health. Yeah, that was one hell of a night.

Was that before they took away the generators?

No, that was not. We didn't have any generators. We had a propane space heater, and that was it.

Did you ever get them back?

Nah.

Do you think you'll ever get them back?

Well, we had a biodiesel generator. They took our generators because they said it was a combustion risk—it was a fire hazard—but the biofuel generator isn't a fire hazard. We were working on using that to create an electrical grid for the entire park. That plan is still moving forward once we get that back. We have the lawyers working on that, because there's no real reason for them to take that from us.

They are right in a certain respect, that having generators in this park isn't necessarily the best idea if there's a way to avoid it.

Tell me about how you became a medic.

Well, there was this action that happened in Union Square. It was the first time we got real press. I don't know if you remember the picture on the cover of the Daily News of that girl screaming after being maced? Right when that went down, I was working in Food. There were two medics, and that bench there was just a pile of medical supplies. There was no real order to it.

That was early on?

That was pretty early. I think it was, like, the second week. Food had everything down pretty well, and I just walked over and was like, "Hey, do you guys need help?" And they were like, "Yeah, we need help." Since then, I've gotten a plethora of street medic trainings, and have become someone who can actually contribute.

Have they been training you in here?

We've been reaching out to a lot of groups—street medic groups—and having people come from all over the country to do training.

What does the training consist of?

We did a seven-hour basic street medic training in the old J. P. Morgan Chase building at Twenty-Three Wall. We did eye-flush trainings for mace and pepper spray. We did a basic first aid one. We did an herbalist one. We did a Narcan overdose training. A.E.D./C.P.R. training.

What is Narcan?

Narcan is the drug you administer to someone who has overdosed on opiates.

Have you been called to a lot of things?

Yeah. I mean, it varies depending on what's going on that day. Some days it's a lot of hand injuries from drumming. [Laughs.] Some days, you just get guy after guy coming in with their hands all bloody, like, "I need to go back out and play!" Other days, after a brutal action or something, they'll come back with sprained ankles, they got hit, they got maced, stuff like that. Most of the time, especially at night, we stay pretty busy, but what that is depends on the environment for the day.

You said you're working the overnight?

Yeah. When I'm here, I work the overnight.

Are you able to sleep?

If I'm here, I'll sleep. I'll work during the day, then I'll do an overnight shift, and sleep the next day. But if it's really bad . . . I went three days without sleep, like, a week ago. Sometimes things just keep coming up, and unless you want to feel like a terrible person in the morning, you can't just be like, "All right, I'm going to sleep!"

It's kind of like in a hospital.

Yeah, something like that.

How did you originally get into the movement?

How I originally got here? People have been asking me that a lot. I'm not entirely sure . . . something having to do with the Internet, I guess.

I found it somewhere on the Internet. Then it started up, and I watched the LiveStream when I was at the job I used to have. I'm like, "Man, this is great! I never thought something like this would happen! I need to go down there! I need to go down there!" And a couple days in, I finally just said, "Fuck it!" I took a couple days off work and came down, and haven't been able to leave since.

Are you from New York?

Yeah, I'm from upstate New York. I used to live down here, but it was too cutthroat for me.

I hear that. Tell me about how you quit your job.

So I took two days off work and I came down here. I took a bus, and then a train. I came down, I spent the day here, and I slept here. Woke up the next day, did it again. Around Saturday or Sunday, I realized I can't leave. I just . . . I don't think I'm physically capable of doing it.

I've been bitching about the state of the world and the state of this country for years. I never thought something like this would happen. Part of what I was bitching about was how my generation were too content with their Xboxes and their reality T.V. shows to ever get up and try to change things. And then they did. I couldn't pass that up; it was such a large part of my philosophy on why things have declined.

That's funny because I used to bitch about your generation, too. Now I'm eating my words.

Give it a little while. [Laughs.]

I'm impressed, though. They did get a bad rap.

[Laughs.] Deservedly so.

I'm an Xer and we didn't do shit, so I can't criticize you guys. We didn't have Xboxes, but we didn't do shit, either.

◆

Did you know people who were down here?

Not when I first got here, but I made friends really quick. It was a lot smaller when I started coming. Most of the people I know now—we've all been here since either the beginning or right near the beginning. Then, it was much more like everyone was here for the same reason. Everyone was here to try to make this work. There was a lot less people just here to party, just here to hang out. We were all busting our asses working ridiculous hours, and we got to know each other and became good friends. So now I know plenty of people here. ❖

Shon

I'm part of the Medical crew here at Zuccotti Square. Street medics. We basically provide medical support for the occupation, for the different marches and demonstrations that are in line with the broader scope of the occupation, and for the ninety-nine percent.

You go along on the marches with your equipment?

Yeah. We're there to treat anything from blisters to pepper spray to baton wounds. We do jail support; when people get out of jail, we're there to provide medical support in case they have any injuries.

In addition to pepper spray and baton wounds, what other kinds of things happen on the marches?

A lot of cough drops being handed out. We keep people hydrated. If they don't bring their own water, we try to have water for them. We've also been able—in some cases, like on the Brooklyn Bridge—to negotiate with the police about providing emergency medical attention. We've been able to get some people out of being arrested.

Are the street medics also active in the park?

Yeah, the street medics do rounds. If there's somebody that needs medical attention, we'll go find them and assess them. We see if they can be treated there on the spot. They might need to come to our clinic here, or they might be rushed to the emergency room.

Have you sent a lot of people to the emergency room?

There's been quite a few, yeah.

I've heard some horror stories about the big snowstorm, and the number of people who had hypothermia.

There were a lot of cases of different stages of hypothermia, but it's a hard number to count. There were wet and shivering people that felt like they didn't need any medical attention. A lot of them did self-care—went to Comfort, got new clothes, dried out, went to a restaurant or something—and got to feeling better. That night, it was easier to count those who didn't show signs or symptoms than those who did.

Were you a medic before the occupation?

A little experience in street medic work, but this is a new type of experience, the occupation. The ongoing occupation is something new in the medical field.

How'd you get involved in doing it?

I found out there was no organized street medic presence here. I did want to come down and help out and be a part of it, but when I found out there was no street medic crew, I came down to help with that.

When I got here there was medics, but most of them had to leave. So then we made a call out to the General Assembly for anybody that had medical experience.

Were there a lot of people who had experience?

I think that night we got seven. We started out with, I think, two trash bags full of supplies, and we put our own personal funds together and got other stuff we needed. We had some donations coming in, and it just started growing and growing. Now we're at the point where we have a really well-operated medical clinic here, with doctors and nurses on staff. We have emotional support and alternative health. Our crew's gotten a lot bigger, and we've evolved immensely.

How many street medics do you have?

It's hard to tell. Right now, I think we have on-site . . . there's four right now. We've got maybe around twenty that have their own schedules and can be here when they can.

How many doctors and nurses would you say you have?

We probably have four doctors, and somewhere between six and eight nurses. We also have other-skill-level people working in the clinic.

And where are those guys coming from? The city?

All over.

Can you talk about why you decided to get involved?

To participate in direct democracy. This is a wonderful chance to experience it and watch it grow, and to work out all the things that come up. We're constantly facing new walls in front of us. We find positive ways to take down those barriers, and to make different pathways from what we experience in our normal lives. That alone is priceless. To be able to have this opportunity in direct democracy is a beautiful thing.

Had you been an activist before this?

Yeah.

What kinds of things were you involved in?

Day-to-day community activism: social justice issues, human rights issues, free food programs.

In New York?

Philadelphia.

Like, soup kitchen kind of thing?

Food Not Bombs. Free food distros.

Have you been involved with food distribution here?

No. I love doing food, and I love sweeping and sanitation, but my calling here is Medic. I haven't done anything else here. [Laughs.]

It seems like a lot of people find a new calling here.
Anything else that you'd like to put on the record?

I think one thing is important: What we've learned from this, we can take to our own communities. I would love to see direct democracy in the form of General Assemblies and Spokes Councils in every neighborhood. That would allow us to work on the issues that directly impact where we live, and directly impact our neighbors.

The Spokes Council just started up, didn't it?

Yep. I think tomorrow's the first one.

Can you explain to me how it works?

All working groups go.

The whole working group goes?

If they're able to. You know, we have to have people on shift here. *They* won't be able to go, but the whole working group that's able to goes. One person is the representative, and it rotates; there's not only one representative. The representative, at any time during the meeting, can be switched out. So it's not a matter of authority, or any leadership taking on that role. It's just a spokesperson, speaking to represent the group, and they'll be with their working group.

So what kind of issues is the Spokes Council going to handle, as opposed to just General Assembly?

Logistics of this park, I believe. What's going on here, things we're working on. Medics will be talking about self care, winterization, other things that have been going on. We'll be able to speak at the Spokes Council about those issues, and address those to the other working groups and caucuses here, which I'm really excited for.

The General Assembly, from what I understand, will be working on issues—the movement as a whole, nationally or globally. Personally, I haven't been able to sit in a whole General Assembly for a long time. I'm glad that I'll be able to participate again, to have the time to talk about the issues and things that we're working on. A lot of working groups—they just meet on their own, work out their own issues, and try to send somebody to the General Assembly to do a report-back. It wasn't effective. So I'm excited for the Spokes Council.

I'd heard, also, that some people who were not in the spirit of General Assembly were shouting.

Oh, yeah, since the beginning. People thought that was their opportunity to get up and say why they're here, and list off all the things that are wrong in the world. The General Assembly had set up what they call the People's Soapbox at the end of the General Assembly to give them time to do that. A lot of people are new to the process. They're really hyped and have a lot to say.

There are some disruptions, and there will be, but the facilitators, especially, are working really hard to correct that, to make the meetings go smoother so more can get done.

Is the Spokes Council closed to the general population here?

No. They can either join a working group, which everybody is encouraged to do, or there's the Occupiers Working Group. People that live here can join the Spokes Council as an Occupier. I think that's great. That addressed a lot of concerns that it was closed.

But I encourage everybody to join a working group. It's a very productive way to plug in to what's going on, have something to do, and help out. We do need a lot of help here. There was just a call for help from the kitchen, to do lunch.

Just today?

Just a few minutes ago. And Sanitation always needs help, I know. There's stuff that has to get done.

I know some people are bothered by the people who are not working and not helping out. Where do you stand on that?

I would like to talk to the people, and find out what are some of their concerns with working groups that they might have an interest in joining. I've talked to some people, and they wanted to join some type of working group, but they felt, for whatever reason, it wasn't a good place for them to be. So I encouraged them to start their own. We really haven't made it clear that there is that avenue, too.

What kind of working groups need to be made that aren't there?

I would like to see a group of people who were homeless in New York City before the occupation started. Let them have the opportunity to put their heads together and see what they can come up with. Some of their ideas could make this occupation better. ❖

Walter II

What brought me here is that I've never felt that the people had a voice. Big Oil has always been telling us what to do. They took out the trolleys when the trolleys were working, so people could buy more cars. It's all about politics—being bought—and I never really felt I had a voice. Kind of depressing. But everybody votes every year, and the same stuff happens, basically. The people's voices are bought.

When I finally had the chance to come down, I stayed for twenty hours straight just talking to people. When it started, I watched it, but I was a little busy. Every day I would read any kind of news articles. I would go to Google News and type in "Occupy Wall Street" and see what kind of articles were being written.

From the beginning, a lot of the articles were slanted, trying to put everybody into one basket of hippies or freaks or something like that. I knew that that wasn't the truth, because usually, when you read an article that's based on truth, you can see some facts. Whenever someone calls somebody a name, it ruins the argument for me. I want to know what your facts are. Don't just hurt somebody because of their clothes or their lifestyle. What are the facts?

So I came down to find out for myself, and the fact is, everybody is down here: directors, lawyers, doctors, nurses, unemployed, poor, drug addicts—yes, people who live a life in and out of the prison system. There's union members. There's one-percenters that I've stood with and talked with.

Really? Who are in favor?

Yeah, she was a woman from Pennsylvania. She inherited her money. She told me a story about her grandfather. Before F.D.R. started the income tax, there were twenty-six plates at the Christmas dinner, and under each plate was a million dollars.

What!

Because he didn't want the I.R.S. to get it. She's a pastor in Pennsylvania. Being a pastor, I believe, has given her compassion for others. Basically, the compassion for others is what's missing for our society to be strong, for any company to be strong.

I think it's not too hard to take care of people. Unions have fought for health care and safety issues, which only makes work on the job safer. Your bottom line will go up because you don't have accidents. When you have to replace the worker, you have to retrain them, and it takes all that money. So for a society to be better, we have to really be compassionate for the poor. We have to help them become better in society, and healthier. The poor have to have health care.

I haven't been to the doctor in a very long time, and it's too bad. I'm lucky and I'm healthy, but if something were to happen . . . we hear stories about people having to sell everything they own once they get sick. If they do survive, they're destitute. This compassion for others is missing, and a lot of it is because of the corporate greed.

The voices of the people haven't been heard for a very long time. The founding fathers wrote the Declaration of Independence; we've never lived up to it, and that's a human fact. When Copernicus said we revolve around the sun, "No, no, no! That's not good enough!" So as humans, we do take a long time to catch up to our ideals. I think this movement is going to change that.

Does your union support your being here?

Yeah, Local Six, Hotel and Restaurant Employees Union, Manhattan. Here [on the table] are the signs for all the unions. In the last four to six years, when Bush came in, he started repealing a lot of the workers' rights, and they said, "Just watch." And then in Wisconsin, they're taking away people's right to collectively bargain, which is slavery in the sense: "You're going to do what I say, or you're going to walk, and I'm going to get somebody else to do it." You know, we're going backwards.

There's many different problems, and they're trying to throw that into the mainstream media as we don't know what to do: "They don't even know what their demands are." If you go to the Occupy Wall Street Web site—I've looked at it—it talks about a lot of problems.

It basically stems from money and politics. They buy the Republicans and the Democrats. Whoever wins, we lose.

In the best possible world, where would you see this going?

I would see this going to where lobbyists cannot lobby any more, and actual real people from the communities are in power, and people can vote and have it mean something, and we protect our food supply.

Monsanto has patented the seeds, and they're putting farmers out of work. That's their business, but now people from that business are in the F.D.A. That's collusion. That's conflict of interest. They're not interests of the people, they're interests of their business, and that in itself is wrong.

But it's been going on. Sophocles, Aristotle, everybody has seen it. We're human. All we can do is evolve and become better. I was thinking about something last night: U.S.A. 2.0. You know, this is just another growth. And it looks impossible. It does look impossible.

I didn't know what anarchism was, but basically, I thought it was people running through the streets and burning everything. No. It's the people, together. People working together is anarchy.

I've heard that it's not necessarily the general union membership, but the people at the top making the choice to support this.

Well, yeah. I think that's everywhere. Everywhere there's people on top telling us what we need to do.

[Walter greets Randy in passing.]

There's a great movie about him. I just saw it about six months ago, and then I saw him down here. I said, "Hey, Randy."

We do a show on Wednesday nights for the benefit of Occupy Wall Street. It's at Nine Bleecker—at the Yippie Café, which is a Yippie museum. Come cover it. There were some great people last week. I was going to perform this week with my group, but I cannot. I'm directing a play. This Wednesday, we open for dress rehearsal.

What's the play?

The play I'm directing is called *Divine Intervention*.[1] It's about a woman who goes to confession. She's sorry for a couple things, but she's on her seventh husband and she's not sorry for that. It's a little comedy.

Anyways, where were we? We were talking about the unions. A lot of people will come to me and say unions are corrupt. There's corruption everywhere, yes. I think this movement will try to have more transparency. Why not? I don't have a problem with that. But the unions are in place right now, and they fight for workers' rights, and it's the best thing going right now for people to get together. Yeah, we can work towards getting corruption out as well.

Do you think the rank and file support Occupy Wall Street?

Well, I think what's going to happen is: You will see in the next week or two some major activity, and the unions are going to call their people out like they did when they were going to shut the park down. So

---

[1]*Divine Intervention*, by Don Creedon, directed by Walter Michael DeForest, Hudson Guild Theater, November 3.

when it's needed, we will show up. There's people waiting for a chance to help out, and when that chance comes, they will arise just like anything. When we need them, they will be there, I believe. I have faith in that totally because it's their vested interest as well.

They've stripped away our powers as people and as workers, and they've given it to the corporations. They can step on our necks and say, "We have somebody who can work for less." It defeats all of our gains that we've made for human rights and workers' rights, health and safety. It just becomes unhealthy, unsafe, and our communities suffer—our families; that's the most important. If we can just take care of our families, we can grow up healthy and wise and productive. ❖

George

Before this whole experience, I was a student at American University.

Where is that, D.C.?

Yeah. I was studying philosophy and international relations. I dropped out last May because I couldn't pay for it anymore. I came back to the city. I started interning for this record label here, Greedhead Entertainment—this rap group Das Racist.

I love Das Racist!

Yeah! I'm Heems's personal assistant. They went on tour, and I kind of just stuck around. I came down here October fifth and I haven't left since, so that's pretty much my story.

I'm Dominican, from very low socio-economic status growing up. Just met the right people, got to the right places, got a liberal-arts college education.

You went to school in the city?

Yeah, I went to public school here. P.S. 87 for elementary school, then Crossroads for middle school on a Hundred and Eighth Street. I was about to go into Stuy, but then we moved to Providence.

Rhode Island?

Rhode Island. Providence is terrible if you don't know anyone from Brown or RISD. They've created this awesome cultural bubble that's bursting with amazing things, but if you're not in this circle, you don't get any of it. It doesn't spill out into the rest of the city. It's kind of sad, hopping back and forth between worlds. It's sad how much is in that bubble that doesn't get out to the rest of Providence. East Side, Wickenden Street—it's all there, but nowhere else. It's just kind of sad.

I went to high school in East Providence. Rhode Island is, like, the bane of my existence. It's a vacuum. It's a black hole—a soulless, lifeless black hole for culture. It's devoid of any substance.

In New York, every place has its own cultural renaissance, all over the city. But if you go to Rhode Island, it's only in that small area of Providence. It was the hardest thing I ever had to do, living there in that soul-sucking vacuum. People are just stuck in this self-centered, vapid, shallow existence, you know? Your *Jersey Shore*, twenty-four-hour-news-cycle-type deal, all over.

But then I got over that. I went to D.C. for school, then I came here, and then I started doing this.

How long were you in school before you had to drop out?

I did two years. I don't have a bachelor's yet. I don't think I'm going to get a bachelor's because I just found out that you don't need a bachelor's to go to grad school.

Really?

Yeah, it's not necessary. I met a woman—she's doing a documentary on this [Occupy Wall Street], and has been following me around for some time. She studied philosophy, just like me. She told me that she dropped out of Columbia, and then a few years later, applied to grad school. She just asked: "Um, I haven't finished my undergrad, but can I apply to grad school?" And they were like, "Yeah! No problem!"

So you could have a Ph.D. but no B.A.?

Exactly. Apparently, they just want you to have that base understanding. So I think I'm going to go for that.

I'm fascinated.

This is much better than undergrad, this whole thing right here. I've learned more in this park in the last four weeks than I have in any classroom in the last twenty years, so I think I'm going to be all set for grad school by the end of this.

I'm actually putting philosophy into practice here, which is so much better than sitting in a classroom reading all these theories and writing papers about them. Instead, I'm like, "No! Let me go try them in an actual open public space!" This experience has been so much more fulfilling than actually just studying philosophy in a classroom.

Tell me something about what work you're actually doing here. Are you working with the Media people?

I do some work with Media. Well, I stopped doing work with Media after my laptop got stolen, because it's really hard to handle any media without a laptop.

Did it get stolen here?

Yeah. It happens. This place is not utopia, by any means.

Yeah, yeah. It's the city, it's the city.

Exactly. So mostly I've been involved in Facilitation and Direct Action, and I help out in all the other working groups.

Is Facilitation different from Nonviolent Communication?

Yes. Facilitation is . . . I guess, the keepers of process. We're the neutral people, there just to help facilitate the conversation and make sure everyone sticks to process—our direct democracy process here. So everyone gets a chance to speak, and no one is speaking over each other, and we can have a conversation. All the facilitators do is just make sure that it stays in control and happening.

When you're facilitating a G.A., none of your personal opinions or feelings come through. It's just, "I'm sticking to process. We're talking about this right now. We're talking about that right now. Someone would like to talk about something else? We could possibly do it later, if there's time." Or, "Wait until after G.A., for Soapbox."

Meetings, too. When you facilitate a meeting, it's just sticking to the agenda. This is an evolution in how we communicate with each other, because honestly, language is incredibly limiting. The way we talk to each other—it's kind of sad that it's taken so long for something more to develop. I didn't realize that hand signals add so much to language and to the way we communicate.

We're not trying to remove the passion from conversation; we're trying to direct it better. People want to talk *right now*, but you have to foster respect for everyone else in the group. Everyone would like to talk about something that they feel is important to them, but we're in a group, and we're trying to have a group conversation. We're going to stick to the agenda agreed upon earlier. We'll move forward through that, and if there's time, we can add things, we can have discussions, we can do all that stuff.

Basically, facilitation is the allowing of conversation to happen constructively, so every voice can be heard and we're not just yelling at each other. That's what happens in the outside world. They meet, they start talking, and then everyone just starts screaming at each other because there's no process to handle all of that.

It's not anything new. These things have been developed over the last forty, fifty years, but no one has tried using them on the scale we're using them. A lot of different movements have used these techniques and processes. Maybe some things were better than what we have, but nothing here is static or set in stone. Nothing's codified. It's all changing and evolving, and we're flexible. If there's something that works better, we'll incorporate it. That's how we grow and change.

What's so special about this is that no movement has had as much press as we've had. We're using all of these techniques. We're using consensus and we're really getting it out there. Consensus has been used for a long time. It has been successful in a lot of movements. The tribes in Latin America used the consensus model—things like the Spokes Council—to come to decisions all the time. We're just trying to bring these things to the rest of the world.

America is the best democracy on record. By no means is it the best democracy or the best democratic system in any way, shape, or form. It's not even a democracy anymore, really, but let's not get into that.

It's the closest, but it could get closer.

A lot closer. But right now, it's in no way functional. I think it was a lot closer after the Revolution than it is now. Now it's just, like, leaps and bounds away from what it should have been.

And it's not just about America. Why I'm really here is because this is what I've been waiting for my entire life. This is it. This is do-or-die. This is a shift in the way we think as human beings, the way we act to one another, how we think of one another. And if this fails, we're done. We're fucked! It's the end! If this doesn't work, I give us, like, two, three hundred years at most. Three hundred years is being really generous. So this is it!

And it's a daunting task. When you really think about it, we're trying to enlighten the entire human race right now—all of humanity.

It's exhausting!

It's really scary, but we have to keep going. We have to do it, take it day by day. Remind ourselves every day that we are just starting out. It's been a month, almost two, and this is just the beginning. We're going to be here for years.

In this park.

In this park, and all over the world. But if this doesn't work, holy fuck!

◆

I love the demands question the most. I'm like, "You can't demand anything of a system that's completely broken. Anything it gives you is intrinsically going to be broken."

The toughest thing for us to do right now is to teach people how to think outside the box. There are those who are in love with the system. Any kind of attack on that system is an attack on their reality, but the world doesn't work the way they think it does. Most of this is education—teaching people that we can live differently. It is possible for another system to be created.

My mother can't even comprehend this at all.

She's not into it?

She's not. Well, she's like, "Oh, cool! You're fighting for this!" She's behind it—like, she's always voted left—but she can't see the bigger picture. A world without a hierarchy doesn't make sense to her. For her, there's always going to be someone on the top, always going to be someone on the bottom. That's just the way the world works. She thinks that things could be a little better, but there are always going to be people that are exploited and oppressed. That's the way it works! Breaking that is the most difficult thing. Allowing people to think—not even to do—to think of the world differently is the issue.

Speaking to that, me and my friend Nicole are working on this really great kind of teach-in involving *Children of Men*.[2]

The movie?

Yes. The D.V.D. actually has comments from Slavoj Žižek, and then this twenty-minute documentary on how all the themes in the movie perfectly apply to the world today.

I've never seen a film just show the world as it is. That movie should have gotten every award. I think it didn't because it just told the truth, and they can't have that. It covered social inequality, economic injustice, the military-industrial complex, the prison-industrial complex. It literally covered everything. Global warming! It was nuts!

The thing about that film is that it doesn't make any judgments. It doesn't tell you, "Look, this is bad!" or, "This is good!" It just says, "This is the world we live in today. You make your own judgment."

So we're using that, and the way that we're trying to build is: We have the comments from Žižek, and we want to show that first because it primes people to look at the foreground and background. Probably a lot of people saw that film, and it didn't have the same effect it had on me because they're just watching the movie. It's a thriller; they're following the plot. But I've never seen an attention to detail in film like that. Those extras should have gotten Oscars. It was amazing!

So the Žižek piece primes people to pay attention to that, and then people watch the movie. At the end, we show the other thirty-minute documentary about how it applies to the world today. Along with that, we have a chart mapping out huge problems of the world and showing how they're all interconnected, because that's another huge problem: People see these issues as separate issues when they aren't. Literally every problem we have in this world is connected to another problem we have. None of them are in a vacuum.

You could get a doctorate based on just making that flowchart.

---

[2] *Children of Men*, directed by Alfonso Cuarón (Universal City, CA: Universal Pictures, 2006).

It's not just me. My friend Nicole over there—it's a passionate project we have because we both feel exactly the same way. We want it to be really representative, like a giant digital web, and you can actually fly through there like a kind of Google Earth-type thing. We're feeling out how to structure that right now—how to be interactive, so people can pick out a problem that's in the world and plot it on the web, and then we can show how that one single issue connects to a myriad more.

That's why it's so easy for people to ignore everything. People are really good at isolating things. "This issue, that issue, don't worry about it. This has nothing to do with that. You care about children in Africa? Okay, children in Africa. That has nothing to do with our fossil fuel reserves in Africa. No, they're not connected." People see that, and then they tackle these one issues, when it's just everything.

That's why it's really hard to come up with the demands. The demands are: everything.

Exactly. I tell the media and the press constantly, "I'm not here to make reforms. Reforms will happen along the way—let's make it better as we progress—but I'm looking to build a new system, completely outside of the one that already exists." That's what I want to do. That's my endgame. Build these occupations, create these communities, foster these relationships with people.

If we come together, we all are empowered to spread our ideas, and to work together toward solutions. They've convinced so many people that they can't do anything: "It's not up to you. It's up to Congress." But it's up to them to get together and think about their world and their localities, to think about how to fix problems locally. We have armies of people who just can't think critically.

What do we do about that?

Therein lies the rub! How do you wake all these people up? We're hoping that our web will help a lot.

I want to have open source schools in the neighborhoods I'm from, in East Harlem. I want to have schools that cover everything from your basic arithmetic and grammar to, like, theories on how to kill communism, free for people to just come in and sit and learn. I want to show people that there's value in knowledge for knowledge's sake. Maybe that'll drive them to start thinking on their own.

We can't just tell people, "Oh, look! There are all these problems!" I want people to feel as strongly as I do about them. I want them to have the drive to learn more, not just come somewhere and have someone feed it to them. It's tough! It's literally undoing centuries of social-ization. How do you begin to do that? I think we've begun to do that, because in this place, ageism has been destroyed.

But in which direction?

In both directions. It's insane! There are those who are older and it's hard for them to not feed the system, but a lot of older people can do that perfectly well. Now, I'm twenty years old here. I'm probably the youngest of the really hard-core activists, but that doesn't matter at all. There are people who have been doing this for thirty years who have been like, "Hi!" We're on the same level. We're completely equal. They respect all my ideas. Yes, I put more weight on *their* ideas because they've been doing it a lot longer. I'm not going to come in here and say I run shit when I don't have as much experience, but that experience doesn't make them better than me.

They share their experience. They help me get to where they are so we can bounce ideas around. I throw out an idea . . . people listen, which is insane! Men and women who are thirty years older than I am, listen. That doesn't happen outside of this space. I can go and walk into an office and talk to a manager, and they're just going to disregard me because I'm twenty years old. That's one of the things that in this space is completely gone. It's crazy!

That's better than college.

This is much better than college. Seeing that—seeing the barriers that are falling as we continue to do this—is why I'm here every day from seven in the morning to three a.m. I don't like leaving this. I have to leave New York sometime soon to go visit people, and I don't think I can. I've never been more fulfilled in my entire life. I'm stretched so thin right now and it sucks sometimes, but then at the same time, I wouldn't want it any other way. It's just amazing.

◆

It's going to take a long time to get people to think on the meta lev-els that you and I are thinking on, but that's my endgame. We did an action recently called Occupy the Boardroom, which was a Web site created by this dude Austin, and this nonprofit he works with, Align. Basically, people send in letters that they want to get to the executives of the major banks. He collected, like, six thousand letters, and we went and delivered them on a march to Bank of America, J. P. Morgan Chase, Citigroup, Wells Fargo, and Goldman Sachs.

The day went like this: There were two marches—a march that hit the Bank of America and Goldman Sachs, and a march that hit Wells Fargo and Citigroup—and then we all met at J. P. Morgan Chase. We handed the letters to these reps, and then we made symbolic paper airplanes and threw them to the top of the building. It was really a festive, fun march.

Everyone on the march wrote a letter themselves. What I wrote was: "My main concern is not with foreclosure, student debt, or economic disparity. It's with you, as human beings, working in these places. How can you come to work here and not see the effect you have on the world entire?" There's a disconnect with reality once you're up there. I don't think all of these people are evil human beings; I think they're just completely disconnected. "Look at yourself. Look at what the system does to you." They're smart, educated people. They're not dumb. You don't get to be an executive at any of these banks being dumb. So they either see it and don't care, or they can't see it at all.

That's the more charitable way of trying to connect with them, as another human being.

Exactly, because vilifying them all the time is just going to make them shut down. Again, there are some of them that do need to be vilified. I'm sure there are some who just are not good people, and completely are okay with everything that's going on. But there have to be some—a few—that just see numbers all day, and they just don't see the people. This is another reason why I love *Children of Men*. It shows that disconnect with other human beings so perfectly. It's technologically great—all these things are fantastic—but there are people in this world.

◆

Another thing we started talking about is Rosetta Stone.

The language course?

The language course. It's five hundred dollars to learn one fucking language, right? It's that much for a reason, because . . . oh, I don't give a shit, I pirated it. I pirated it in every language. It works beautifully! It is magnificent how well Rosetta Stone works. It's really, like, the golden tablets. I feel like John Smith, like, "What? This is language?"

I feel like it's so expensive for a reason, because to learn those languages would destroy so many barriers between people. The second you meet another human being and they can't understand you, you automatically categorize them as unintelligent. It's so much easier to dehumanize them—to see them as less than you are—because they can't understand you. It's so difficult for the people who need these languages the most to learn them and to access them.

The people who can afford that five-hundred-dollar language program don't even need it. Anyone they're dealing with is going to be speaking their language anyway because they have enough money to spend five hundred dollars on a language program. I think I'm just going to start pirating Rosetta Stone and giving it away.

I don't have a headset. It's really difficult to do it with my laptop mic, but I was practicing German with my step-dad's headset for a week, and I picked up basic German. I've forgotten it since—its been a few months—but I was just starting to think, in basic terms, in German.

I had a French trip in high school, and I didn't speak shit after taking French for, like, seven years. Some German girl staying in the same house spoke fluent French, and they're like, "She's been taking it two years." So it's a weird American problem.

Oh, definitely. But even then, in Europe you're only going to get that education if you are middle class to begin with. Like, the Roma aren't getting that education in France.

This was, like, the late eighties.

Less disparity, yeah.

It's definitely heated up.

Everything is going to shit! And everyone—they're just coating over it. "It'll be fine!" As of now, the damage we've done to the climate is irreversible. We can only slow it down at this point.

And people are still fucking not even paying attention. Going forward with their, "Now let's go for natural gas through hydrofracking!" It's like, "Fuck water! Who needs water? I want some gas!"

And it's like, "Say what?" You have incredibly intelligent, super smart chemists and biologists and engineers working to do this stuff. They're really smart people! I can't do that! The engineers to decide all these pipes, and the chemists that need to come in to make these chemicals to break up the thing . . . "I can't do what you do."

And that's what they came up with.

"What are you doing? What is wrong with you?" It makes no sense.

What about this pipeline from Canada?[3]

Yeah, the tar sands.

The superpipeline!

Yay! We went on an action against this thirty-centimeter pipeline they wanted to put through the fucking Village, one of the most populated areas in the world. This company, Spectra Pipeline, has the worst track record for safety in, like, the history of pipeline companies. A pipeline in Southern California that they had blew up; killed, like, eight people; destroyed, like, eighty homes; and did more than fifty million worth of damages. And that area is so much not as densely populated as the fucking Village! And not only that, it's going to pump radon gas into your stoves, so that's just, like, lung cancer for everyone. It was FERC, the Federal Energy Regulatory Committee, that the pipeline has to be approved by. They have never denied a permit to build a pipeline.

We got there. We came with, like, two hundred people—the largest amount of people at a FERC public hearing in the history of FERC. The second largest was seven.

So people don't go to those things.

No.

They're not publicized.

They're not. They put this on this Web site, on this page in the middle of nowhere . . .

---

[3] The Keystone Pipeline System originates in Alberta.

You have to know that you're looking for it.

Exactly, to find it. No one knocks door-to-door in the neighborhood that it's going to be put through. They don't tell these people. And they wanted it to connect to Con Ed's infrastructure. Con Ed's infrastructure is decrepit. Like, "No, that's not good!"

So we went to the public hearing. They brought what we had to say to Washington, and if they pass it anyway, I'm lying down in front of a backhoe. I'm literally not going to let it happen. That's what we're trying to get people to do here. It is completely okay for you to just say, "Fuck you! I don't want this!" You can definitely just go, "No!" On marches, I've straight-up told cops, "No!"

You can do this! They've indoctrinated people into thinking that you can't, that you have to listen to them. "If it goes through here [at the hearing], that's it, the argument's over." No! You are a person with a voice. And as long as you're willing, and you can stand, and you can say something, that's the power you have. It's so powerful. They've convinced you that your voice is not powerful, when it is. It's the most powerful thing you could use now, because voting is just a completely arbitrary process. Voting does nothing. This Electoral College doesn't work—another thing that's just completely broken. I don't know how shit stayed together after 2000 and *Bush v. Gore*. ❖

November 2

Maria II

Occupy Wall Street en Español is a group of Spanish people. We all come from different countries, and we are participating in this protest against those companies that are "occupying" our countries. They're taking our lands, creating monopolies in our countries, and that's basically our protest. Also, we're against the immigration policy, and against the economy that's buying our politicians.

Also, the media. It's controlled by the governments, and also by these companies. People are not well-informed. If we don't have the right information, we can't choose who's going to govern our countries. That's basically the problem that we are facing now.

What corporate interests, specifically?

We have a few corporations that we're against specifically. Right now in Peru, Exxon, the gas company, is a huge problem. We're going to eventually bring pictures of what's going on in those countries. The economy is going down not just here in the United States. It's everywhere, especially in those countries that are not governed well.

How did you get involved in coming down and occupying?

Me personally? I watched it on T.V. I live in Brooklyn. I've been living here in the United States for six years. I watched it on T.V., like, the third week they were occupying, and I just got interested and came here. I took a few pictures and sent them over to my friends in Mexico, so they could know exactly what's going on, and so they will have the real picture of it. I explained to them what was the reason for us to be here, for them not just to see what the media was letting them know.

I just feel for them. I feel like I need to be here both to support the cause, and to represent, in a way, my country and the problems that are facing them right now.

We were talking earlier about the sleeping arrangements for your working group. What did you guys come up with for that?

We're going to start a schedule so we can switch the days—who's going to be sleeping over which space, you know? We're going to be here Monday through Sunday, and we have a huge group.

How many?

Right now we're over a hundred.

Oh, wow! How often do you guys meet?

The meeting is every Sunday at seven o'clock.

What's with all the cops out here today?

I think it's because during the day, there's more people here, so they just want to come down and see if there's any conflicts. They're just trying to protect the people. It's okay. We're cool with that. As long as we respect them and they respect us, everything's okay.

Tell me about the experience of occupying. How has that been?

It's been great. People here are very, very solidary. We help each other. We're very organized. We recognize people. We protect ourselves; we have a security group, and it's watching also the Medical tent there.

And yes, I like it. I really like it because we all share the same cause. We're together in this. ❖

November 3

Jordan

I was on the road in Philadelphia when I heard about Occupy Wall Street. I was on my way to New York, and then back to San Francisco, where I'm from. I figured I'd come here and see what was going on. As soon as I got here, I realized that I wasn't going to go back to San Francisco—within, like, a minute of being here.

That was also really influenced by what happened on the Brooklyn Bridge. I've seen these kinds of things start up a lot. The feeling here is similar to the antiwar protests in 2004: "We can do anything!" That fizzled out, but here it's really sustained. So when everyone got arrested on the Brooklyn Bridge—after this being around for two weeks, seven hundred people got arrested—it really showed me that this was serious. Then when I came here and actually checked it out, I completely gave up all my plans.

I would say that I've been looking for something like this probably since I was fourteen, when I first started talking to people who have a critical analysis of capitalism, of the way our country is structured and the way our society is structured. There's an artist, Seth Tobocman, who sums it up really well. He made this piece that says, "You don't have to fuck people over to survive." That's a real fundamental aspect of what this is about.

The standards that we have in this country, in my opinion, are designed to keep us feeling insecure and always wanting more. And the way in which we get more is by subjugating other people. Up until now, I've been trying to cultivate better standards for myself and the people in my community, so that we're screwing over people less.

I would like the option of living in a culture and a society that isn't based on oppressing other people in order to have our day-to-day stuff. I feel that that's impossible in the United States right now, and it's impossible globally for someone who's privileged like I am. Obviously, we can't get rid of that privilege, but we're trying to create dialogue around that, and create something different.

What have you been doing in the way of living differently?

I was doing Food Not Bombs when I was in high school. We collect food that grocery stores throw away because it's past it's expiration date, or because it's an apple with a little brown spot on it or something like that. And then the food gets cooked and served for free as a demonstration against food waste. It's not a food production problem in the world, it's a food distribution problem. There's no one who needs to be hungry. There's enough food for everybody. So there was that.

I live in collective houses with a lot of people. We share space. Recently, I lived in a room with three of my friends. People would ask me, "How do you do that? How do you manage in a room with three other people?" But they are really good friends. I don't need my own personal room 24/7. I'm from San Francisco, so rent is really high. Sharing space is a way of mitigating rent. When I pay less rent, I need to make less money. I can work a job that's part of the system less, and I can put more time and energy into community projects.

In San Francisco, I was part of this collective called the Bike Kitchen. It's a volunteer-run spot. People go there and learn how to fix and build bikes. We collect scrapped bikes and old bikes from people who are throwing them away, and then it's a tool workshop. No one gets paid to be there, so that's part of creating a different kind of culture. And Occupy Wall Street is, in my mind, a big wake-up call trying to announce that culture to other people.

Everything that's going on here is built on the shoulders of lots of other movements that have been going on and lots of other work that people have been doing. This is a big expression of that—for many people, an introduction to that.

That's true. I think there's a bike collective here in New York.

Oh, yeah. Time's Up! does a similar thing. Those bike collectives exist all over the United States, and in other countries as well. That model is something that has been reproduced a lot.

Are there other kinds of things that run like that?

Totally. ABC No Rio is this really good resource in New York that's been around for many, many years. They have a photography studio, and screen printing, and they have shows there. They have a zine library in there—like, independently published things. It's a collectively-run thing. People don't get paid to be there, and you pay what you can to use those services. It's like A.A. meetings, in many ways.

That is a different way of interacting with people. Ultimately, I think, a healthier way for us, as humans, to interact. It's definitely healthier for me than buying all my own stuff, and having my own place, my own workshop—like, my own screen printing workshop.

Financially, it makes sense to share that kind of equipment.

Exactly.

You can't necessarily have a photography studio on your own.

Especially my context in San Francisco, where rent is really high. So when you can have fun by spending less money, then you don't have to work as much. When you don't work as much, you have more time to do things that are ultimately fulfilling.

A lot of us have a job that is a means to an end, not something that we inherently enjoy or believe in. I've been in that position myself. I don't want to trade forty hours a week of my time in order to have all of these material goods. These things don't bring me as much happiness as building my own bike and going on a bike ride. Obviously, there's layers and layers of privilege inherent in my situation. Even if I don't have a job—even if I squat, and I never pay for food—my existence is still fundamentally based on the oppression of other people.

Why do you say that?

If you live in the United States, your existence is based on the oppression of other people historically, in the form of slavery.

I was recently in Guatemala, so this is a good example. In the fifties, there was a democratically-elected president who wanted to do a lot of land reform, but United Fruit Company owned most of the land. The top people in United Fruit Company were also involved in the C.I.A., and in the cabinet for the presidency at the time. They created a campaign to say that what was going on in Guatemala was a communist threat. They ousted that democratically-elected leader and put in a dictator. The dictator removed all the land reforms. People were really poor. They had absolutely nothing, so they created a civil war, and there was a civil war in Guatemala for thirty years. The problems that existed during that civil war still exist in Guatemala today. The whole political system is entirely corrupt.

People in Guatemala are subjugated so that United Fruit Company can turn a huge profit. Every time you eat a banana, it's typically coming from some really screwed-up situation down there.

That's one of many things. We create all these oil wars. We have this weird situation where we have these borders that we don't want people to cross, but at the same time, our economy is entirely dependent on people working at wages that United States citizens don't want to work at. We're willing to subjugate these other people because they were born on the other side of a line that we drew in the sand years ago.

I cannot escape that. Every second that I live, that is a part of my existence. It's a part of all of our existences, and we need to come to terms with that. When I think about it that way, it's not worth it for me to try to participate in that system. Having my own room and having a flat-screen T.V. and owning a car is not worth it for me, when I look at the real cost of those things.

◆

What's going on here [at Occupy Wall Street] is an attempt to base a culture and a society on the idea of mutual aid and respect for each other as opposed to insecurity and fear. What capitalism thrives on is creating insecurity and fear in ourselves.

A really base-level analysis of this is general advertising. We're a captive audience to a lot of advertisements. In order to secure money to pay for our shelter and our food, we have to move through places where advertisements are, and they catch our eye. The people who create those advertisements create a culture that says that one type of body is good. So, like, skinny is good, fat is bad. That creates insecurity about our bodies that I actually don't have any control over. I was born into this body. I didn't pick this body. I can work out, I can eat a bunch of junk food, but regardless, I was born into this body.

There's also the huge class ramifications of the whole vilification of the poor, the overweight poor.

Right. We create this scenario that thrives on building insecurity in us in order to create a "need" for certain products. If you read about the history of advertising, that happened at the turn of the century as products were being made more and more efficiently. There was a time when advertising was designed to sell you a product based on the merits of that product. Advertising was text-based. It was information: "You should buy this." What advertisers began to realize is that it was more effective to sell a lifestyle or an idea with their product.

Products were being made at such a rate that they couldn't be sold fast enough. They were being made well enough that they would last, and you wouldn't need to buy any more of them. There wasn't enough of a need for all these things that were being made. So advertising went from informing someone about what exists to trying to create a need for that thing.

"You will be more attractive if you wear these clothes." They tell us what attractive is, and the problem with that is that you have to make a certain amount of money in order to then be attractive. Not all of us can be making that amount of money, so it creates this cutthroat system, right? But who's to say what's attractive?

What I like about what's going on here is that we're redefining those standards. This has been going on in the do-it-yourself anarchist community for a long time, this rejection of traditional standards of beauty and body image. The gender binary is part of that as well. We're creating something that's more human and more accepting, something that's based on compassion and love.

That's my fundamental reason for being here is that I want to encourage other people to think critically about capitalism, and about the images that we're told to believe in. It was really liberating for me to critically examine those things, and then release insecurity I had about my body and my place. I still carry those insecurities, and it's going to be a long time of undoing all that learning, but it's been really liberating for me to realize that. I want to encourage other people to look at that, so that we can make a choice. The way capitalism works is that it just takes and takes and takes and takes. There's no space that's left for an alternative, you know?

Describe your day-to-day experience here.

Well, in a day here, I swing between being completely inspired and excited about this place to being completely dejected and frustrated. There's a lot of awesome things going on. Every time I have an idea about a way this place can be better organized, I find out that three other people have already had that idea and are talking about it in a group, and I'm totally invited to join that group and talk about it with people. So there's a lot of people here who are really committed, and thinking really creatively, and willing to try out new ideas, willing to make mistakes, willing to be wrong. People are making themselves really vulnerable, and that's exciting, you know?

Also, seeing a lot of people who are willing to be homeless is really inspiring to me. That's what I'm doing. I'm sleeping on the street, and eating food out of the garbage can. It's really inspiring to see people who are willing to do that because this is so meaningful to them.

I don't say those things to elicit pity. Those are all choices that I'm making, and this is worth it. This is more fun than having those other comforts, even as winter approaches. People are like, "What do you do when it rains?" And it's like, "Well, you get wet." So now I'm soaking wet. Whatever.

Some other highlights I'll touch on real quick. The Oakland Solidarity March was a highlight for two reasons: One, we approved to send Oakland twenty thousand dollars and a hundred tents to help them rebuild their camp after the police raided it, and also to help them bail people out of jail. That was exciting to me because there was less of this greedy ownership over the money that we've been donated here. People are starting to realize that these resources aren't ours at Occupy Wall Street in New York; they're all of ours. That's exciting because it really challenges state power. It challenges police power. It's like, "Okay, you can go and bulldoze the camp. That's fine. We're going to put a bunch of money in and rebuild that camp."

Point number two is: That night we had a big solidarity march for Oakland. We walked off of the sidewalk and into the street, and we marched against traffic. We split up into several groups and marched all through Manhattan, and people were really stepping it up. At one point, the police tried to corral a bunch of people behind an orange net, and we ran up behind them and grabbed the net and tore it out of their hands.

Wow, really? When was this—yesterday?

This was a week ago yesterday. The night that Oakland retook Oscar Grant Plaza, which is the place where they're at.

People were getting de-arrested. I was in the process of being arrested by an officer. I was blocking a motorcycle cop from cutting us off. He pushed me over. I tried to get up; I got pushed over again. I was in the process of being arrested and someone grabbed me and yanked me away. Then the police tried to grab my feet, and a bunch of other people grabbed my arms and pulled me into the crowd.

Later that night, I did Community Watch here. Not to toot my own horn, but the point is: I'm doing something to protect people. The police aren't doing anything to protect people. They're doing things to keep us in line. People are really starting to step up to that, so that is a real highlight for me.

Also, that happened in a really nonviolent way. I don't consider tearing away a police net violence. People weren't attacking the police. It was just like, "You can't take our people." I wasn't the only person who got de-arrested that night. It happened to a lot of people. It's really exciting to see that kind of stuff happening because it's us saying we have some autonomy, and we're taking responsibility for ourselves, and we're serious about this.

And then all of the projects that people are putting together here are exciting. We're gearing up for the seventeenth—the general strike here—and a bunch of unions are going to take over some bridges, and we're putting out a public call to shut down Wall Street. The call is: The Stock Exchange will not open on the seventeenth!

We're doing a bunch of Direct Action trainings up until then, just to introduce people to direct action. What it's going to mean if you're blocking the streets. What it's going to mean as far as getting arrested, you know, blah, blah, blah. Dealing with tear gas and all that shit. And I'm getting the feeling that people are really willing to do that to make this big statement. All of those things are really, really exciting.

One of the downsides is the way this camp functions. Not a downside, but just a recognition of how far we have to go. We don't have leaders here, which I think is great. It's really important that this is a leaderless situation, and collectively organized. But based on inherited ideas of power and oppression and hierarchy, there are leaders that emerge here, and people that are listened to. We're trained from our culture to look for leaders, and we're also trained to fill those roles. So some of the hierarchy that's based on gender divisions and racial divisions and sexual orientation divisions is getting reproduced here.

Typically, a lot of white men are people in power. The media prefers to talk to those people. So there's not a strong gender analysis. We're really caught in this gender binary here. We're not acknowledging trans people. We recreated systems of hierarchy because the police are in our heads and our hearts, and so firmly ingrained in our beings. It's going to take a long time before we can break them out.

The police as a more metaphorical—

Yeah, exactly.

The Man, so to speak.

Sure, the Man is in our heads. That system is taught to us as normal. That's why the General Assembly is such a messy function right now. It took me a long time before I realized that I can go to a consensus-based meeting and not say anything, and still participate in the meeting. I go to lots of meetings. A lot of times I may say, like, two sentences, because my ideas are being voiced by the group consciousness, you know what I mean? It takes people a long time to realize that, because consensus is so different. I've been involved in consensus-based processes for a long time, so I feel like I'm more used to it. For a lot of people, this is brand-new. That's just a hurdle we have to clear.

There's also been assault here. Women have been raped here, and the way I look at that is: We exist in a culture of violence, and we're building this within that culture. As we unlearn that culture, it still exists here. Those atrocities happen throughout New York every day, so it's no surprise that they happen here. But it is really disturbing. My understanding is that it's happening in a population here that is using substances irresponsibly. I used to be a mental health and substance abuse counselor, and the way I see that population is as a consequence of the society that we're trying to change. An unacknowledged consequence of capitalism is that people are in these positions.

We have free food and clothing, and there's zero bureaucracy to access services here. We have free medical. Of course people are going to come here, because to go to a shelter or any other service . . . I was telling people, "If I still had my job, I would send my clients here because they don't have to deal with any bullshit. You don't have to deal with any sort of humiliating anything. Just show up, you're not judged, you're given what you need." Obviously, we're attracting those people here, and we're trying to come up with ways to deal with . . . not the people, but the problem behavior that sick people bring.

One idea is that we don't serve free food all the time. What I'm a big fan of is that each working group has people within that working group who get food for the group. What the kitchen does is maintain the food storage. So if I'm doing food for my group, I go to the kitchen before our meetings, and I make sure that we get a bunch of food prep for everybody. And there can be a group of people who only occupy and live in this camp; I'm not saying that they have to do something that I deem useful or not. The point is: That's how to get services in this non-hierarchical, horizontal decision-making process.

That is a way of integrating people with problem behavior into our culture, and modeling a different kind of thing for them, saying, "You can hang out here and not be judged and have everything for free and I love you. You can do that, but if you're going to be a part of this community, you have to engage with people respectfully. And that means no putting me in danger by bringing the police in here because you're using drugs irresponsibly." That also means not assaulting people. If those people get pushed out of this park—if they get pushed into the criminal justice system . . . I'm not saying we shouldn't use that when we have a real threat right here, but the criminal justice system creates the people in that scenario. It keeps people there because it's a profit-making thing for the people who run it.

That's the disheartening factor: There's all that stuff going on, and there's the ways in which we recreate hierarchy. I just need to remember that what we're fighting against has been ingrained in people's minds for generations. For many people, this is, like, one day old. So that's a long road to walk, but it's what I've committed my life to.

◆

What working group did you say you were in?

I'm with Direct Action. That's the main group I spend my time with.

So you plan the actions?

Yeah. The way Direct Action works right now is: It's like a hub. People show up, and they bring ideas they have for different actions, like this [flyer] came out of Direct Action.

This is a great idea.

Yeah. Or, like, Bank Transfer Day is Saturday, so that's a thing that Direct Action's working on. Direct Action's working on the seventeenth. They planned the Oakland Solidarity March.

It's like a hub. You show up with your action idea. You're like, "I want to do this action. My group wants to do this thing." And that gets workshopped and people discuss it, people join you in planning it or whatever. Official days of action that O.W.S. puts on go through the Direct Action Working Group as, like, "This is what we're doing today."

Do you guys plan the teach-ins also?

Mm . . . we may plan some teach-ins, but there's an Education and Empowerment group. They're an Outreach group. I mean, anybody plans teach-ins. We don't only do that, but we may do that.

The Occupy the Boardroom thing—that was you guys?

[To Ari.] Occupy the Boardroom was people from D.A., right? With the letters and everything?

Ari: Yeah, some of those jobs—Austin and Align have been planning this from a while ago—use this network that was set up for people sending letters to the C.E.O.'s who destroyed their lives. They came to Direct Action, and we coordinated this whole action together, and made it the Occupy Wall Street Event of the Day that day by getting consensus in Direct Action.

Maybe you could talk a little bit about some of your upcoming actions you have planned?

Jordan: Seventeenth, general strike. Groups are participating nationwide, shutting down bridges and occupying their cities. We're going to shut down the New York Stock Exchange. It's not going to open. The open call is: "Come down here and take part in a big march that surrounds Wall Street and doesn't let people in." Within that, there's going to be all sorts of little groups that are doing things that might be more high-risk. I don't even know what those are, but they're going to happen. The middle of the day is going to be filled with teach-ins, and people are occupying the subways. They're riding from all different boroughs, having little General Assemblies in different subway stations, and Soapboxes to tell their stories. Then there's going to be a big meet-up in Foley Square. There's going to be marches from there to occupy different bridges. So that's coming up on the seventeenth.

On the thirtieth, there's a big meeting in Manhattan between people in the Department of Defense, Wall Street financiers, and aerospace contractors.[1] So the people who make, like, drone planes and stuff like that. They're meeting for two days at Madison Square Park, and so we're going to shut that down.

It's a conference?

Yeah. So we're going to shut that down because that is a real prime example of what I said, like, "Why are our tax dollars going into building these weapons and creating these wars so that these defense contractors can turn all these profits off of killing people? That doesn't really produce anything good for us." And there's going to be teach-ins associated with that. What I'm trying to organize to go along with that is a regional convergence of different Occupys, all converging here the weekend before, for us to meet and greet. And then we all shut that down together with thousands of people in New York.

That sounds wonderful.

Yeah, I hope it happens. That's what we're moving towards. So those are two big things that are coming up.

Oh, on the eighth, this guy is scheduled to be deported, and he has committed no crimes. He's a community activist and a father of three. It's all bullshit. They're going to deport him because they're racist or something like that. I don't know why they think it's okay to do those things. So there's going to be a big march to his hearing, and then I think the idea is that people are not going to let anyone leave that building until he is not going to be deported.

And then there's Stop Stop-and-Frisk. There's this policy in New York City called Stop-and-Frisk which predominantly targets youth of color. Something like ninety percent of youth of color who are stopped

---

[1] The 17th annual Aerospace & Defense Finance Conference was held on November 30–December 1 at the headquarters of Credit Suisse Americas.

for Stop-and-Frisk aren't doing anything wrong. They're being systematically traumatized by police. So a bunch of people have a little teach-in about it, and then they go and sit down in front of a precinct, and then they get arrested and taken away. It's happened twice now. Cornel West was part of the first one, in Harlem. They did another one in Brooklyn two days ago, and we're going to keep on doing that to raise awareness about it until they stop that policy. ❖

Mike

Around the second week, I learned not to take anything personal. Just let every day be, and learn from this organic movement. Every day's new, so every day I wake up and I literally put on my thinking hat—put on Michael—and say, "Okay, you're going to go through that tent door now and everything's going to be different. It's going to be flooded with snow or something." This is an organic, ever-changing franchise that we're working on. Acknowledging that we don't have the kinks perfect yet helps me deal with it on a day-to-day basis.

So how's it going for me? It's going extremely well. That's just a personal decision—kind of a mental personal coping mechanism—because I'm very, very organized, almost to an O.C.D. level. Further than that, I'm a biochemistry/Spanish major, which requires a lot of organizational and other skill sets that you just don't normally need.

Are you at school this semester?

Yeah, well . . .

Took a leave?

No, I didn't. I'm still working on papers right now.

How's that going?

It's not going. [Laughs.]

You're not trying to write papers in your tent, are you?

Well, yeah. I can get emails on my Blackberry and I can type on my laptop, although it dies every now and then. I have a really nice light—a photographer's light. I'll show it to you.

Have you been going to class?

No. I'm currently working on a huge paper that will give me credit. Originally, I took this semester off to work, and I did work before the occupation started. I took a kind of semester abroad—an independent study. I'm working on some pieces by Federico García Lorca.

What's the paper?

This is an idea I have for Lorca . . . it's more than an idea, at this point. I'm talking about his history, his life. When Lorca first started writing, he would write about, "Oh, the countryside! How beautiful and how orgasmic and nice and lovely and fun!" Once he came here to New York, he was like, "Oh, New York! How fun and how orgasmic!" So I'm like, "Dude, make up your mind!"

I go to school in Wisconsin, and I'm here in New York. It's kind of that similar paradox where you have countryside, "Oh, zone out on my bike," and here in New York, "Oh, the train and the smell of smoke. Love it!" So yeah, it's that kind of weird thing, and I'm just seeing how his poetry or his art changed, or became better or worse or whatever. It's really just a survey of his work, and his transition from countryside to New York and back.

But it also has personal ramifications.

It has a little bit of personal, and I think that's my experience for being able to do it. Just that little bit of personal tone I have that allows me to write about it. That's what I'm working on with Lorca.

[A photographer snaps a picture of the baby.]

What's that for?

Photographer: [Inaudible.]

Mike: [Laughs.] "I do that on a daily basis."

That's so fucking disrespectful!

Yeah.

I mean, I don't care if he takes a picture of the baby. Obviously I don't care, otherwise I wouldn't bring the baby down here, but, like, you don't need to be a dick about it.

Just asking to be polite is not a big deal, you know?

It's not a big deal. If he asked me, I would have said yes.
Okay, let's forget that and move on. We were talking about the ups and downs . . .

So yeah, that's one of them! [Laughs.] If you're going to do this for the long term, you just have to zone yourself out so much. I've come to realize that this is not my home. I do not live here. I currently just, you know, occupy this space. None of this belongs to me, so if the cops came and took everything, I wouldn't be totally traumatized by it. The stuff that I need, I try not to have them here, and if I lost my laptop, that's one thing I'm willing to risk losing.

You have it backed up?

Yeah, I store most of my stuff online. My important information I store online, so I could access it anywhere. That's because I travel. So the deal is: Yeah, I just make these kind of conscious decisions that I'm going to make it not bother me. Regardless of what happens during the day, I'm not going to let it throw me.

It's a very stressful environment. The drums beat, and I don't get much sleep, and all the pressures I get: "Are the cops going to be coming to kick you out right now?" And people—just dealing with people on a day-to-day basis.

But it's such a good vibe. It's weird to me that some people bring a lot of hostility in.

Yeah, especially now. It's become a show—a tourist environment, almost. People who are not quite in the loop with what's going on are not doing this kind of open-ended journalism that you're doing. Just, "Why are you here! Three questions, yes or no?" They get this kind of surface level, and they think it's okay to smoke, and they just throw their cigarette butts on the floor. To some people that live here, it's like, "No! That's our back yard! Please don't do that!"

Hostility does come through, and I think it's from not understanding, not having a clear idea, really, of what's going on. Or some people come with malintentions. And if you're looking for that one shot that's going to buy you a thousand bucks on the cover of the *Daily News*, then you're going to run into problems with people.

"I'm still a person, see?" Especially if they're a little snotty. I don't mind taking a picture for someone or talking to someone, but I'm a person, so, "Hi!" you know? "I wanted to know you. I don't care if you take the picture."

So every day I wake up saying, "Whatever happens, happens. We'll deal with it as we go along." And just from working at this table—I work at Información en Español—we have our own little changes that come up on a day-to-day basis: "Oh, my God! What did I do with this document, this paper, this very important thing?" It's a problem-solving-skills kind of deal. Anyway, it's still a movement, you know?

◆

Can you tell me about when you first decided to come down here, and what your reasons were?

Honestly, just curiosity.

Were you in New York?

I was here in New York, and then curiosity killed the cat, so . . . I passed by and I saw . . . I think it was Chris. He was being hauled off by the cops, dragged on the floor. I was like, "Whoa! Cops can do that? No way! Cops don't do that in Wisconsin!" The local sheriff comes in at two o'clock and kicks out all the college students because bar time is over. He's, like, the cool sheriff guy who looks out for everyone, you know? Everybody knows him, Officer Pete, you know what I mean? That's the kind of environment. I was riding my bike without the lights on, and he's like, "Mike, I'm going to get you on that!" The cops are not this kind of hostile. I mean, I've been near it before, so I know they're kind of N-Y-P-D—like, television cops—but the ones that I've seen are the ones in Times Square that take pictures of tourists, not the ones being super hostile and weird.

So curiosity brought me here, and then I saw stuff happening, and then I started having these conversations, and then I realized that, "You know what? I'm never going to have another opportunity to do this." I'm only twenty-one—I'm still pretty young. I eat healthy, and health things are going pretty good; I might not get sick. Weighing all the pros and cons, I decided that, "You know what? Maybe I should get involved with this and spend a week." And then a week became two weeks, and then two weeks became . . . I don't know how long I've been here anymore.

So you were here from, like, the first week?

Yeah, from day four. I don't think I slept that night here . . . I didn't, but after a while, I started spending more and more time, and then eventually, it just became home.

What was it like at the very beginning?

It was more . . . almost survival mode, and people were pulling on their skill sets a lot more. During the first couple of weeks, you knew exactly what to do. Somebody needs to be at the Welcome Table? Okay, fine, let's just sit there and tell people where stuff are. People need help in the kitchen? Okay, fine, let's go help in the kitchen.

Now it's organized itself into a movement. The kitchen has a face, the Información en Español . . . not that it's less inviting, but it's more organized. And it's rolling, so one thing we have to work on is integration. What should happen is: Anyone who sits in that chair knows exactly what to do because there's a booklet that explains everything. So that's what happens here.

I'm still a kid, and this is probably the most fun I could have while doing something positive. I don't know that, being in New York, you're going to ever have an opportunity to do something like this, you know? Most people just get on the trains, work the entire day, and then head on home. So you're never going to have the chance to make some kind of social impact.

And I think what we're doing here is important. It's a big deal. It's kind of a big deal.

I agree.
Are you planning on staying through the winter?

Technically, I have to go back and finish school in January. I might stay through Thanksgiving. I might even spend Christmas or New Year's, but then I really do have to start winding it down.

You could come back in the summer, I guess?

Well, no, I'm bringing what I've learned to Wisconsin. They already have an Occupy Wisconsin, but I mean, it's a franchise. You could just bring it anywhere. I could bring it to my own little small town.

Right, of course. What are some of the things that you've learned that you would bring elsewhere?

Something like this, you don't take mental health into consideration. All the things are awesome, you know? We have our own Internet, Media, LiveStream, everything! I think having a kind of a buddy-system mental health kind of deal—people looking out for each other—would help a lot. Exhaustion is a real huge deal here, and you don't want people who are very active getting exhausted or becoming disillusioned, because: "Oh, no! That's not what's supposed to happen!" Kind of spoiled-brat disillusioned, and I suffer from that.

Another thing is that here in New York, people are getting embarrassed because homeless people, drug dealers, and sexual offenders are finding this spot very lucrative and very attractive. I don't think that's something we should be embarrassed about. That's society's problem. We're just a movement, and we're trying to fix those things, anyway. It's sad that those things might have been in the park, but I don't think that that's our problem. We protest things we don't like; I could protest those as well. Instead of an outreach, we could do an inreach, and protest things inside the park that we don't like.

The media's like, "Oh! Sexual offenders in here! Homeless people!" Yeah, but if you go two blocks, you could find that, too! If you just step right out of Zuccotti Park, there's probably a homeless guy by Trinity right now, you know what I mean? It's not our problem, that's society's problem. But *we're* going to fix it, anyway. Just watch. That's what my spin would be for the media. ❖

November 4

Laura II

I want to hear about your experience of facilitating.

What encouraged it is that I want to go back to my homeland, Canada, and help the Occupys there. In particular, Edmonton reached out to us for support, so I was thinking, "Well, hey, I kind of miss Canada." If I involve myself in how this works—see how the kinks are going in the original, big movement—then I can bring that knowledge, that bit of expertise, up there. Not to run the show, obviously, but to have an idea of how it's working somewhere else, in a place where they've tried to evict and we're still here, and where we deal with a lot of problems.

It's a different environment. Edmonton's going to be smaller. Like, this is Manhattan . . .

I didn't know they were occupying up there.

All the Canadian cities—all the major ones—they're all occupying.

So that was my motivation for getting involved in Facilitation. I just went to one of the meetings. They're talking about whatever, and during the meetings, they ask if you want to facilitate. I hadn't done the training. I was like, "I know the hand signals, but . . ."

It's two facilitators, and they try to have it so there's at least one traditionally marginalized voice there. So, like, women or colored or whatever. And they really try. If it's two white guys, they're like, "Oh, we're really trying to avoid this," which is great. Every night at the G.A. as well, they have this . . . what do you call it? "Step up, step back." So the step up is: If you're a traditionally marginalized voice, we encourage you to step up.

In society, we're subconsciously taught—from ages before we can remember—how to act. One of the most general examples is between men and women. Boys are taught to be aggressive and assertive, to get out there and do things. They're more inclined to take risks, to put their necks on the line. And then women are encouraged to keep it back—just think, observe. They're both good qualities, but it ends up in a dysfunctional power dynamic. So this is encouraging all those women and other minorities to overcome that. We're saying, "Get up and put your voice out there!" We're encouraging those people to come to the Facilitation meetings. Well, we encourage everyone to come to the Facilitation meetings and become a facilitator.

The training is really interesting. I'll tell you a little bit. It's all about direct democracy and consensus, which is a totally different form of democratic process. Generally, what goes on in the world is "majority rules." To give you an example, let's say you have ten people and six of them want something. They convene and decide whatever, and then there's four people who might just be totally fucked over. Whereas consensus can be frustrating—it's a little lengthy and it goes back and forth—but everyone has a chance to have their voice heard. Everyone might not get their way, and you can reach a point . . . like, it happened last night where you're trying to put through a budget, and there's a thing called blocking—have you ever been to a meeting?

I have.

Let's say someone blocks, and it's, like, one person out of twenty. They are not removing the block ever. There's nothing that can satisfy them. They feel really passionate against it. If it's just that one out of twenty, it's "almost consensus." Sometimes there's that one person or a couple of people, which sucks! It would be great if we could overcome that, but in reality, some things need to go through. You could argue forever about it, but what we've decided to adopt is a ninety-ten. If there's ninety percent consensus, then it'll still go through. If not, it's either tabled, or . . . or just, like, forgotten about. It just doesn't go through.

It's much more inclusive than majority rules. This whole political ideology is different to what the norm is. I think it's really great that they're trying to teach it. So it's not just about facilitating, it's about trying to give power to this other way of having society talk with each other. It's a lot more like a dialogue, and it's a lot less argumentative.

And it's still got kinks. I don't know how to argue for why ninety-ten is still okay if someone's really upset about something, but that's what they've decided to adopt, and I think that's definitely a lot better than fifty-one percent.

So that's the Facilitation meetings, and it's really informative. Not super in-depth, but a crash course in this political science ideology.

Do you know where this consensus stuff originally came from?

No, but the guy that was teaching it had, like, three degrees in political science. I believe that lots of societies—egalitarian societies—have gone on that basis. When there's enough resources for all the people, there's a shift from the dominant hierarchies to an egalitarian society.

◆

Okay, so I got the facilitation training, and I was just going to start out as a timekeeper. We met up here, and at that point, they only had one facilitator: a white male, not a traditionally marginalized voice. So they're looking around, and they're like, "Well, what are we going to do?" I was like, "Well, I would really love to. I know that I don't have experience, but it's not too complicated. And we're a team, so if I'm not living up to what I'm doing, this other guy's done it before."

I think that's a good argument for why [affirmative action] works. Most people would say, "What if some white male with good criteria comes in, but a woman who doesn't have the same criteria gets picked?" What it does is, like, I did fine, right? There's a job to do, and I'll learn. Maybe someone else could have done it better, but . . .

It's a systemic problem. Obviously, if some people are taught to be a certain way their entire lives, they're going to be somewhat better at it. And so if you go on the basis of who's a little bit better, then they're just going to still constantly be on top. You can, on principle, recognize that a woman could do it, but if they're never given the chance . . .

I read an article about it recently. It was about Norway or Sweden or something. They have a much higher percentage of women or minorities that have to make up a board of directors. Over time that it's been in place, the percentage has gone up. And they've got, like, really great companies. In Canada and the States, it's a much lower percentage, and people still argue about it for the same old reason: "What about the qualifications?" But you need to give them the chance. Maybe it'll be a little shaky at first, but we'll probably all be okay. It'll force those companies to look harder for the minority people that do qualify. And if they are a little less qualified, it gives them the opportunity to get the experience they need so that they can be as qualified.

◆

Maybe you could talk a little bit about how you got down here.

I came down to New York to visit my friends in September, before the occupation had started. I didn't know about it. I'd maybe seen, like, "Coming up!" but it wasn't something that was in my conscious mind at the time. Then it started happening. My friend goes to school here, so he knew it was a big deal. I was doing the tourist thing, checking out the MoMA and the Guggenheim, blah, blah, blah. But my friend is doing an exchange term here. So he's like, "What do you think of this?" I was like, "That looks interesting." We visited it in the first week, and we thought it was pretty cool.

Then I went home for a bit and I read more about it. I had another friend—also from Canada—who was occupying. I was talking to her, and she was like, "How are you not occupying?" You know, making me feel bad. I'm just like, "Oh, I don't know." So I decided to come back down. My friends said that after Thanksgiving, I could come crash on their floor again. So I was like, "Oh, what a great opportunity to hang out in New York for free some more." So I came back down, and I was going to check it out right away, but then I got sick. But after I got better, I came down to check it out some more.

I'd seen it in the first week, and then a couple of weeks later. Anyone who saw that transition . . . it started out as this amorphous mass of people and things going on. There was a little bit of organization, but not too much. Like, there was a table for taking donations, and an area for making signs, and groups of people who were interested in similar things. I remember people saying there were meetings for Arts and Culture, and meetings for this and that, but there weren't tents or tarps set up, or really solid space. It was a lot more loose at that point.

Then I came back, and it looked almost like this. Less tents, but there was the library. There was the whole Info thing where there's a bunch of computers and cameras. Everything looks like this is turning into a really solid space of information and things going on.

My friend was working in the medic tent, by the way.

Had she been a medic before, or was that a new thing for her?

She's a massage therapist, so I imagine that's what she was doing. I don't know if she's still here, actually. I haven't seen her in a while.

So okay, where was I? I came back, and it looked super cool. Particularly, the library caught my eye, obviously. I was just like, "Wow, this place is so great! They even have this library!" I came over and I was checking out the books, and I was like, "Oh, these look really cool." Just one of those new faces: "What's going on? How does this work?" I asked people, and they're like, "Yeah, just take books."

When I tell people that now, they're so amazed. I was the same way. I was like, "You can just take them? That's incredible!" I took some books and started reading them, and I came back down to volunteer. I realized that this is something I really want to support—more than monetarily. I'd given a bit of money before, but I think you need volunteers as well as money. I came down, and they just put me to work. Then I just . . . I don't know, I guess I sort of fell in love a little bit. I kept coming back, and now I'm sleeping here! [Laughs.]

That does seem to be a lot of people's story.

I wouldn't be here if I could still stay at my friends'. They had to move into a smaller place, so that's when I moved to a tent. Actually, I'm more comfortable. Their place was really shitty. There was mold and I'm mold-sensitive, and occasionally they'd come home drunk. So I'm getting better sleep here, as much as I complained before!

Are you planning on staying for the winter?

I'm thinking that maybe I will go up to the Edmonton occupation and help out there, seeing that they are asking for support. I can kind of act as a liaison. Maybe we can start more of this web effect between the different occupations. Globally, that's really important because a lot of the same problems are showing up.

I recommend *Shock Doctrine*,[1] by Naomi Klein. She goes through the whole history. It's been going on for decades—arguably longer, de-

---

[1]Naomi Klein, *The Shock Doctrine: The Rise of Disaster Capitalism* (New York: Metropolitan Books, 2007).

pending on what you want to focus on. She picks specific events and people that have, through the past several decades, shown a pattern that points to a systematic way of being that our society has adopted. It's been going from country to country. It was going to other countries first, and then has been more slowly put in place here.

Well, let me tell you a little bit about what her whole theory is. If there's an economic system that creates disparity, people usually can see that. So a politician wants to put it in place, but the people are like, "No! That's going to suck for us! We know that's not good! We don't want that!" But then if there's some sort of disaster or something, whether it's economic or geological or whatever, and the general population is kind of in a state of shock, it's a lot easier to put those in. She analogizes it to electroshock therapy, which is all about the *tabula rasa*: Cause such shock and terror and trauma to the mind that you erase all the bad things done to it in the past—all the things that are wrong with it—and then you can put in the proper way of being. It's the same thing. It's like shock therapy, but for economics.

Okay, so your economic system is flawed because it's not unfettered capitalism. You're too fucked up to accept it, so we're going to shock your country, which they did first in Chile, she says, and then to Argentina and the Southern Cone, and Central and South America. It's like Poland, and like England with Thatcher. Same thing here with Bush and 9/11. It's basically about the nation being in a state of shock, where even if they kind of recognize it, they're too scared to look out for their own well-being. It causes terror, and it splits people up about what they're going to do, and how to fix it.

[To passer-by.] Are those donations?

Passer-by: Yeah.

Laura: There's a donation bin right there. [Points.] Thank you!

That's exciting [the donation].

I know. We've gotten really good books so far today. A guy brought a bunch of books by Derrick Jensen. Do you know him? He's a writer, but, like, advocating eco-terrorism. His new book I haven't read. It's called *Deep Green Resistance*,[2] I think. Something like that. But I read

---

[2] Aric McBay, Lierre Keith and Derrick Jensen, *Deep Green Resistance* (New York: Seven Stories Press, 2011).

his book called *Endgame*,[3] which is about the problem of civilization. I won't go into him too. I'm only halfway through *Shock Doctrine*. Why did I start talking about her?

You were talking about how it's global.

Oh, yeah. It's a global movement, and I see things in the government in Canada right now that are really scary—that a lot of Canadians are worried about—which is why *Adbusters*, I'm sure, put it out there. Have you looked at the guy who runs *Adbusters* and what he says about the whole thing?

No, we're just talking to people who are actually in the park. He's not occupying, is he?

I don't think so, but they put the call out. It's so funny: They put out a picture—in Canada—that says, "Hey, go to downtown Manhattan, and bring your tent," and look at what we have.

There is an Occupy Vancouver, of course, but it's not as strong in Canada. I think population has an effect. There's just not as many people, so it doesn't hit the same. But we haven't had any violence. In Vancouver, the mayor's talking about, like, they're not going to try going in by force, and they're not going to try and set deadlines. They never wanted to tell them to put their tents down. It's a bit different in Canada because it's so much colder and snowier.

Well, Vancouver doesn't really get snow. It's a rain forest climate, actually. It snows, like, once or twice a year, and the entire city shuts down. And we all make fun of Vancouver for that because they're like, "Oh, we got some snow!"

Well, we're like that here, you know? We get very upset when there's, like, an inch.

◆

Is this your first political activity?

I think probably my first thing was when I was, like, twelve or thirteen. We boycotted Esso ... I think it was about the type of gas they were selling, or how they were extracting it. Anyway, it was for environmental reasons. This was, like, twelve years ago. I was there because

---

[3]Derrick Jensen, *Endgame* (New York: Seven Stories Press, 2006).

of my family. My aunt is head of the New Brunswick Environmental Network, so she's, like, the staunch environmentalist, feminist, vegetarian type. She would get us involved in these kind of things.

And then when I was thirteen, there was this group called Climate Change Caravan, which was about raising awareness. They biked from B.C. all the way to the East Coast, Nova Scotia. And because of Gandhi, they did it vegetarian, and entirely realized on donations. It took about four months, I think, in total. I didn't go on the whole thing, but we joined them for one week. I biked from Ottawa to Quebec City.

That's wonderful. You went with your family?

Yeah, that was with my aunt, my mom, my aunt's boyfriend, and a whole bunch of . . . mostly university students and hippie types. I'll say "quote, unquote" because, like, I don't really have a problem with the word too much. I call myself a hippie. I love people on the planet.

I don't see it as a negative thing, either, but I think we're in the minority with that.

Words—the ones that aren't politically correct—can convey so much. That's the annoying thing with political correctness, though I recognize the need for it in some ways. Language, I think, does have a very subconscious kind of effect. My mom's a counselor, and a big part of therapy is telling people to rework how they think about situations.

People don't look too different walking down the street. The difference between someone who's depressed and someone who's not has a lot to do with the thoughts in their head. You're walking along, and you're like, "Oh, I have to work! My life sucks! I can't do anything! I'm not good at my job!" and they might just look perfectly fine. Lots of people think like that. Other people are just like, "Oh, it's great out!" whether it's sunny or whatever. I mean, that's super simplistic.

But it's absolutely true that your attitude is important, and the language you use.

Yeah, the language and how you think about it. My mother talked about the difference between the word "wish" and the word "hope." Like, "Oh, I wish I had a better car," as opposed to, "Oh, I hope that something good happens to me." It's a fine line, where if you really look at language—the exact meaning of words, what they relate to and how they fit—it's so subtle, but it can make such a big difference.

I think it's important. So I do totally agree with people who are like, "Yeah, we should try and use 'she' as the general pronoun." Actually, a lot of books that use "she" are written by psychologists, who are very aware of that. If you ever read any psychology books, it'll all of a sudden be like, "Hey, they're saying 'she,' and they're not talking about a specific she." And so what that does: If you're a woman, you identify a whole lot more with this general sense of, "You are part of the greater group." You could think of yourself as the "he." ❖

Sebastian

This interview was conducted at Charlotte's Place.

There's a lot of people who thought they were liberal before they were tested. There's a lot of people coming here who would probably argue until the nth degree that we should have more social care in society, but they're now probably the same people who are wandering around going, "We have to get rid of the parasitical element of our community!" There's a huge number of us—who are much less vocal—who are trying to make a new society which is going to be better than the society out there. A society that can actually serve the needs of people who have had very, very hard times, and are basically coming here because we have support for them.

I'm pushing to formalize our social care. "Is this a soup kitchen, or is this for occupiers?" Well, what's the difference? If you feel like you want to be here, and you're part of the underclass that is rebelling against this supposed one percent, wouldn't you be welcome? Why wouldn't we want to do every effort to support you? Why wouldn't we have a Drugs and Alcohol Counseling? Why wouldn't we have all the things that we desire in the world?

There's so many mentally ill people here. That's because there's so many mentally ill people who've been left in the streets. People are saying, "Oh, the police are bringing ex-cons and homeless people here." Well, if I was a conscientious policeman, I would do the same thing. Where else would you take them? The society hasn't got no room for them. It's completely left them behind.

As an occupier, I can help care for them. I'm happy to do so. And this is a continuous balance against the people who are walking around saying, "We have to get rid of these people!" That's why I say it's a microcosm of society outside. We're acceleratedly learning all the lessons of what society has meant. There are those who think we need to police, and those who think we just need to get to know people better and understand them better. Outreach or policing, you know? It just depends which way you look at it.

One of us is always up in the nighttime to protect our stuff from theft, because we're in the middle of New York, and why wouldn't there be theft? But instead of taking that position of defense, we take a position of getting to know everyone who comes through the park. You know, making time to talk to people, and you meet some incredibly interesting people wandering through the park at four in the morning. Some of them are in need, but a lot of them are just curious. They get out of work at four in the morning. They may be talking a bit loud because they had a couple of drinks, but they're not bad people.

You might say about a person: "Oh, they're a heroin addict!" The fact that they're a heroin addict is one reaction against their particular position. It's a way of coping with their position. When a homeless guy pulls a knife, it's generally because he's lived in an insecure environment his entire life, and feels threatened very easily. It's because of insecurity. A homeless person pulling a knife is a very different emotional thing than an educated person from college pulling a knife, do you know what I mean? Judgment is a really, really poor tool to use; compassion is a very, very powerful tool to use.

Maybe more difficult, though.

Yeah. Well, you're not encouraged to use it, I guess.

I notice, though, that Nonviolent Communication seems to be invested in some of these ideas.

I'm not a fan of Nonviolent Communication. I think it can be so easily misused as a kind of passive-aggressive—

Really?

Absolutely.

Although isn't that your tent area?

No, they put their table up in our tent area. People come to us about it all the time, and I'll act as if I'm one of them because I want an excuse to talk to people and play with people. But most people who are from the Nonviolent Communication team are . . . basically, like, they come a couple of hours—if that—a day. They just left their table there, and a few of us have taken it over. They're there sometimes, but . . .

The nonviolent communicators have a very clear understanding in how to patronize. But P.C.-ness is not part of street life, do you know what I mean? So the minute they come across someone who's violently communicating . . . nonviolent communication shouldn't be an opportunity to correct people. It should be a way of communicating on a higher level with people, regardless of their interaction with you.

I haven't had very many good experiences with Nonviolent Communication. It's an offshoot of P.C.-ness, and P.C.-ness is the enemy of honesty, as far as I'm concerned. And it gives one social group advantages over another. So say you went to college, and you can understand very easily the tenets of nonviolent communication. It's very easy for you to sit in front of someone who's from a street gang and go, "Oh, you see, what you're saying is wrong. You know why? Because you're not communicating in the right way." It shouldn't be about that.

In its purest essence, like all utopian things, nonviolent communication is incredibly helpful. The tenets of nonviolent communication talk about the fact that you must always try and understand where someone is coming from. The empathy angle of nonviolent communication is incredibly important, but it's very, very easy to put the empathy to one side, and be technically nonviolent-communicating. P.C.-ness, if you use it as a technical exercise, has no humanity or compassion in it. It actually is violent and not at all communication. So nonviolent communication has to be put in context. There's certain tenets that go over the top of it. And they are in the training, but they are fundamental, and if you move them out even slightly . . .

For instance, you have to try and understand that what someone says to you may not indicate their intention. Cultural differences are massive in communication, massive. When someone says something like, "You people," or even uses what you would consider a racial slur or something like that, it doesn't necessarily mean that those are hateful or hurtful intentions in themselves. People are just raised that way.

People just hear that language, and they speak that way. The more rules you learn about what's good and bad communication, the more your judgment can be inspired, you know what I mean? The more you know how right to communicate, the more you can judge someone who doesn't communicate right, and that would actually put you in a less compassionate standpoint. So like all tools, they need to be used very, very responsibly.

I'm fascinated, because I'm having a continuous misunderstanding of the area you're in. You're not really a working group.

No, we're just a highly rebellious group of people who consider that living in a certain way is appropriate and good, and living in another way isn't. For instance, they started a Community Watch program in the park, but in our area we decided to opt out of that. We don't consider that wearing a badge and all this stuff is going to improve our relationship with our community. So we actually do the same duties as the Community Watch, but we hang around in our neighborhood and welcome people to our neighborhood. We try and keep it positive and friendly so our neighborhood is somewhere people can come. The fact that we have got the Nonviolent Communication—the coaching area—is actually kind of ironic and applicable.

One person who's been fundamental to getting our area working who you should talk to is Joey.

Yeah, I've talked to him a lot, but he doesn't want to go on tape.

Right, okay. Well, Joey's from Cincinnati. He's from the street gangs of Cincinnati. He's got, like, stab scars on him and stuff. But he's an incredibly kind and—you know, if someone who's vulnerable comes to our camp, like a woman with a child, or a homeless person . . . he was the person who invited Mohammad to come and live with us. On the front end, he's the most, "Yeah, whatever!" aggressive kind of character. He's actually got the best heart. And if some hipster comes along who wants play the guitar and hang out in the area, he'll be less welcoming to them. In his own way, he's controlling the diversity of our camp by looking after people who need looking after, see what I mean? He's been a real linchpin of keeping things positive.

And then there's Stacy, who's an incredibly practical person in our area, who wouldn't have necessarily the same kind of reaction to someone who was, like, a homeless drug addict or something. She wouldn't necessarily be as kind as Joey or understanding as Joey, but she's much better at making sure things are in order and clean. She's a worker. And we all play a role in keeping it going.

But I'd say Joey is fundamental. He's both tough enough and loving enough to make something positive out here. You can't just be loving. There's a saying: "Without courage there can be no other virtue." And I really, really, really—I don't know who said it, but I really live by that. I think that if you're afraid, forget any other virtue you might think you're going to inhabit; you're not going to inhabit it. You have to have courage. The ones who are afraid—who are insecure on the streets because they have never interacted with street people—they are the least virtuous among us, in my opinion, because fear is not something that leads to virtue.

You're area seems so cohesive, but you all just met there?

Well, it's cohesive because . . . I don't know. There's, like . . . I think Joey really did it, I have to say. You know, the first time I lay down next to Joey, he was in pain because he got arrested on the Brooklyn Bridge. He had this bruise, and I had some painkillers that someone had given me at Medical. At that time they didn't have any doctors, so they couldn't give out painkillers very easily. This doctor had come by, so I'd taken the opportunity to get some.

I gave them to Joey. Our first interaction was one of giving; me and Joey, both recognizing in each other that we come from a position of giving. And before two minutes, we were thick as thieves. Then it was like, "Well, who else is in need? Who else needs giving to?" And this has been natural for us both, and other members of the area.

We have a homeless guy living with us now who—you know, he has the issues that a lot of homeless people have. If you are judgmental and you are unable to cope with that, you won't stay in our area. Diversity is always healthy in an area. It always keeps people who are bigoted and self-interested away.

How long have you actually been occupying?

Just over a month. Me and my wife came here together. I've been here since, like, soon after I heard of it. From the beginning it was a media blackout, so no one heard about it. My wife heard about it through social media probably ten, twelve days in, something like that.

What made you guys decide that you wanted to come down?

Well, we wanted to come because we support the movement. Social justice is something that is really close to our hearts. We think about it all the time. My wife—the day George Bush managed to change the law so that corporations could give as much money as they wanted to government campaigns and lobbyists—she cried that day. She's politically aware. I'm more socially aware. Together, this is the movement that we've been waiting for for many, many years.

As far as what made us come here rather than Occupy Portland, we saw a video of the girls being pepper-sprayed by the police. But my reaction to that was slightly different. I watched it from every angle, and I saw a girl screaming in the face of a police officer that he was a fascist. It felt like she was repeatedly, abusively screaming in this guy's face. And then shortly after that, she ducks out of the picture—I don't know if she gets arrested—and these other girls who've been quite peacefully standing there get sprayed in the face with pepper spray.

It was a very clear indication to me of what situations are like when there's hatred and violence and everything negative in the world. And I considered that this would be a good place for me, as a Christian, to come, and somewhere where I might be needed. As arrogant or as conceited as that sounds, I felt like I could be positive here. And so I came here to bring peace. And I've done pretty well, although I do get kind of angry sometimes. [Laughs.]

Would you tell me a little bit about how your faith relates to your participation in the movement?

Anyone can see that in our society, all the sinful characteristics of a personality—greed, vanity, pride, independence—are encouraged a hundred percent from the top to the bottom. I don't know how you can sit back while people suffer and call yourself a Christian. It doesn't make any sense. If there's a movement for social justice, and as a Christian you're not involved, I just don't understand where you're coming from. And I would have to say, I believe that you didn't read the Bible.

What is the reaction from the religious establishment?

I would prefer that my church was more actively involved, but my church are very, very, very considerate about not being political. While this movement is seen as a political movement, they can't be officially involved, they feel like. Other churches in New York feel the same way. Whether my church is right or wrong, I don't judge. I love my church and I trust them, and I take their leadership and their understanding.

They've been supportive of me financially. There's someone on the phone I can reach to talk through things. I've got a support pastorally here by a really wonderful guy, who's really insightful and understanding. He runs international projects, so he understands cultural differences. He spent a lot of time in Vietnam, and he's just a really good person to talk to—very loving, very understanding, very measured, very considered. They're an incredibly wise church, and I love them, so . . . It's called Imago Dei in Portland, Oregon.

I don't know much about churches. Is it Catholic?

No, it's nondenominational, but I'd say its ethics are post-evangelical. The evangelical movement is about going out into the community and making sure Jesus's message is spread. The post-evangelical movement found that to be not satisfying. The post-evangelical movement is more about going out into the community and being Jesus's hands and feet. It's not about preaching, it's about doing.

So this is very much in line with the way my church operates. I'm a record producer full-time, but I volunteer on the weekends as a homeless ministry when I'm in Portland, and I volunteer in underprivileged schools and all that sort of stuff. Being part of my church means being active in the community. It means going to people and teaching them about Jesus not by talking, but by doing and supporting and guiding.

Here in the park, I don't think I've ever felt closer to God. I just feel like I'm doing exactly what I should be doing. There's so many opportunities to reach out to people. Like, loads of Christians see my "I hold the fruits of the Holy Spirit" sign, which is the way the Apostle Paul said you can recognize a real Christian from a fake Christian. Real Christians produce these wonderful fruits in their lives compared to people who use the name of Jesus, but then produce all sorts of misery and suffering in the world. So he was warning against that, and that's the early, early church—like, the first ever Christian churches—and he was warning about the same thing we suffer under now, back then. The fruits of the Spirit was his way of showing you how you can recognize them, and they're all opposite to the American characteristics. They're all, like, meekness rather than pridefulness, long-suffering rather than immediate gratification. There's always love and joy and peace, and it goes on. It's the famous wedding speech. It goes on saying, "The greatest of all these is love," and all that stuff. It's from Galatians.

Because of that sign, Christians come and talk to me. I've helped Christians relate themselves to the movement a great deal. On top of that, we attract loads and loads of people in need, like homeless people, so I've had a hands-on opportunity to work with people as a caring, compassionate person, and just be supportive to them and take care of their needs and all that, which is deeply satisfying.

And then there's also the opportunity to be the balance against the people who consider that anyone who has a different lifestyle to them is in some way a parasite on the camp who needs to be ejected.

For me, if you're a heroin addict, it's not fun. You don't choose to do it out of some sort of, like, "Oh, I've got a list of options: work in a bank, go to college for another four years and get my doctorate, or go become a heroin addict." There's a reaction against pain and isolation, and just being in a situation where you're deeply unsatisfied spiritually, emotionally, physically, whatever it is that leads you to that kind of decision-making. The only answer to that is to care for someone, and be compassionate, and improve their living situation unto a time when they feel ready to live a different life. If that's what they want. If not, then you don't judge. That's not your job, to judge people.

But there's a lot of people who just aren't understanding enough. They've had certain privileges in their life which left them blind to what it's like to live without privileges, whether they're a white male from a good background, or whether they've had all sorts of disciplined upbringing. People grow up in a culture where language of judgment is supported. I don't think you can wander into a park and shout out at the top of your voice, "We have to get rid of the parasitical element in this community!" unless you've heard that somewhere before—in the right-wing press, or in your family, or wherever.

Maybe people act like a liberal while they're at college, and then they come out of college and revert back to whatever understanding they have about the world. But the idea that this is a left-wing, liberal camp is ridiculous. There's a huge element of people who are just as un-socialist and uncaring as the outside world.

I am not personally a socialist or a conservative or a Republican. I have more in common with libertarians because I believe that any power structure, when allowed to become too powerful, is going to create evil in the world. There is no un-corrupt power structure, and the best thing you can do with power structures is to bring them down and get rid of them.

That goes for the church, too. Community church should be—like, you can have links and support networks throughout the country, but there should be no centralized power base in a church, which is probably why I'm Christian and not Catholic. Power corrupts.

What I think the church should do is—basically, I don't think it's about what the church does. It's about what individual Christians do. And I think that that is the problem of this whole world. People want a list of demands of things we want someone else to do, whereas everyone in the park is well aware: It's not about what someone else does, it's about what *you* do as an individual. I want individual Christians to respond to this society the way they should, which is to reject it, and to start to build a new society where we actually do care for the people that Jesus teaches us to care for.

When I saw how you guys were taking care of Mohammad, it just really blew my mind. And Joey told me about the doctor who didn't want to take off Mohammad's shoes.

I watched a nurse clean Mohammad's feet. He had trench foot. I mean, have you ever seen trench foot?

I've never seen it, no.

Trench foot is . . . it smells of death. It's dead, rotting flesh. So I saw this nurse—this dear, dear nurse—clean his feet, and I was blown away. And then a couple of days later, I found this other situation where I was like, "Okay, now it's my turn to step up."

And you did.

And I did. I don't know . . . you have to go there. As a Christian, you have to go there. It's actually biblically required for you to wash your brother's feet. Jesus does it in the Last Supper. He goes around and washes everyone's feet, and everyone's really upset with him, like, "You're our lord! Don't do that! Don't do that!" And he's like, "I'm showing you how to be someone's lord. I'm showing you that it's actually opposite to what you imagined, that in fact, the greatest among you will be the humblest, the smallest among you will be the most prideful and arrogant." He teaches that economy. When you start to take that seriously as a Christian is when you start to really understand Christianity. There is nothing else in it.

The whole capturing of Christianity as being something that's about moral values is ridiculous. Jesus would go up to somebody who has a terrible history and a terrible past, and he just loves them without any judgment whatsoever. He's our teacher, and we should follow his ways of being. And that's a hard thing to do, so they distract themselves in every way possible so that they don't actually have to respond to the way he really wants for us.

Mohammad's feet are getting much better, by the way. He's still got a really big problem with his little toe, but the remainder of his feet were really swollen, and they've gone down now. A lot of the sores have healed, so he's in a much better situation. And this is his fifth sober day. He's laughing and hanging out.

He had a bit of misery and suffering involved in those couple of days. When you detox, you have all sorts of problems with diarrhea. You have to get the right medicines so that your brain doesn't get damaged and stuff like that. It was a serious business, but we couldn't get him to trust enough to be taken off to hospital. He was like, "But I'm happy here! While I'm here with you guys, I don't want to drink. But if I go off somewhere else, I'm afraid I'll want to drink!" So we just said, "Well, let's do your little detox here, then, shall we? Why not?"

He's been living on the streets. For us, the camp is chaotic; it's just stressful to the ultimate. To him, it's the comfiest, most secure community that he's been in in many, many, many, many years.

I actually saw him one of the first days I was interviewing people, at the food table. He was cursing them out. Now I see him looking so much happier and so much better.

When I first met him, he used to shout at people all the time. He's gotten used to that as a way of life. He's been so abused. He's had years of life where he's been woken up in the middle of the night by a bright light in his eyes, and a policeman kicking him and saying, "Get up! Get up!" In the middle of sleep, day in and day out. Drinking, every day, half a liter of vodka in order to get rid of pain he's got in his shoulder.

Last night, he said it was the first time he's slept without pain. We've made him comfortable, and his body is relaxing. He had injuries from his time in the Soviet war, you know? If you're living under that kind of pressure to hit out and to shout out . . . behavior is always a reflection of what's going on in someone's heart. It's not like he's a bad person.

He'd shout at someone—anti-Semitic things, things that in some places he'd learned to put his satisfaction of hatred. Or he'd shout at the police, whatever, trying to protect his territory. I'd say to him, "Well, that is unacceptable! If you want to do that, then you're back out there. If you want to stay with us in here, that's not how we roll." Just strong communal pressure. "If you enjoy the fruits of this community, you won't abuse people, because we believe in peace and love, and that's not how we act." After a few days of saying that to him . . . now he's remembering who he was. He says, "I've always been a very kind person." He tells stories about his childhood and his mother. He's back in connection with who he is when being able to not have stress. Any one of us can be an asshole when we're under stress.

I know that very well.

I know that, too. No one is beyond that. If people could have even a day or two walking in the shoes of someone who's homeless—and I'm not talking about meeting them and serving them soup and then saying goodbye, but actually living with them—it's incredibly, incredibly distressing. Most people would be a wreck in a couple of days.

Me and Joey were having a laugh one night because it was so cold, and Joey went off to get a bottle of whiskey for us. He had a terrible cough, and the next day he said, "I woke up at three in the morning, and for the first time in my life, it was a logical decision to reach out and take a swig of whiskey. My cough stopped and I went back to sleep, and I woke up this morning thinking, 'Oh, my God.'" Do you know what I mean? And you judge someone for being an alcoholic? You just try living on the streets and being talked down to and abused in that way.

Not to mention, Mohammad got through 9/11 in New York as a Muslim with a huge beard and continuous abuse from people walking past. He talks about the one conversation he'd always have with the police when they were waking him up: "Oh, have you talked to your friend Osama bin Laden recently?" Osama bin Laden isn't even Afghan; he's from Saudi Arabia! The pressure that these guys live under, you know? And at the first opportunity, the first support network, the first system, his desire immediately went to stopping drinking.

People are so quick to judge. People might say, "Oh, you put an alcoholic in a flat, you give them everything they want, you put them on welfare, and they still drink." Well, it's because, actually, what humans are missing is not a flat and money and food. It's community. It's love. It's the thing they've done the most to destroy in our society. Independence is a terrible, terrible lie of our culture. The more independent you are, the weaker you are, the more vulnerable you are, and that's exactly how they want the underclasses to be. Independent, alone, without faith, without hope. And that's the situation most of us live in, even within our nuclear families.

If you had to go next door to see your neighbors and say to them, "Please, we're hungry," you're taught by your society to be ashamed to the point where you might not even do that if you're in need. And that's a very, very sad thing, and it's been designed for us. You only have to look at societies around the world.

The first thing that the English did when they wanted to suppress the Irish uprising was to ban all dances, all social groups, all sporting events. They were banned. No people allowed to get together, because people together are powerful, and people alone are weak. And that's what they want the world to be like.

It's something people are missing about what's going on here.

Communities are self-correcting, and this one's halfway through. This one's growing and changing all the time, and there's bad elements to it. In my opinion, the bad elements are not the homeless, drug-addicted people; it's the other people. So I have a very different viewpoint to some. Maybe a gangbanger who just got out of jail has come to the park because they want to be part of this movement. He's not the bad element, it's the people who think that he's the bad element just because he's got a tear tattooed on his face. The bad element, to me, is the highly educated, highly—

[Laughs.]

You know, the supposedly liberal element that's running around talking about who is to blame for whatever problems are in the camp. They're the destructive element. They always have been; they always will be. The judgmental, the unkind, the intolerant have always been the thing that's weakened our society.

You're so well-spoken.

See, this is what's funny. You told me that the reporters who say nice things are going to slam you. Should I say something hostile? [Laughs.]

[Laughs.] Well, no, you haven't said anything, which is good. The reporters—they lead you. They go, "Oh, yeah, yeah, yeah, yeah. Well, have you heard about this? What do you think of that?" You know, "I heard there was a rape here. Did you hear about that?" Oh, well, I hear there's a rape in every single homeless community in the entire of America on a regular basis.

When I feed homeless people, someone turns up every week or so beaten to within an inch of their life for their possessions. Poor people robbing from poor people because they're desperate and vulnerable. If that stuff happens in this camp, it means we are involving the people who most need us, the people we're fighting for the rights of the most. They live that lifestyle and they have that reality. It's hard for people to understand when they've been sheltered. But it's easy for someone like Joey—who comes from gangs in Cincinnati—to understand.

I think that people who are sheltered believe that they deserve the things that they've been given.

But compassion and empathy has to extend to everybody. There is nobody who thinks what they think independent of their community, their society, their media, their government. That viewpoint—that you have what you have because you deserve it or you're entitled to it—in some way is basically taught to you as a child. No individual person is to blame for their worldview. If you're privileged enough to have met good teachers in your life, then you're lucky. If you've met bad teachers in your life, you're unlucky.

The guy who's going around saying everyone's a parasite is in a state of absolute panic. He's got no peace, he's got no joy, he's got no love, and that's a horrible way to live. So you have to have compassion for those people.

Here comes my wife.

[Catherine arrives.]

We've pretty much covered your experience of the camp—what would be the word you would use?

From a legal standpoint, it's best to describe it as an assembly.

Okay, your experience of the assembly. I think that we've also covered why. Would you like to say anything else about that?

Well, we talked about why I occupy as a Christian. Why I occupy as a thinking person is the same as most people. I think the Federal Reserve is a highly, highly immoral industry, and I think that the government is highly, highly corrupt. The corruption runs through every element of our society, and it's acceptable in our society as well. When the police can be given, like, four point six million by the Chase bank to improve security, and then a few days later they arrest seven hundred of us on a bridge in Brooklyn, that is a proof beyond all proofs. The ten-day media blackout is a proof of the corporate interest in the media. In the current state of democracy, if you have money, you have more of a say than if you don't have money, and that is not democracy.

I like democracy. I like the idea of it and I support it. I don't necessarily believe it's possible, with such a large, powerful and corrupt government, to actually run a democracy, so I'm ready for them to give up power. The American government has allowed itself to become the same way as the royal families allowed themselves to become: in the interest of the royal families and not the interest of the people.

So if the president and the Congress want to be a tourist attraction, we could have people visiting them. Maybe some time in about the next fifty years. We just have to slowly take away their power. We can try and improve them, but . . . I'd like to impeach Congress, basically, based on the corporate interests. You shouldn't be allowed to have corporate interests. It should be illegal, not acceptable. If that's not the case, I think we can keep them as an institution, because I'm sure that their wigs and stuff—do they wear wigs?

Catherine: [Laughs.] No.

No wigs.

Catherine: Some of them probably wear toupées.

Sebastian: We should get them some wigs. It would help their tourist appeal, because that's what I think they're good for, really. We need to have small governing bodies in our towns and cities. The states, obviously, should have more power than the federal government. That's obvious if you want to keep things safe and un-corrupt. From a political standpoint, I'd like to take money out of politics completely, so I'm with everybody else on that. But that wouldn't be enough necessarily to keep me sleeping in a park—maybe it could be, I don't know. It's hard to separate yourself from being a Christian.

And what was the other thing you asked about? My background in activism? I'd say my background in activism is a hundred percent tied to my background as a Christian, which is a small proportion of my life overall. My load in my life has been to seek my own glory—I was a musician all through my twenties. I was seeking gratification and glory. I'm thirty-three now. My late twenties into my early thirties has been a time when I've been redressing that balance in myself, and finding happiness in that.

I do mural projects in schools in Portland, and I try and improve the environment of underprivileged schools. I think that's activism. I think that's the kind of activism we need more of. It's great to fight the beast, but the beast will crumble if we don't support it. You can't lose a game you're not playing, you know? So if you decide to be poor, and you decide to give what you do, as far as your time and your energy, to helping other people, the beast won't survive. If you choose to go and buy expensive goods at corporate stores and indulge yourself in all sorts of ways, then the beast will continue to grow. There's a very strong amount of activism in your personal choice about how you live. Not that I'm judging anyone's personal choice about how you live, but I'm just saying: If you don't like the way the system is, you don't have to have it. It's your system. ❖

Jonathan

My name is Jonathan. I'm twenty-three, and I live in Park Slope. I'm a music producer by trade; I went to school for sound engineering. I'm back in school for political science. I go to Queens College.

I saw a few footages on YouTube when it was first starting, around the seventeenth, the eighteenth. I finally had a chance to check it out—I think the first time was the twenty-first. The initial message was pretty catchy: the ninety-nine percent versus the one, and the one percent controlling a lot of the wealth and the power for the ninety-nine percent to have what's left over.

I care deeply about that, and personally, I'm also here because I'm antiwar. I would love to see all the troops come home from everywhere. We're not safer being in a hundred thirty countries. People argue that that is our security is being everywhere, killing people before they kill us. I think that one casualty will create one more family hating us and our policies.

What do I do? I drum with Pulse, the drumming working group. But I also participate in Sanitation, Comfort, and Direct Action. We plan marches and demonstrations.

That's what I do.

What's been the the good and bad of your experience here?

It's good that it's so open, and it's bad that it's so open. I mean, what comes with it being so open is: We're not in control of who comes or what comes, or what agendas are being pushed. I'm all for feeding the homeless—I think it's awesome—but then we also have a little problem with junkies and dealers. And they need help, too, but I don't think they can get the appropriate help here. Unintentionally, we've sort of created a safe environment for them because the cops don't come in here. So I joined Community Watch. We walk around late at night, and we have a little sticker that says "Security" or "Community." That's something I'm concerned with: people who are a little destructive.

The positive I sort of mentioned. It is that anyone can come and share their ideas. You know, I've learned so many new perspectives, and I've learned about so many different things I didn't know about just from talking to random people. It's a wonderful thing.

Does Pulse have a sleeping spot? Do you camp in the same area?

This area, basically. This big tent. We keep most of the equipment here. A drummer sleeps there. [Points.] Another drummer sleeps there. I sleep up the park, almost on the other side. I don't sleep with a group, really. I just have my own little tent.

Are you guys still having problems with theft?

Yeah, we still have some trouble. I mean, I just had an argument with a fellow drummer because I brought a lot of equipment and I'm not here all the time. I don't bring it for me, I bring it for the group. The conversation ended with him yelling and saying, "You should be here to watch it!" And that just makes me think, "Oh, maybe I should just come with, like, one drum for myself, and leave with my own drum when I go." But I don't want to do that. So I'm thinking about that, how to solve that problem. ❖

Matt

This interview was conducted at Charlotte's Place.

Now Sebastian set me straight today. I thought your area was the Nonviolent Communication Working Group.

No, it's not, but we are affiliated with the Nonviolent Communication Working Group. A few of the folks in the camp are with that coaching table, but only three or four. I think the number was higher, and then a couple of those guys left, so I think it's down to three or four now.

How many people would you say are actually in that area?

There's three . . . five . . . eight . . . ten . . . fourteen or fifteen, something like that. It's hard to say exactly who's there and who's not, but I'd say fifteen or so. It's grown as folks pop up who need places to stay.

Can you tell me the story again about getting your stuff stolen?

Yeah. I'd been here for . . . I might have spent three nights . . . yeah, about three nights in the park. I had a tarp, and I had a sleeping bag and a pad, but no tent, and I was doing pretty well staying dry; I got a little bit wet one night. I was camping in a space kind of adjacent to the . . . whatever the community is called, and I had met a few of them.

Then I went to Brooklyn to visit a friend and sleep in a warm spot, because it was raining and cold that bad night. I spent the next day just sort of wandering around Brooklyn and sightseeing a little bit, and

then when I came back, all my stuff was gone. I had a shoulder bag of
books, and my banjo, and the clothes on my back. My sleeping bag and
my mat and . . . everything was gone.

It started out unintentionally. The folks—they were just cleaning up
and straightening up, and they'd set my stuff in a "We're not sure who
this belongs to" pile, and I think it walked from that pile. So they didn't
steal it—they didn't intentionally put it out to be stolen—but you know,
from that pile of stuff that they weren't sure who the owners were, my
stuff just walked away from there.

But from that point, they took me in and said, "Here's a spot in a
tent." And actually, my sleeping pad hadn't gone very far. And then I
went to Comfort and got a sleeping bag. I started staying in the tent
where I've been for the past ten or eleven days, something like that.

**Maybe you could talk a little bit about that group, because it seems
like you guys are pretty tight-knit, and you have some kind of
interesting energy happening over there.**

Yeah. Sebastian and Catherine might be the only two people who came
together. Everyone else has been added, you know, sort of piecemeal.
Mm, I don't know . . . there's a little bit of a common denominator—a
radical faith aspect—between some of the folks. Loren and Joey are
both Catholic Workers, and Sebastian is here on—he might not agree
with calling it this—a mission call. I came here to see what church folk
were doing on the ground, and Stacy is also here for some faith-based
reason. So there's a little bit of a common denominator between a third
or a half of us, something like that.

I came here to see what, if anything, the church was doing on the
ground because Zuccotti Park is where the church is called to. It's not
Trinity. It's not Saint Paul's. It's Zuccotti Park, and I wanted to see
what was going on there.

It's been interesting. There's a lot of seminarians from Union who
come in and hang out with us,[4] and there's some Protest Chaplains.
The church activity amongst the park is sort of grassroots. There's not
a Chaplain Tent. Nobody's handing out tracts or anything like that.
Well, there's some guys preaching on the street corner, occasionally,
but most of the church's activity is grassroots, which I find encouraging because it's coming from a personal, organic level.

---

[4]Union Theological Seminary in the City of New York.

Could you tell me a little bit about radical faith?

Yes. A growing interest of mine is this intersection of Christian faith and social justice. I feel like that is the scriptural call. It is to pursue—yes!—to pursue justice at the cost of economic stability. It is to forswear the state and all of that sort of thing. I feel like that message is all but entirely lost in the mainstream American church. I know that's a lot of the reason why Sebastian is here, pointing out the discrepancy between mainstream American church practice and what our scriptural precedent is.

He characterized his church as post-evangelical. Is that something that's familiar to you?

I know of it, but I don't identify that way. I grew up in the Methodist Church. I have been working and attending church in a Mennonite Brethren sort of Anabaptist community in Virginia. So I would say I have a growing Mennonite affiliation, but not officially.

So Mennonite is like Amish, is that right? I'm a little ignorant about the—I'm Jewish.

[Laughs.] They're related, and old-order Mennonites resemble Amish folks in their practice of radical simplicity. No electricity, no cars. Horse-and-buggy, rural agrarian work, and rural-based communities.

So it intersects with a lot of the kinds of things people are saying who are affiliated with Occupy Wall Street.

Yeah, but I'm feeling a conflict in being here myself. From my experience of what environmentally sound life has to look like, the city doesn't work. I think, all green energy initiatives aside, New York City is inherently consumptive. Urban gardening and wind and solar and all of that is great, but I feel that there needs to be a stronger rural-community rejuvenation, and that's what I feel called to. But I also feel called to be a part of this kind of social movement. So I feel like I'm here for a time to be on the ground at the center of this movement, but it's not my place long-term.

I came here from a farming community out in Missouri, and it's just been sort of system overload, culture shock. There's always too much stimulation, and it's just . . . it's crazy.

I understand. If I go away for the weekend, it's hard coming back, and I grew up here.

Yeah, Manhattan makes me crazy. Brooklyn's not so bad. I've got a friend in Brooklyn. I met her on the train on the way down here, and I went out to her apartment the other day to get a shower and do some laundry. It was amazing! People live out there. There's, like, a soul to Brooklyn that is absent from downtown Manhattan.

So the conflict I'm feeling is: How long do I stay here? It's all up in the air because I'm just sort of traveling around indefinitely. I've got nothing I have to get to. At the same time, I'm not going to hunker down and pull through the whole winter, but it's just because the city makes me crazy.

How about an Occupy in a slightly more rural area?

Right, that would be good.

You're coming from an intentional community?

Yeah, I'd been visiting for the previous month at an intentional community in Northeast Missouri. That's Amish country, although this community is not Amish.

Do you mind me asking which one?

The Possibility Alliance. Their project is—I think it'll be five years old in April. So pretty young, as their experiment goes.

And it's a farm?

Mm-hmm. Petroleum- and electricity-free, so candlelight at night, and wood heat.

That's nice.

Yeah, it's wonderful. I spent the month sleeping in the barn loft and waking up when the roosters crow. Coming from that to sleeping in the park was a huge, huge shift.

Well, just the light can be very disconcerting.

Yeah. The first night I got here, I just walked around town until, like, two thirty in the morning because it was just so overstimulating.

Did you grow up in a more rural environment?

No, I grew up all over the state of Virginia. My father is a Methodist minister. The Methodist church keeps its ministers moving about, so it was four years here and four years there. I didn't grow up in any one place, but it was always small-to-medium towns. I guess the largest city was forty thousand folks.

What does your father think about what's going on here?

I talked to my folks the other night, and they're not surprised that I'm out here. They're a little bit skeptical. They want to know what I'm doing, and they want to know what everybody is doing. "What's the point? What are you asking for? What are your demands?" It's hard for me to answer because I'm asking the same questions.

Okay, we're all here. We all have valid grievances, but where are the clear solutions? They're here. You just have to find them. Because of the horizontal leadership structure—or lack of leadership structure, intentionally so—there's no spokesperson. There's no clear set of demands, but it is a place where any number of folks can come together and talk about their grievances and pursue solutions. It's not easy to point to, but it's happening all the time. That's tricky to describe to your parents, who want to know, "What are you doing exactly?" Well, I'm not exactly sure, but there's tons of important things going on.

The social construction here is really important. The consensus model, I think, is great. The N.Y.C.G.A., the General Assembly here, is pushing its upper limit for size to still be effective. I'm really down with the General Assembly model, but it tries my patience for getting things done. I like the Spokes Council idea.

Did you go to the meeting?

I missed the meeting—I was with a different working group—but I like the idea. I'm hopeful for the possibility of the Spokes Council freeing up the G.A. to talk about real broad, ideological, movement-based things because the time won't be consumed talking about budgetary things and logistics and money.

So that's what's going to get separated to Spokes Council?

As I understand it, Spokes Council is specifically for logistical things, while General Assembly is for ideological, Occupy-movement issues. The General Assembly was getting bogged down with day-to-day working of the park, and spending too little time on political things. Its whole purpose is to be a political body. I think they're both really wonderful models that are applicable and important for any community, whether it's a town community or a city community or an intentional community. I think that horizontal structure is really important and really beneficial. So for me, just seeing the self-governing policy at work has been really helpful, both for its strengths and its weaknesses.

How big would you say General Assembly has gotten?

It was in the mid two hundreds the night that the Spokes Council proposal was passed. The fifth time that it was proposed, it finally passed. It wasn't on full consensus, so they counted the votes. It was seventeen blocks and two hundred something affirmative votes, so in the mid two hundreds that night.

What percentage of the park shows up for those, do you think?

I would say a third or a half. And it's hard to tell if that attendance is based on involvement in other things that are going on at the same time, or if it's just apathy. I'm sure it's both, but as to what percentage, it's hard to say. There are some folks who are active in a working group or something that aren't compelled to join the General Assembly, just because of its pace. It's during dinnertime, and they get impatient.

Which working group are you involved in?

I've been to some of the Direct Action trainings. I'm involved with them to a certain degree, and I was working with Sustainability folks when I first got here. I've sort of fallen off with that. And now I'm trying to have a look at some of the different environmentalists, like the Earth Summit, and the Environmental Solidarity Working Group. They're meeting at the same time, so . . . [laughs].

That's problematic!

Yeah, it makes it a little bit tricky, but I'm trying to hear more of the environmental conversation, because we must go through thousands of plastic forks, knives and spoons every day. The waste in the food line of disposable utensils and plates and cups is really disgusting. ❖

November 5

Daryl

My name is Daryl. I didn't originally plan to come here at all. I was
skeptical about the movement, and I had just moved back into the city.
After living here for a while and working, I went traveling. Then I went
back to Las Vegas, where I'm from. I'm a writer. I do freelance writing.
I decided to come back here and get started on my career again.

I heard this was going on, and I was like, "Do I want any part of this?"
It didn't seem like it was very focused. I'd done some activist work a
couple years ago. I got really discouraged, and felt like there was no
energy or anything. It didn't feel like anything was moving forward.
But with this . . . I was seeing that this was sustaining itself. After the
Brooklyn Bridge march, I felt like maybe I should come down.

Also, I didn't have a place to live. I was living with somebody, and
I knew that I needed to be out soon. I was thinking about subletting,
but then I started to feel that maybe there was a little bit of alignment
[with Occupy Wall Street]. I wanted to be part of this movement. I
wanted to be part of a community and live somewhere, and they need
people here to try to advance the cause. So you know, I prayed about
it a lot, and I came.

One of the first nights I came down here, I just wasn't sure if this was
really the smartest thing for me to be doing, given, like, the weather
and everything, you know? I slept down near that flower bed over
there. I was just sitting there, and this woman in a business suit came
up to me. She extended her hand to me, and she said, "Thank you."
I had done nothing, really, to deserve her thanks, but I felt moved all
the same. I shook her hand, and I said, "Thank you," and she went on

her way. And then it started raining that night, so I felt like, in terms of an answer to my prayers, I got that I was doing the right thing, but that it was going to be difficult, so to gird myself for that.

Then when I came down here to camp, there was no space. I sat over in that flower bed again. You know, coming out here was a leap of faith for me. I consider myself a reluctant Christian. I believe that all religious and spiritual traditions have truth in them; there just happens to be one set of symbols and stories that appeals to me the most. So I started praying, and I was like, "All right, God. I'm going to sit here, and I'm going to wait. I'm just going to let the spirit move me where I need to go." And within a few minutes, someone said, "Hey, this space right here just opened up!" I was like, "Okay," and I moved in. Mike was over there, and he was like, "Hey, do you need cardboard under there?" He hooked me up, and made my experience here completely dry and water-free when it rained again. So I definitely feel like the spirit has been working with me, helping me to face the challenges that I have to face in the days from now on.

How long have you been out here?

A week.

But you came down before that?

I came down once, just to get a feel for it. Then I came on Friday, and then it was the day of the storm. I was going to stay, but my friend was like, "Come crash at my place." So I did, and I came back on Sunday. From Sunday on—that's when I've been staying.

Can you talk a little bit about the ebb and flow of your days?

I wake up. I check my tent out. I try to see how I can further secure it, because as you can see, it's in a walkway. It gets bumped into a lot. The other day it was really windy. My tent had blown completely aside, so I weighted it down with bricks on this end and a chair over there. I need to re-duct tape that. I thought I was moving, but it turns out I'm not.

Sometimes I'll take my pack, and I'll leave and go to my friend's place; shower, check email. Then I try to get back here around five or six, and I get dinner. I talk to people about why I'm here; I feel like I'm doing that a lot. I'm trying to figure out what I want to bring to this movement, just in terms of my strengths and skills. Mike and I are both Christian, and we've talked about reaching out to some of the peace churches—like Mennonites, maybe the Quakers—and just seeing if there are any institutions that will help support the movement and be more of a presence.

I just talked to someone with a Mennonite connection.

Really?

I'll introduce you to him.

Yeah, I'd love to meet him.

He's not from New York, but he might have some insight into what's going on around here.

Sure. Well, I know that Judson Memorial Church down by N.Y.U. had a quote . . . it was like, "O.W.S. is not simply a jobs issue or a bank issue or even an immigration issue, but it's a spiritual issue about what is happening in the United States."

◆

I think that all my activist work has really come out of when I started doing meditation and studying mysticism. I started feeling as if I really believe in "do unto others as I would have them do unto me," and the idea of being compassionate towards other people, and being peaceful and loving. Then, I can't just simply be silent in a world that is not at peace, that's destroying the planet each passing day.

I feel like that's where the change is going to have to begin; it's going to have to begin within ourselves. We can pass all the laws that we want, and those are definitely helpful—I mean, during the civil rights era, people didn't want integration to happen; it took a law to come in and make things happen—but the ultimate ideal, for me, is that people need to look into their hearts and see that, "Look, we're all on this planet together, and we're all sharing the same space. We need to work together to pull ourselves out of this . . . this hellhole, otherwise there's not going to be anything left for our grandchildren."

Before I came here, I was working with Picture the Homeless in the Bronx. We were looking for buildings to reclaim—to occupy—and it was really hard getting a group together. A bunch of people showed interest, and then not everybody showed up. We found a building, but then we weren't able to get into it. And while I was doing that, I was actually being paid to protest, if you can believe it, by . . . it was a union, to boycott Amish Markets.

Really? What's wrong with Amish markets?

They had stolen a bunch of money from their employees by not paying them back pay.

Aren't they supposed to be, like, religious dudes?

No, no, not the Amish! They're not the Amish!

Oh! It's the name of a—

It's the name of a chain. They're not actually Amish!

I was like, "What?"

Not the Amish people.

Not the people themselves, note to self.

There was a campaign from September 2009 to January 2010 by the U.F.C.W. I was doing that, and I also went to a couple of antiwar protests. Obama had decided to do the troop surge in Afghanistan, and that's a lot of what people were out protesting. I guess I got discouraged really quickly. I wasn't staying anywhere, and I was hoping to find a building that I could occupy. I ended up spending a night on the subway. I was completely exhausted, and I wandered into Grace Church, on Broadway. I sat there, and I realized that I'm not going to be any good to the movement if I'm exhausted and hungry and tired and whatever.

So that's when I decided to go back home. I was focusing more on my writing career, and feeling, you know, "I'll let somebody else do that. I need to be behind the computer knocking the stories out."

But then you decided . . .

Here I am, yeah. I think writing is important, but I found that I needed balance. It was getting to the point where my characters were living lives that were more interesting than my own. Thoreau has a really good quote, which is, "One cannot really sit down to write until one has stood up to live." And I feel like the stuff that I write is always a reflection of the life that I'm living. I want to write about things that are happening in the world, and to do that, I need to be in the world, and I need to actually live a life. My life is really more important than my art. So it's about finding the balance between doing this, and then taking the time away to work on stuff and reflect and all that.

◆

What I think is an issue—what concerns me—is drug use, and people here who need treatment, who need help. I don't know if this is necessarily the place to be able to get it. That's really what concerns me. When that need—that addiction—starts to take hold, the sort of behaviors that can manifest destructively . . .

Regardless of why people are here or what they believe, we're all here together. We're part of a community, so it's definitely something that concerns me. But I don't think I'm the only one that it concerns. We'll work it out. We'll work it out.

As you were saying before, people need to form a more cohesive group in order to make it through the winter.

I've been here during the winter, when I was doing the protests against Amish Markets. I was standing outside when it was, like, ten degrees, and it can get even lower than that. It's very taxing physically, emotionally, mentally, and you can get frustrated. You can get depressed. You can get angry. And I can just see that leading to lots of conflict.

The other day, there was almost a fight in line because somebody was flashing a flashlight in somebody else's eyes and wouldn't stop. That almost led to a fist fight, you know what I mean? That's not what we need. What we're doing is too important to let bullshit like that throw us into a tizzy.

Already, there are people who want this thing to fail. We already have enough working against us between Wall Street and the weather. I mean, the weather alone is enough, so in order to survive, I think that we're going to need to come together. It's not to say that we're not going to have disagreements, that we're not going to have fights, but I just think that we really need to be of one mind and one heart to be able to make it. It's going to be really tough, and we're going to need to have to be there for one another, in a way that I don't know if we're quite there yet.

What would be the way to move in that direction?

Don't know. Well, for one thing, we need to kind of know each other, even if it's just knowing the people in our respective neighborhoods. That's why I've been trying to introduce myself to anyone I see.

I definitely feel like I'm part of a community here. There's a bunch of us in this block, and we look out for one another. If we see somebody who's futzing around with somebody else's stuff and we don't recognize them, we're like, "Hey, do you need something here?" And then if someone needs something, we try to be there for one another.

That's something we can at least do within certain sections of the park, if we can't do it in the park as a whole. I think that's the beginning is to know who your neighbors are, make friends with them.

Do you feel like people don't necessarily know their neighbors?

I'm sure people do, but I don't know. I pretty much stay in this section of the park because it's more peaceful here. I mean, I go down there, obviously, to eat and walk through, but . . .

What would be interesting would be to have representatives from each neighborhood come and meet and discuss various issues that are concerning us as a whole.

That's a great idea.

I kind of think it is too.

You should bring that as a suggestion.

Yeah, I should.

G.A. would be the place, right?

Well, I think Town Planning might already be on top of that. They took a census to see how many people are living in each tent, and they set up that [big tent].

Is Town Planning a new thing?

I think it's new.

I'm having a hard time keeping on top of everything. There seem to be new working groups every day.

There's a lot happening. You really need to be plugged in to the working group thing to know. I haven't really been. I've just been focusing on getting myself settled and forming a routine, and also just working. I work part-time on the weekends, and then there's a blog that I'm trying to get off the ground, too. So there's projects of my own that I'm trying to work on. I'm related to this, but I don't directly get involved in the official General Assembly thing that's happening over there.

I would like to get more plugged in, because I feel like there are things that . . . I just got up one day and I saw that [tent], and I was like, "What the . . . ?"

That just happened yesterday, right?

Somebody decided for that to go up. That's my fault for not being at the General Assembly or in a working group. Considering this whole thing is about us having more political say and more political power, it would probably be a good idea for me to take more of an interest in what's happening politically in the camp. [Laughs.]

[Laughs.] I read about that this morning in the paper.

Oh, it was in the paper?

It was in the paper. But it's funny, because I was here yesterday and I didn't see them working on it at all. I guess they had to put up a frame?

I saw the frame going up, and then the next time I saw it, it was up fully, so they move fast.

That's the Women-Only Tent?

Yes.

So Town Planning is responsible for the big tents?

I think so. They're going to be in charge of that, and maybe of dividing the neighborhoods up into sections and whatnot. And hopefully, out of that will come a congress, if you will, of people who actually speak for the community that they come from. That's my hope. I'll try to plug in and see if it's heading in that direction. Otherwise, I'll have to get my ass to a G.A.!

Well, keeping warm and doing all the basic stuff seems to be a lot of work here.

It is. I spent the better part of three hours figuring out if I was actually going to move from here to there, and then finding support to lift my tent up off the ground so that when it rains, the water won't collect. There's so many things. There's never a dull moment.

And then the beef jerky people came through and threw jerky at us. There's so many distractions here.

Yeah, the beef jerky thing was a little wacko. I don't know what's going on with the beef jerky.

One thing I think is that not enough people know about mic check, so I can never hear what the announcements are.

[Listens.] Yeah, that's a problem.

You know what I mean? It's not really that helpful, is it?

Yeah, you say, "Mic check!" and apparently, the mic's not working.

No, the mic is really not working.

The mic is broken.

Is that for today, that big puppet? [Points.]

Yeah, they're going to Foley Square with the puppet. That's Obama. ❖

November 6

Scales

At the occupation I go by Scales. Before I was at the occupation, I was a dancer. I still am a dancer. As an aside, I don't really like the idea of someone being a painter or being a dancer; you just are. But I was a dancer before I was at the occupation.

Professionally speaking.

Professionally, yes. But the problem was that that was very connected to people having the money to pay for your services. If no one wants to buy a dancer, then you're not going to get any work. So I was feeling sort of, you know, the economic problems of the United States in that sense, but that wasn't really the reason I came to the occupation.

I came to the occupation because I wanted to be productive. The most important thing to me is to be productive—as productive as possible—in things that actually matter, whether it's art or politics or just talking to people or . . . I don't know, building something, whatever. I knew that I could be productive down here within some sort of construct of the occupation, which is why I joined the library.

So to answer your question, "How does why you came here differ from why you're here now?" I came here with sort of a loose idea . . . like, I knew that this was a space where I could be productive within a system that I believed in, but I didn't really know how. And then I got involved with the library. Once I got involved in the library . . .

First of all, I'll say that I'd never cared about libraries before I came to the occupation. I rarely ever went to libraries; I didn't think they were important. But now that I'm here working in the library—literally running this crazy outdoor library for free social media—it's taught me how important it is to have that space. It's important to have space that's free for people to have access to literature and access to media and access to . . . just books. A lot of people don't have Internet access. I hope that eventually, we can create a working computer lab within the library, too, but I don't know.

There's something very special about the idea of providing people with the tools to educate themselves. That's what I think this occupation is about. It's not about, "Here's the party line," or, "Here's what I believe," or, "This is why we're here." No, this occupation is a learning experience for everyone, and I want to make sure that people have the information and the tools to educate themselves.

Give me an update on the library. How's that been going?

I mean, it's been going pretty well. I was quoted in a different newspaper where I mentioned that the library was sort of this immaculate conception. It never really started, it was just here, which is sort of true. You know, the library started out just as a pile of books on a tarp and someone called it a library.

But when there's that source of literature, people often bring more literature. They're like, "Oh, there's some books! I'm going to bring more books!" So people brought more books. People came and said, "Maybe I should organize them into bins!" They did that, and it just snowballed, and now it's really big and huge.

Now we're getting books from publishers. We're getting, like, hundreds of copies of the same book! [Laughs.] It's not that helpful, but it's great. Naomi Klein's been down here. The creator of *The Vagina Monologues* has been down here.[1] It's been great.

It's definitely been an interesting experience working in the library because it's not just working in a library, it's building a library. It's also sleeping in a library, which I never thought I'd do. Two months ago, if you'd said, "Hey, you're going to be sleeping in a library . . ."

"With no ceiling . . ."

"Sleeping in a library with no ceiling, and being a librarian there," then I would have been like, "No." But I like it. It's nice.

What first drew you to the movement, politically speaking?

---

[1] *The Vagina Monologues* was written by Eve Ensler.

To be honest, I was here on the first day and I was very skeptical. Like, I didn't come back for about a week after the first day because . . . because of all the reasons that people come here and are skeptical. Like, "Oh, it's disorganized! They're not saying that they have any necessary goals! All these people aren't here for a unified reason!"

But the more and more I wasn't here, the more and more I said to myself I really need to be here. I really need to inject myself into that system so my voice can be heard. That's when I realized all the value of that "disorganization" or that autonomy between people. It's not just, "Here's what we want! Here are our demands!" We are all here for different reasons, but we're all unified because we're all angry.

When I realized that, a lot of my reasons changed. I used to be a Marxist, but now I sort of consider myself a nothing. I don't know what works, but I know what doesn't work. That's why I'm here, because this is a community-building exercise, and we're figuring out what works within this application.

So to sort of synopsize your question—because it was a good question—my political views before I came were very concrete, and since I came here they've become much looser. I'm here to figure out what works, and I'm going to learn what doesn't work at the same time. And I don't care what people do as long as they're not hurting others, and I think that's a very concrete statement. Certainly, I've been trying to inject that into the system as well.

◆

I think that there's a lot of centralization going on here, which I don't like. I believe in the freedoms that people should have to do whatever they like as long as it's not negatively impacting anyone else. I know that's sort of a broad statement, and there can be discrepancies within it, but I'm sure you understand what I'm talking about.

What about the centralization are you not into?

I have a lot of problems with the centralization. I'll give an example. Before the library was part of Finance and pooling our funds with them, we were an autonomous entity, which is quite important for a library. A library needs to be a neutral zone. It can't be censored. If someone brings us . . . I'm having a brain fart right now. What's that book by Hitler?

Mein Kampf.

Yeah, if someone brought us *Mein Kampf* . . . I don't like *Mein Kampf*, but we'd put it in the library because you have to give people free access to literature, regardless of what that literature is. You can't be censored. And that's why I really didn't want to get in bed with Finance. Now we're in bed with Finance. It's not necessarily a bad thing, but I don't think it's necessary. I don't think all this centralization is necessary. I don't like the idea of having to go through the G.A. for every single proposal because I don't think it promotes a sense of community.

I've always said: If I want to go and check up with Sanitation or figure out what they're doing, or if I need something from them, I know a lot of people from Sanitation because I've taken the time to get to know my neighbors. If I need to talk to Info, I talk to my lovely friend Cynthia over here. If I need to go to the kitchen, I know people from the kitchen. I can do that.

I understand that there's a place for the G.A. as a space for everyone to get their voices heard. I don't really think it's functioning as that right now because there are just so many people. It's not really their fault, but I don't think this massive centralization and homogenization of working groups into, like, a structure is necessarily conducive for becoming a community of neighbors, you know what I mean?

So you're not into the . . . what is it called? The Council?

The Spokes Council.

I keep calling it the super PAC, but that's not it.

You know, you'd be surprised, because I'm not as against the Spokes Council as you would think, specifically because I see the Spokes Council as something to fix, in a way, the problems that we're having with the G.A. All the things that I like about the Spokes Council are things that I hate about the G.A. The thing about the Spokes Council is: Now we can make decisions in a G.A. form, but in much smaller clusters, which I like because then more will get done, and more will get done faster. So I like that about the Spokes Council.

What I don't like about the Spokes Council is that I feel like the structure of it is very . . . I think it's very neutralizing to those that are not the spoke. And I realize that the spoke is rotating, and again, I want to say that I'm not against the Spokes Council. I like the Spokes

Council, but there's some things that I don't like about it. I guess what I'm saying is that it's necessary at this point because of the problems we're having with the G.A.

What is the spoke, exactly? Maybe you can just explain that.

So the spoke is, basically . . . I would describe it as the speaker. The spoke is always rotating, so it'll never be the same spoke unless you've gone through all the people in the working group. But basically, I would describe it as, like, bowling pins. There would be the front bowling pin, and that would be the spoke. And then the rest of the bowling pins, which are the rest of the working group, are behind the spoke. The spoke is representing the working group so that their voices can be heard in organized fashion. And of course, to make sure that there isn't this crazy power structure like, you know, a Speaker-of-the-House situation, the spoke is always rotating.

Each meeting it's a different spoke.

Each meeting it's a different spoke.

◆

You're also involved in Info?

I mean, I'm involved in a lot of working groups. Info, I sometimes do cover for Cynthia when she's not around, but my major focuses are within S.I.S.—Shipping, Inventory and Storage—and of course, the library. I occasionally help with Comfort when laundry needs to be done and things like that. But majorly, it's S.I.S. and the library.

S.I.S. and the library are basically the same entity because without S.I.S., we would have this crazy influx of books that we wouldn't be able to deal with. It's very important to have that storage facility. I tend to go over there and do cataloguing, and then bring books back. I help with any organization that needs to be done there as well.

How big is the storage space?

It's big. It's really big. It was donated by the teachers' union. It's supposed to function as a bank, but it's not, obviously, right now, because it's a storage facility. It's quite large. It definitely fits a lot of stuff.

So it's fitting your books. It's got the books and the Comfort stuff.

There's a lot of Comfort stuff. This is why S.I.S. is so integral to this movement right now, because we are getting such an influx of donations that we can't physically deal with it at this small park. We need that storage facility, and at S.I.S., we just make sure that it's organized and that it's distributed to the working groups appropriately. That's basically what S.I.S. does.

That's what I do at S.I.S. is make sure that things are organized and are going out to the working groups that need them at the times they need them. Like, if I send people blankets at twelve o'clock in the afternoon, then that's kind of stupid because no one needs blankets; no one's sleeping. But if I send them at eight o'clock, then people need them. So you know, that's the idea is that we need to get them rolling at the right times to the right working groups. I'm not going to be sending books to the kitchen, you know?

Logistics.

It's difficult logistics, and I think a lot of people at S.I.S. get very pissed off, because you know, people tend to come into S.I.S. and just be like, "Oh, we need this, blah, blah, blah," and they just take it. And I don't really think that there's a problem with people necessarily taking stuff, but there needs to be a structure in place so that people don't abuse the system. We're not rationing anything. We have plenty of everything, but we make sure that it's going to the right places at the right time and in the right quantities.

And also coming in. While it's coming in—while we're getting all these donations—we make sure that they're organized properly.

It seems daunting, trying to keep everybody in all the supplies they need.

It's very daunting. No, absolutely. We get so many donations a day. We got three hundred boxes of down comforters the other day. Yeah, they're piled as high as the sky. It's crazy.

Where did that come from?

I don't remember the donor, but they came two days ago. We also got some donations of tents and things from this Alaskan guy. We get lots of donations. Yeah, it's wonderful.

Can you tell me a little bit about your background beforehand?

I'm a hip-hop dancer. So I guess . . . I don't know, I guess I'll give you my most recent background. I went to college for about a semester, and after that, I was like, "Fuck this! I hate college!"

Fair enough.

I went to a community college. I know everyone has their different experience in college. My experience in college was that I was yelled at by adults all day, and I was like, "This is kind of stupid. I'm not learning anything, and I'm not here for the right reasons." And so I left, and then I moved to New York.

Where were you located before that?

I grew up in Pennsylvania. Lehigh Valley, around Allentown area. It's a suburb of Allentown. So then I moved to New York, and when I came to New York, I got a job as a go-go dancer to pay the rent.

Is that good money?

It depends.

It's tips?

It's tips. I'm not going to go into the logistics of go-go dancing.

Whatever you want to say or not say . . . I'll just ask, you don't have to answer.

The thing about go-go dancers is that it's based on the idea of freshness. Fresh faces, fresh this, fresh that, and there's an art to it in the sense that you will get lots of tips in the first two months, but then people will get bored of you. What I did in go-go dancing—and this is why I sustained my income—is that I would constantly be changing my look. I would have different outfits, different hair colors, different everything. The joke with other go-go dancers is that I had a different hair color every day, which I didn't. But I went from brown to red to blond to red again to blond to everything. Yeah, lots of different outfits, lots of different sort of fetishy things, whatever. And I worked at a bunch of different clubs, which was interesting because that's sort of what brought me into the dance world.

I didn't come out of go-go dancing and say, "Oh, that was fun! I felt so hot! Yay, I'm a go-go dancer!" I came out of it and I was like,

"Wow, I really like dancing. This is something that's really important to me, and I really like the art of it." So then I started pursuing dancing professionally. I met Marina and the Diamonds, and I started working through that. I did that for a little bit.

Dancing's a very hard thing to pursue. Especially if . . . I'm quite a good dancer, but on a resumé saying, "Hey, I just starting dancing and I have no ballet training," it's kind of like, "Oh, I don't think I want you." But I was able to get work by going through the back routes. I didn't go to auditions. I would go literally to the artist and be like, "Hey, give me a job." And that worked out. But then after that . . .

I still want to pursue dancing, but I came here, and when I find something that's interesting . . . I live my life in a sort of mercenary way. If I find something that's interesting enough, I'll put a lot of time and effort into it. I thought that this was important, so I came here, and now I'm doing this. I think a lot of people here, by the way, have similar stories. There's a Canadian girl at the library, and she came to New York to get her yoga license, but then she found this and she was like, "Oh, well. This is kind of important. I'm going to do this."

And you know, in terms of after occupation, the things that I've learned will be of benefit to me in every conceivable way. My skills in organization have become better. I built a library; that's kind of crazy. The skills that I've learned here . . . I don't want to say, "Now I'm going to put this on my resumé! Yippee!" That's stupid. That's not the reason I'm here. But I will say that I've amassed a tremendous wealth of knowledge by being here, and that's really important, and it will definitely help me later in life regardless of what I'm doing.

Hopefully, the Revolution will come, and then . . .

That'd be fabulous.

The most interesting thing is: People can have their little projects here, and they can really get it out. Like, I'm working on this project called Occupy Runway. The idea behind it is that we are going to construct garments out of tarps and spare blankets and tents and things from the occupation—garments that are inspired by the æsthetic of it. In the end, it's going to coincide with spring fashion week. We're going to do a march down Fashion Avenue, and each model's going to have a sign. So that's what I'm working on right now. That's my little side project, but I wouldn't be able to do that outside the occupation. I can do a project like that specifically because I have the support of my brothers and sisters at the occupation. Yes, I'm only hoping I can pull it off. I can draw clothes, but in terms of making them not fall apart, I'll probably need to recruit F.I.T.'s help or something.

I would imagine you'd be able to find people who'd be into working on something like that.

Yeah, regardless of anything, if they're not into politics, it's a huge P.R. thing. Any student would love to do that because they'd get their name out like that.

I mean, this is definitely a creative environment. Oh, we have so many creative people here! I think that everyone is creative; Picasso said that everyone is born an artist. I really do believe that, and I will say that being here brings out that creativity. That's why we're here: because we're such creative entities. This space is conducive for having creative thoughts, and I've definitely been quite creative here—creative and innovative.

Innovation is important in a space like this where you have to be innovative to not die. Like this [person propping up the Media tent]: He's being innovative with a broom. ❖

Cynthia

When you spend the day here, you really understand the workings of it. The biggest misconception is that there's no organization, no leaders. Me and my friend Eric just came back from our coordinators' meeting at nine, and we were saying that in our opinion, the organization is sort of centralized/decentralized. That means there's tons of information, not that there's no goal. The goal is, essentially, equality in this abundant world. It is centralized here in the park, but with so many different concerns to that goal.

It's not just specific to New York or America; it's the abundance of the world. It's also a way back to the spirit and soul of humanity, meaning equality, human dignity, fairness, democracy, voices being heard.

It's those voices that may have been on the fringes, that were not about to be heard. And it's not just race, because it's white, Mexican, African American . . . it's everything. Also, there's a class that hasn't been as educated that we're trying to include and allow a voice to.

We have our General Assembly every day at seven. We also have our working group meetings and our occupiers' meetings. Many people are intimidated by the word "meeting" because they don't know how to voice themselves. They're afraid they're not going to learn properly how to be heard, or they get frustrated because they're not being heard. So they hear "meetings" and they want to stay away. That's what I mean: It's decentralized because we want to include everybody's voices. We are really working hard to do that.

Today I work at Info/Outreach. I've been here thirty-three days. I'm living here. I've worked in our Comfort, our kitchen, and our Sanitation. My thing is outreaching to communities—not just passer-bys and tourists, but also our communities here within the park.

Being here in Zuccotti Park is an important stance. It's not a fight; it's a stance. It says that we are here. We're not leaving until we get some changes within our socio-political-economic system.

Our current systems, since before the economic meltdown in 2008, have been not working. So we voted with President Obama. His whole platform was changes, and we feel that we haven't gotten the changes from his presidency. We gave that opportunity. He said, "Changes are coming. Changes are coming." These changes have been an issue for many, many years in our socio-political-economic system. People put their hope in Obama's changes. We thought it was a new era. I personally believe that he did try through struggles, but it hasn't happened.

Since the changes haven't arrived yet, I think, collectively, something happened with us as humanity, as a people, as all peoples. We've been waiting. We've been waiting. We've been waiting. They pushed it back to another agenda, pushed it back to the next agenda and the next agenda. And now, for some reason, you can just witness—what is it?—fifty countries all over the world now standing up for humanity, for dignity, for equality.

It's a universal upwelling.

It *is* an upwelling. My point is: It's been a long time coming, and the most beautiful thing that happened was that collectively, the peoples of the world are standing together. That's not happened in our country since the civil rights movement, where they said, "This undignified behavior is not working for humanity." So this is the special thing about it: collectively, everybody standing together.

This outreach that happens within the park—how does that work?

There are several of us who realize the importance of reaching out within our community. We are trying to reach out to people not just from working groups. We are all about compassionate, dignified equality for *all* peoples. Not all peoples who gather here know how to make the changes happen, but they want to be involved.

People are drawn here because they feel protected. They don't really know how to fit in, but they're drawn here. It may not seem like it. It may seem like they're just here hanging out, but it's because they're not included yet. They're intimidated to come to our meetings, our working groups. This was a big discussion today.

It's not just about race; it's not just about people of color, or Latin people, white, black, whatever. It's a certain type of people who have been on the fringes of society. They've just been on the wrong side of our society. They have been, maybe, outcast because they've been institutionalized, either mentally or for addiction to drugs or alcohol. They've been let out of the prisons or mental institutions, and they're thrown into these homeless shelters.

In essence, political leaders like our mayor and so forth of this city are saying, "You have somewhere to go. You have a homeless shelter. We provide you this." Well, those are more dangerous than prisons. People don't want to go there; that's why we have homelessness.

But the one percent—for instance, our Mayor Bloomberg . . . what he said the other day, that we defeat our presence here because of all the homelessness, all the drugs? Those happen in the streets whether Occupy Wall Street's here or not. That's been ongoing. I mean, it's silly. Does he think he's the mayor of Walt Disney World? This is New York City, one of the toughest cities in the world. These things have gone on and will go on whether Occupy Wall Street's here or not, but because we were getting these people here—homeless and runaway kids and drug addicts and alcoholics . . .

I take it upon myself to go into these areas within our camp. People are not aware of how facilitation works in our meetings, so we're inviting them to come to a Facilitation Working Group meeting. You can facilitate in meetings, or just be a part—a voice. Or at least, just have an awareness of what you choose. You can actively be in our meeting. You are invited. You are welcome.

So there's small pockets of us who are initiating that on our own, as individuals. We're getting together and making a nice introduction and report with many people here within the camp, not just here where it's nice and clean, at the library or in Info/Outreach—see, this is pretty—but all throughout the camp, wherever we can include people.

We say, "Hi, I'm Cynthia. I work in Info. Do you know about the meeting today? It's going to be at four o'clock." A lot of people here in our park, like in society, do not have access to computers or fancy iPods or cell phones or smart phones. You can't just give them a flyer, or say, "Go to N-Y-C-G-A dot net." Chances are, they won't read it. They may not have the capacity to connect with it because they feel like, "Ugh, it's just another paper thrown at me."

So on a human level, that's what I mean about coming back to the spirit and soul of humanity. Olivia, you know, we're interacting as human beings—in the eye—and that's what we do here.

That's what we feel is very important. If we're saying the ninety-nine percent . . . which I feel, personally, is a terrible tag. I feel like here in this park, we are one hundred percent. We are one hundred percent, so I don't really like that victimized ninety-nine percent, myself. That's my personal opinion. I don't really like that. We're saying we're the ninety-nine percent? Well, ninety-nine percent is not just a certain educated class that's doing the meetings. Ninety-nine percent is: Everyone should be included, if you really have that heart.

That's what our coordinators' meeting started to be about. It got a little too much on that subject, because the coordinators' meeting every morning is just report-backs for every working group. It's for any urgent or vital information that's currently going on, but it started to get into that discussion. So it will be a breakout group, which they started discussing after that meeting.

A few of us decided to just go throughout the camp and talk: "Oh, this meeting is about this and that and the other," or, "The way it works is like this," or, "Direct Action is a group of people that works on protests and marches." Telling people these kinds of things—really verbally communicating within our camp—so that we can grow this with the people who showed up here. The stance of the people here is so important, and as you know, the symbolic stance of being here . . . if this park goes away, we don't have Occupy Wall Street, so we need to build this up thoroughly. We're doing that. We are working on it.

How are people reacting to the outreach?

I'm saying outreach, but we do—

Inreach.

Right! Yes, exactly! People that I outreach to, and other people . . . it's great! It's sort of like, "Okay, thank you." You know, some people are a little hardened, so they won't say thank you, but you can see in the face and in the eyes how they start to soften. It's a beautiful thing, because people don't want to admit that they don't know what's going on. You can see in their face it's one of those a-ha moments. You can see in their face when they're like, "That feels so good!"

At our meeting, we also talked about the vernacular of speech. Everyone has a different vernacular. We have a group here who comes from the streets, and we have a group here who comes from a more educated class. So that's also inreach/outreach that we're doing, to try to connect those two vernaculars so that we can all relate. Some people who are more expressive or more passionate—they're not yelling or being forceful. They're not being angry; they're just talking, and we have to allow that. We have to be open. It's not for us to say, "No! Talk when *we* want you to talk! Have a meeting the way *we* want you to have a meeting! Compose yourself! Don't do this, the way *we* don't do this!" No, no, no, because some people who talk like that can be passive-aggressive, and it's not a good thing. It's actually a real wall.

This really is a beautiful challenge. It's the most beautiful challenge because if we can make this work, we're proving so much about the beauty of humanity.

How do you take what's being learned here and bring it outwards into the bigger world?

We do have an Outreach group. In fact, they have a meeting today. What they do is they have, like, a luncheon, and they invite people from different boroughs to hold their own G.A.'s. They learn how we facilitate G.A.'s. They learn how to gather a stronger voice. And we're spreading this, through the outreach program, to all the boroughs.

You should probably go. It would be interesting for you to see that. Everybody's invited. That way you can actually talk to other people, and that would answer that question, "What would it be outside the occupation?" We all really do want to hear each other, help each other, spread the knowledge and education. We really do want to grow as a society of humanity. That is what's happening. That's what's happening throughout the world now.

In the beginning, we had this wonderful world map, and we put pins on all the places that are being occupied. We have since lost it, although it might be in our S.I.S., because you know, we've had snowstorms, rainstorms, evictions and cleanups, and it's gotten a bit lost. Smithsonian museum representatives have come down to acquire it when our movement is done. That and our map of Zuccotti Park. I love the Smithsonian, and this is really history.

That's why we're making a book, to set down the real history. The press has been pretty skewed—not accurate at all.

Of course, the *Post* and Fox. Bill O'Reilly—who's a cotton-ass—said on his program the other day, "There's going to be murder!" You know, there's a murder on the streets of New York, in all the boroughs, probably more than once every day. But that is a city. That has nothing to do with us being here. We are actually providing a lot more safety to the streets that has never been in this area.

We just had a harm-reduction group coming in. They're making us aware that the people who come here—you know, the addicts and the alcoholics—they need the help. There are areas here that have been able to help them, to assist them, to give them that compassion, and to at least make it safer for them, so they can hopefully get out of that addiction or that phase in their lives. We have our medics here to treat the homeless—our medics, our volunteers, our nurses, our doctors, our psychologists on staff. We have acupuncturists.

For the mayor to say something so ignorant . . . it shows him to be out of touch. He is a part of the one percent that we are actually making a stand against.

Someone described him as "the hammer of the one percent."[2]

---

[2]Douglas A. Muzzio, in: Kate Taylor, "Demonstrators Test Mayor, a Backer of Wall St. and Free Speech" (*New York Times*, November 3, 2011).

So the harm-reduction people were trying to link you guys into the services they have in the area?

Yes. We have our guy Stephen, at the library, that works with Scales. He is an ex-addict, and he has had a wonderful doctor who helped him through it. Now he's clean. He's wonderful, he's productive, and he's great, so he's trying to help other people. The doctor brought his colleagues and representatives—who were all over the boroughs, like up in the Bronx—to come down here to hand out pamphlets, and to have a meeting with us. They know we have this issue with people being safe: Do they feel safe as they come here?

That's something that the press and media don't like. They just like to say that people are gathering here causing trouble. No, they're gathering here and feeling safe because we have Community Outreach, Community Watch, Nonviolent Communication, safety class, . . .

I've done many night watches from two to four in the morning. Around the coffee, partner up. We go around and we do this in such a way that we make a presence within our community, to prevent any kind of unsavory acts. I love that I just said "unsavory," but you know what I mean. So our presence here, actually, is a very good thing. It's an educating thing. It's a knowledge-is-compassion thing.

The people that are against it—the *Post*, Bill O'Reilly, Fox News, all the other news that are saying these negative things—it's really embarrassing for them as a human. People are getting fed and clothed and a place to sleep. There are a lot of compassionate people here. That's what I meant about the beauty of humanity: There's so many beautiful, compassionate people. The Empathy table is for everyone.

It's really an amazing thing, but you know, at the same time, please understand that this is incredibly, incredibly difficult work. It's very, very hard work. I've been here thirty-three days, not only getting used to sleeping outside because of the noise and the weather and so on and so forth, but actively getting up and doing Community Watch, and thwarting fights and issues like that.

And then just our passions and our emotions. We sometimes fight or we argue, but they're friendly arguments. We make up within our groups. Our passions, our emotions . . . we're like, "Aagh!" because it's very difficult work. Sometimes you feel like you're making so much progress, and then some fool will come and rouse up people and get people to work against, and a lot of them are paid to do this.

Really.

I know that for a fact because someone from our group was sitting at a café, and there's a gentleman here . . . everybody knows him. He's a black guy. He has this beard. He comes almost every single day, mouths people off talking about, oh, he's a one-percenter. He spreads these just terrible messages, and someone heard him say—in a café, talking with someone else—that he's paid to be here, to do that.

I worked my first days here in Comfort, and I know for a fact that the guy I helped—he was so sweet—said he just got out of Rikers. He was holding up his pants because they didn't give him his belt back. There's apparently some new system where you have to sign something to get the rest of your things back. I don't know what that was about, but we gave him a belt. Not only gave him a belt, but new jeans, new clothes. We kept him warm, gave him a place to sleep, and he marched with us. We told him as much as we could about what it was about. I can't say I've seen him here again, but I know that these people are coming.

We hear that they're let out of jail and told to come here because it's safe. In Tribeca, there's a homeless man who's been there about twenty years. We know for a fact that the police woke him up, told him to come here. We know that for a fact because he told us that. He actually was a very intelligent man. It was his choice to be homeless, and he wasn't just some crazy rabble rouser, or a harmful man.

So we know in those three instances that, yes, people are told to come here. It is safe here, and we do take care of them. We have the compassion. Can you imagine what a beautiful society this would be if everyone did that?

Every time I come here, I wonder why this can't exist outside.

We're hoping it can. That's what the outreach is about: to get past these borders, to get the word out to the boroughs. And it is being spread out throughout the world now. It's really good! Exciting!

Would you tell me about your background in activism?

I'm not an activist. I've never been an activist. I've never marched a day in my life for nothing. I've been in New York over fifteen years. I do hair and makeup for film and television. I came here—I was actually on my way to Chicago for about a month or so. Before I left, I came down here because I heard about the seven hundred arrests on

Brooklyn Bridge. Then I heard about the Union Square pepper spray night. For some reason, something triggered in me. "I've really got to see what's going on there."

All my friends and my clients were like, "Don't go down there. You'll get arrested." I didn't have that fear. I just knew I needed to see what it was about because it was happening in my back yard.

So I came down here on a Friday night—I think it was the thirtieth of September—asked questions, went around . . . I can't even say what happened. All I knew was I had to come back. I stayed in a hotel a couple of days because I gave up my apartment. I stayed for three days in a hotel to decide, "Do I really want to come back here, or do I want to head back home to figure out my own situation?" I decided, "You know what? Let me come back here on Monday and see how it is." So I slept here Monday, and I've been here ever since.

I said to myself, "The day it feels like something that I don't believe in—which is being a total anarchy/violence movement—I'm out. If I don't see a good in it—I don't see a potential in it, a hope in it—I'm going back." And you know, I haven't taken a project in a month, and I have three more months of work. I get into the union—the hair and makeup union—which is very important to me because it means I get my benefits, and I get to actually be working on films like the Batman film that's here right now.[3] Right now I work on indie films. So I have been putting that off. It's a little bit stressful because I know I need to get back to work—I really need my own situation—but it's so hard to leave because I see it grow every day.

When I give up hope, then all of a sudden a new group is coming up with something that I thought, "Oh, man! I was just thinking we need that!" So I just see it growing every day, and every day it's harder to extricate myself. I feel like I want to be a part of it. I want to be here when we get that . . . well, what I'm hoping is we get a message to our leaders that we voted into office—who are making our laws for us and working for us—saying, "We want a public discourse with y'all, and we want to show you what changes we are now going to make." That's what I want to see. Will it happen? You know, will money be out of politics any time soon? No, but I want to see a big push towards that. I want to see an inkling of that before I leave.

---

[3] *The Dark Knight Rises*, directed by Christopher Nolan (Burbank, CA: Warner Bros. Pictures, 2012).

We see that in the little ways. We have a lot of diligent people who are part of what they call the one percent. They don't have to check the bank accounts; they have the money to offer. They have the donations, they have the heart, and they are believing in this. When I see that, it's like, "Yeah, those are the people who have the contacts with the politicians and the lawmakers, who have the influence with them, who know them, who have dinner with them." That they're on our side is sort of an inkling towards opening up that public discourse.

Let's make changes for our society. Let's not say we have no money for keeping the mentally ill in institutions. Let's say we do have the money. Let's find a way to get them the help they need. Let's find a way to keep Social Security and medical benefits. Let's find a way to get better-paying jobs. People have these terribly low-wage incomes. They're struggling to keep their heads above water, barely able to get work, barely able to pay for the MetroCards, you know, because they have a family. I'm single, I make good money, and *I'm* struggling. It's a disgrace. Right now . . . I think it's tomorrow, we have No Fares for the Unemployed. We have that going on. I want to see that!

Oh, I think that's great!

Isn't it, Olivia?

I think that's great.

Thank you! Those are the inklings of hope that I see. When I give up hope, and I see something like that, I'm like, "Okay, I can stay a little longer. I can help to keep the movement here, and keep pushing that along, and keep other people coming here, and encouraging other people."

◆

A lot of my friends and family don't even know that I'm here. Of course, my parents do, but . . . Clearly, everybody knows that the occupation is here. I mean, it's been fifty-something . . . what? Fifty-two days about now? Everybody knows we're here, so I don't want to force it down anybody's throat. My clients, who some are the one percent—not necessarily my family members—I want them to ask me what it's about. I want them to come with an understanding before I present it to them.

For instance, I have a very, very good friend who's husband is a banker. They're not necessarily the one percent, but she had no idea that I've been down here all this time. She didn't even know I gave up my apartment to be here, and she's been a dear friend of mine for fifteen years. She's very successful.

We had dinner and we talked about it, and it was interesting to see her viewpoint because she was initially very angry, not knowing about me being here. So that's why I'm saying I don't really talk to people until I know that they want to talk about it. It's a bit of a delicate matter. Like, my friend . . . when she allowed me to talk about it, I engaged in a conversation, and I could say she left with more of an understanding of what it's about. She just heard all these negative things like you and I are talking about in the media and the press. She just thought it was no system; just terrible, like, a bunch of homeless idealists and hippies.

And then she knew I was here, and she knows that that's not me. She knows I have never done this kind of thing, but she does know me as this friend who—I'm not a traditional kind of girl, you know? Some educated people work in the corporate world, and some educated people have chosen not to work in a corporate world, and I guess that's what I meant about my friends and myself. They know that I'm a little bit more of that kind of a free spirit type of person. I haven't finished college and I don't work in an office. I'm more of an artist.

It was nice to engage her, and it was nice to put that word out. Slowly, I'm getting to my friends, to my family. I guess my point in saying this is: We have still got a ways to go because even within my own self—my personal self—my friends and family still need some education on this, still need some dialogue on this, and still need some awareness. We still have a long way to go, but we do have Outreach, and it's helping along the way.

Personal outreach as well as reaching out to strangers.

Absolutely. I just—for me personally, I just don't want someone to engage negatively, because it's such a sensitive issue right now. It's very difficult mentally and physically to sleep out here. I'll be honest, six days I slept in a hotel because my friend had a hotel room. One day I got really sick, and I slept at a friend's house. But I feel more connected sleeping here because then I understand what it takes to make a stand here. Where to wash up, where to go to the bathroom, what we need in terms of winterizing, and being here in Comfort. When you disconnect with that, then you disconnect a little bit with the movement.

Is there anything else that you would like to add?

People are really putting their blood, sweat and tears into this. That's what I would really like to tell people. There's a lot of blood, sweat and tears from a lot of beautiful people. It's pretty great. It's pretty amazing. It's pretty amazing to be part of it, just to be part of it.

I feel very fortunate, even though some days you'll see me losing my cool, like, "Aagh!" I lose my cool when people put us down. Like, "Oh, yeah? Well, you don't have this? Nice going!" Okay, well, our legal team is not here because it's one a.m. Our press are not here because it's two a.m. We don't have the information for you because it's three a.m. and I just got off Community Watch. We haven't cleared the pathways because we can't account for people who come in and . . .

When people do that, you'll see me losing my cool. You will see me losing my cool. ❖

Evan

I wasn't here until the twenty-ninth of September. I had been moving out of my place in Brooklyn because I had lost my job a number of months before. I'd come back to New York from Berkeley. I lived in Brooklyn for eleven years, and then . . . it's a very long story.

My background's in construction management. I went to school for architecture, design/build carpentry, the whole bit. Got into, finally, green building—working as an owner's rep for a developer here in New York. That was until Thanksgiving, 2008. I went to Brazil for seven months. Came back, tried to be a real estate agent because there were no other options. I thought I would be able to get closer to acquiring buildings and doing some development—like passive-house stuff, and brownstones in Brooklyn. Anyway, I just ended up doing rentals in Manhattan and was miserable.

Then I went back to Berkeley for a while. Applied to the ecological economics program at Berkeley in the Energy and Resources Group. I didn't get in, but it started this process of examination of what's really going on, and coming to be disappointed with the sort of green building effort and everything—how it's been co-opted.

Read a lot of conspiracy stuff about the Federal Reserve, and about the Bush family, and the C.I.A., and J.F.K.

I came back to New York for this job that was just with a regular developer. Real sort of nasty people, but it was a good-paying job. At that point I was broke, so I took it. I moved back.

I got fired after two months, but I had already started this currency project. Before I even left—like, February—is when I first thought of it. And then I hooked up with a Slow Money showcase in Brooklyn for entrepreneurs looking for financing. I met someone who was also working on a currency project, and we started working together.

So me and him were working on this project, and fast forward again to a point where I couldn't pay rent anymore in Brooklyn. I was moving out, and I went down to Philly; I have friends in Philly who I was going to stay with for a couple months. I stayed there for about a week, but then my project partner was coming back up here. Here is the place to start experimenting with alternate currencies and stuff like that.

So I came back up, started working on that, and got involved in everything from biodiesel generators to meeting-minute templates, tent distribution and planning, fund-raising mechanisms . . . all of it. I'm spread thin right now.

Yeah, you look like you're carrying the weight of the occupation on your shoulders.

There's a lot of people down here who have a lot of ideas but aren't very accountable. A lot of that is actually being there when they say they're going to be there. People are left hanging, but I guess it's to be expected. It's incredibly chaotic here.

What were you saying about alternate currency? You mean literally currency?

Yeah. I mean literally, currency can be anything. Currency is just information. It's information about energy, resources, abilities and skills, whatever people have to give and whatever people want. It can be numerical. It can be qualitative. It can be quantitative. It can be any of these things.

What we're working on is a Web site where there's a gifting platform. People can build profiles, and describe their wish lists and their
gift lists—you know, their ability, what they have to offer—and make
that information searchable and available. So start to free up the information pathways. We have a lot of blockage. A lot of people want
to help, but they don't know how to get involved. And there's a lot of
people who need things down here that aren't getting them.

So it's not like barter, exactly, but . . .

No, a barter economy is a misnomer. Barter is very limited. Barter depends on the fact that it's a two-party transaction, and society doesn't
exist with two-party transactions; it exists in a collective. So you need
some kind of credit system, basically, that people can give to. The
credit system can be based off of reputation. You know, recognizing
that this person has given a lot. And also, people who receive things
write thank-you notes. It's rebuilding the commons: sharing, trust, all
these things.

You're planning to implement this within the park?

Well, there's a lot of outside donors. That's the first priority: Make
what we're doing down here more transparent by growing a project-
building page, with project teams, direct donation and direct support,
crowd-sourcing—all these things.

And then investigate the broader social implications.

Yeah. Right now the Federal Reserve, otherwise known as "dollars,"
have a monopoly on our issuance of currency, something which Jefferson warned of way back in 1822, I think the year was. If we give
monopoly to our currency, people will end up homeless in the streets.
That's what we have because it's artificial manipulation of the supply.
    What's happening now—it's happened many times before—is: Put a
lot of money out on the street in the form of loans because that's how
money is actually created. It's out of thin air. It's loaned into existence, and when they stop loaning and continue to call in the loans
that they've already issued, the supply of money goes down. If everything is commodified and only exchangeable through dollars, what
will happen is that there will be scarcity. It's a false scarcity, but it's a
false scarcity that's used as the primary instrument of oppression.

My long-term thing is to take back control, to have communities be able to make and manage very robust currency systems: pooling resources, investing in local organic food, everything else that's good for the Earth—restorative as opposed to destructive.

Seeing as this is something Web-based, what about communities who are not wired?

Well, ah, there are different systems that aren't Web-based, but I think that in order to really overcome the obstacles, we do have to use the best tools of communication that we have.

[A passer-by hands Evan a flyer.]

Passer-by: Use social network to create jobs.

Evan: All right.
So I think that's a hardware issue that can be solved. It's not that hard to solve.

It's interesting. It's both practical, and has a utopian quality as well. How were you introduced to this as an idea?

Depression over conspiracy. Realizing how deep the controls go and how they're sort of hidden. Understanding how money works—having that education—and just realizing that that's why the government is on its knees now. People look at corporations, but corporations are just sort of the henchmen for banks. It gets down to old, ancient issues of usury, that somehow money has the right to make money just because it's controlled by one person. Judaism dealt with it, Christianity dealt with it, Islam dealt with it. All throughout history, the idea that the owners control by extracting the bounty as they distribute the money . . . it's inflation. So it's an ancient issue.

How would money function if it didn't . . . replicate itself?

Have you ever read Louis Hyde? *The Gift?*[4] It describes it pretty well. There are a lot of other books, but that's probably the best and most accessible. It has the idea of the increase of the gift. The gift must keep moving, and basically, what profit is is what people extract.

---

[4]Louis Hyde, *The Gift: Imagination and the Erotic Life of Property* (New York: Random House, 1983).

I guess one of the best metaphors is a bucket of barley. A bucket of barley is given to somebody, and then they plant the barley. The barley grows, and then you have, say, two buckets of barley that you harvest from that one planted barley. It's a spiritual thing. When people give their good spirit, there's a natural increase. It's a feedback loop.

What interest does is that it takes out the material aspect. It takes it out, separates it from the spiritual and the social, and destroys social fabric. It's like, "I'm going to protect myself now." It's fear-based.

The structure we're working on is that these entrepreneurs—local organic food producers—need cash to increase, so you give them a zero-interest loan as a gift, right? But the idea is that you give the gift back. The expectation is that if you have a bounty, you return it to the community—to the collective—voluntarily. If you do it voluntarily and it's not forced in the form of interest . . .

Interest takes it's money whether or not you have a bounty, you know what I mean? It frames the situation as: "All right, I give the bank its piece and I keep my piece," as opposed to, "I return what was given to me to the collective, plus more." So it's sort of a voluntary system. I don't know if that explains it.

It would be individuals who would give the loan?

No, it's a collective. It's a pretty complex system, and it's kind of hard to explain without diagrams, but everybody loans to everybody. Everybody owns everything. I guess unincorporated association would be the best legal framework for it. Everybody is a user. Everybody is an investor. Everybody is potentially an issuer of currency, and all currency is a promise to . . . I can be a carpenter, and I'll say I can build four tables. I just put them out there. I will build four tables for everyone, and I get credit on the system.

It's a lot of accounting, so that's the quantitative aspect. It's a spectrum between quantitative and qualitative. There's gift circles, like couch-surfing, and then there's the informational form of it in terms of WikiLeaks. People just collaborate. It's the commons. But then there's also time banks, where everybody's hours are equal to everybody else's, and they count the hours. There's local exchange trading systems, where they're more sort of job-based, or sort of discrete: "I will build a table—I don't care how many hours—and this is how many units of alternate currencies." And then there's local currency, like

BerkShares and stuff, which is basically cash proxies. They serve as a way to keep dollars from flowing out of a town, back to a centralized location. It's to decentralize dollars, and you have to sort of work with all of the different realms that are already happening.

Is this something that has been tried anywhere?

Yeah, tons of times. There's time banks everywhere. There's local exchange currencies, LETS . . . a lot of this is happening in the Transition Movement in Britain— Transition Towns. But I don't think anyone has ever tried to do a combination of all these things. That's what we're trying to do with Slow Money—local organic food investment and stuff like that. It's a local organic-food-backed currency, essentially.

What is Slow Money? Is that like Slow Food?

Slow Money is this new movement. Woody Tasch wrote a book and came up with this concept.[5] It's still usurious. I mean, it's just lower interest rates. It's still, like, we want return on our investment. It's money making money. I remember, going back, there's two kinds of people in the world: people who work for money, and people who have money working for them. The idea is to discard the whole idea that money—capital, amassed capital—works for any individual or entity, you know what I mean? The increase of the gift is shared, otherwise you stripped the community of its collective spirit.

So no hoarding, basically.

No hoarding, yeah, and no usury. Go to Wikipedia. Search local currency, alternative currency.

How do you get people who have money to loan voluntarily? It seems like the people who might be more open to this don't necessarily have the resources.

Everybody has the resources. Everybody has resources to give. It starts with people knowing themselves and discovering themselves. That's what he's trying to promote.

The monopoly currency system tries to value everything in dollars. In terms of people who have money, they just need to give it up. It'll

---

[5] Woody Tasch, *Inquiries Into the Nature of Slow Money: Investing as If Food, Farms, and Fertility Mattered* (White River Junction, VT: Chelsea Green Publishing, 2008).

solve a lot of problems for them. Believe me, I've worked in high-end residential construction—high, high-end Manhattan residential construction—and I see how unhappy people are. So you know, just give it. It needs to be cleansed. Absolve the money of its sins because it will continue to infect people and make them greedy, more greedy. ❖

Gypsy

Could you start by telling me a little bit about yourself and how you came down here?

Uh, random leftover Deadhead, blah, blah, blah. I watched our country fall apart since Clinton left office. Well, there's been a bunch of disgusting crap since they basically killed F.D.R. so they could drop the bomb, but yeah, that's a bunch of conspiracy theory. Clinton had it almost fixed. Since the Georges Bush—King George and King George the Second, whose entire resumé is bankrupting six corporations, getting fired from the one before he could bankrupt it, and then being given the biggest corporation on the planet and bankrupting that. It is! I mean, this isn't conspiracy; it's the front page of the newspaper!

I feel bad for President Obama because whether or not he has good ideas or is a good person, he's fighting against . . . what? Six hundred and eighty-seven assholes who just really want to ruin our country and make money. I'm here because I've had it, for years. You know, "If you're not mad, you're not paying attention!" Earlier this year, I wrote a thirty-two-page paper that I thought was a hundred percent or close to it, and started sending it to politicians. It was on thirteen or fourteen things wrong with our country and how to fix them. I didn't write and bitch; I wrote with answers, because if you point out a problem and don't have a solution, you're an asshole. Just shut up.

So I wrote thirty-two pages of solutions, as I see them, that could work. "Please use it as a framework to make something better." Then I had to go see my mom, and I had to come through New York. I planned on staying here to see what it was, see how it worked, see where it was going, help if I could. I'm still helping.

Around here, they like to say, "Oh, anarchy! Let's do everything backwards and wrong!" Every time something works, "Let's dismantle it so somebody else gets a chance to try their hand at it!" The things that feed you, clothe you, keep you alive, keep you connected, keep the movement going should be in permanent structures—tents that are good; we don't have permanent structures, of course. They're getting all that backwards. So if I can get this camp pulled together and talking to each other—or if I can watch it happen—that's when I'm going to go ahead and see my mom this weekend. So vicious rumors: By the end of this week, I might be leaving. The tents are here; it's just logistics now. But for some reason, they want to give the tents to the transient people and leave our permanent facilities flapping in the breeze.

All right, that's my bitch that has been going on for a couple of days. Now about the movement, I wrote this paper. I came here. My hundred-percent paper has turned into seventy-five percent of a damn good framework to start a conversation on how to fix it all. You got an email address, I'll send it to you.

Okay.

Something needs to change. A lot of things need to change. It's been built convoluted on purpose, so there's no one problem, no one answer. There's a dozen problems and three dozen answers. [Matt] Taibbi in Rolling Stone actually said it best. He said you can't take a picture of a stock broker on a telephone, selling stock in a company that moves it's money to China, exchanging it for Italian lire and buying a shipping company to ship something here, which puts an American company out of business, and that guy lost his job. There's no way to take a photo of that, and that's actually how it works.

I got a three-hour lecture the other day on the way banks work and the way trading works. I still don't understand it. I'm lost on all the terminology and I just woke up, but your mortgage becomes a sellable option. As far as the market is concerned, there's two mortgages, and they're trading on both of them. The simple reality is: They're trading on the options of twice as much money as what was actually invested or has collateral behind it. And then all of a sudden, somebody misses a payment. The insurance company pays the guy who lent the money, the civilian loses everything they have, and the banks go havoc.

With 401(k)'s, they got rid of any kind of pension. I think there

should be a national pension fund. Five percent of everybody's paycheck goes to it. No matter how many jobs you work in your life, you
have a pension. But they put 401(k)'s as an option, a tax-free option
for individual investment so you have a better retirement. And then
the corporations saw that since you were paying money for your own
damn retirement, they got rid of pensions.

Then the Walmart model: Never hire anybody full-time. You don't
have to give them benefits or anything else. Now every corporation in
America is taking that model. If you need them an extra day, you can
get that eight hours without paying them overtime. As far as business
goes, that's damn smart, you know? It makes a lot of money, but you're
screwing over the people below you.

My idea is five percent of everybody: from the Georges Bush, Warren Buffett, Jimmy Buffett, [laughs] . . . I want to meet Warren Buffett
and say, "Man, I love your music!" and just see what he says. "That
'Cheeseburger' thing is really cool!"

Five percent goes to the local hospital. You break your leg, don't
go to the insurance company; the hospital's already doing that paperwork. If you've got to send that paperwork to an insurance company,
it triples the price of your hospital visit. They send it back to the hospital, and there's all that duplication of effort, and no real reason except
to make money for a corporation that shouldn't exist to begin with.

Five percent goes to Social Security. Everybody, even the Georges
Bush. Five percent of their income will go to Social Security every time
they get paid. When you retire, if you're worth more than a million
dollars, you don't get a check. George Senior is worth what? Six point
three billion dollars? He gets a Social Security check every month, and
he cashes it.

[Laughs.] How much Social Security does he get?

I actually used to know, but I read that, like, two years ago, and that
many numbers start falling out, so . . .

Well, then take George Bush, who's, "Oh, ho, ho! I'll give myself
minimum wage as my paycheck, and I'll leave it all in the corporation."
Well, guess what? In the sixties it was, "Power to the people!" This
should be, "Profit to the people!" You have your corporation or your
company or whatever. When your profit sheet comes out, before your
stockholders get anything, you will take thirty percent of the profit of

your company and share it equally amongst your employees. It will be taxed again at the thirty percent, which is five for the hospital, five for Social Security, ten to the federal government.

There's no more medical expenses for anybody. Your five percent paid everything you will ever need. Five percent goes to the state for highways and all that, five percent to the pension fund. That's thirty percent of your check. Right now, if you make ten dollars an hour, you make four hundred a week, and you bring home three hundred and ten. This way, you'll only bring two hundred and eighty, but all your medical's paid. You will get a Social Security check that's a hundred fifty percent of the national median, with food stamps. The feds get their money for highways and bombs and everything else. The state gets their money for highways and bombs and everything else. And you will have a pension when you retire.

Sounds good.

The corporations have to give you thirty percent to begin with, which gets taxed again. They've made their contribution. Thirty percent of their profit goes right to their employees and gets taxed again. Everybody contributing. That's my way to fix taxes and make hospitals. There's nine other points in this thing. Social Security, food stamps, banking and lending, make it illegal to advertise prescription drugs . . .

Oh, God. I wish.

One point three billion dollars for research and development, three point seven billion for advertisement. Eighty percent of the budget for making and selling pills is advertisement. Make it illegal, your pills will cost twenty percent of what they do now.

Et cetera, et cetera, et cetera.

I'm a consultant—restaurant consultant and a business consultant. I build shit. I relax by organizing. I'm going to try to make this camp a functioning camp that feeds its little army, clothes its little army, takes care of it without a bunch of waste and bullshit. I have the bigger picture also, so I'm pretty busy.

Yeah, I'm hanging out, living in the park, doing eighteen hours a day with my evening security duty and everything else. Nine o'clock meeting, ten o'clock meeting, I've got to go play guitar on the sidewalk so I can buy my own cigarettes, so I'm not leeching off the movement.

If I make that much money, I will buy my own food so there's more food, you know? You got to feed the Revolution before you can feed the people. You got to take care of yourself, if you can. We're not trying to create a welfare state, but I would love for Mayor Bloomberg and everybody in the country who's looking at us and saying, "Oh, what a disreputable bunch of whatever, blah, blah, blah, blah, blah . . ."

Bloomberg is intentionally sending his homeless people and his recently released convicts here, and we're feeding them, we're clothing them, we're housing them. We're doing it, and he won't! So we've actually beat their system. Send us more homeless people. We'll feed them, we'll clothe them, we'll house them. We'll prove that you can't do shit and we're good at this. And keep sending me busloads of people from Rikers Island. We come into a riot squad situation, I'm putting them on the front line. You fight with a motherfucker that'll stab you. Send us more of them. Send us busloads of people from Rikers Island. I'll put them right on that gate when you go to come in here. Send us killers! We'll put them right on the gate. Come on in, dumb-ass!

"Oh, I know what we'll do! We'll send them people that will kill us!"

Send us a few more! Send us the gang members, send us everything! They will come in here, we'll feed them, we'll clothe them. Come in here now! The happy little hippies are taking care of the people that'll shoot you. Send us more. And then send cops down here against, you know, whatever gangs and recently released convicts and ex-military. Send us all of them, then come on in.

Send us the hard motherfuckers. Send us the homeless. We will feed them. We will clothe them. That's what we're here for. We're here to prove that we are decent people, and we're doing better than the government will ever even try to.

Well, it's definitely true from what I've seen.

But we have internal stupid shit. We are building semi-permanent housing for our transient population. If there's a snowstorm, rainstorm, protest in another city, they might just get up and leave. Our kitchen is never going to get on a bus and go to Albany. Our information network that hooks up to the world is never going to get snowed out and go home, but it's flapping in the tarp because—and I just got done with this argument—"Oh, we're supposed to run ourselves on an anarchistic system!" this and that and the other. The people who keep preaching that don't know what anarchy means. Anarchy means we don't need a leader because we all think the same thing and we're going to go do it. Try to find me three people in this crowd that agree to anything! And if someone does not agree, it is not anarchy.

We're trying to set up the Medical tent right here. Everybody's on board except these two girls, and they're over there bitching, "Oh, anarchy this! Anarchy that!" I said, "You know what? This is anarchy!" If we'd had a little bit of hierarchy, chain of command, organization, this would have been done six weeks ago, and I wouldn't have been standing here telling you we're going to move your shit to put up a hospital. Total anarchy! You love anarchy? This is anarchy! Shut the fuck up, we need a hospital!

Max: Do you need help talking to people about moving?

Gypsy: No, actually. I got that all together. We just had the two that wanted to whine, but they're good for the morning.

What are you trying to put up?

Gypsy: Our First Aid tent has been sitting there, and in between these two trees will be a sixteen-by-sixteen on the sidewalk, so if you need an ambulance, it pulls right up to First Aid; wheelchair access, this and that and the other. Everybody's on board except two girls who want to whine, and they got, like, a one-man tent and a tarp pole. "We're not moving anywhere!" Bet you do.

This is the ladies' tent, right?

Gypsy: Yeah, and if it had come to a vote, I would've voted to go ahead and put up a ladies' tent. But now we got these two new tents. One is for Direct Action, who doesn't have any equipment or anything, but they got a tent.

Max: But they tend to live on-site.

Gypsy: Get a tent! You're going to freeze to death!

They don't have a tent at all?

Gypsy: They have their tents. Now they got a big tent that they are not going to move into, bet. But the other one is for—and I'm not homophobic; I'm not prejudiced against anything but stupidity—but we have a tent that's for the transgender population that we have here. As they're walking around with signs saying treat transgender equally, they're generating themselves as a special interest group that needs a tent. You're equal! Buy your own goddamn tent and go to sleep! We need this for the kitchen!

Max: Are you press?

I'll tell you who I am when I—

Gypsy: [The kitchen] is flapping in the breeze!

Max: We can get tents. We're doing another order today.

Gypsy: Actually, there's apparently four more down there now.

Max: There are four more.

Gypsy: Uh, to house homeless people . . .

Max: No. Money was given by specific people. So Medical paid for—

[A heated argument ensues.]

◆

After the argument died down, the interview moved across Rector Street to Steve's Pizza, on the west side of Liberty Plaza, where Gypsy proceeded to vent the lid of his take-out coffee using a hunting knife.

There you go. We have a political movement that is now here trying to overthrow the fifty men that own the planet, along with the largest corporation and military on the planet—their goal is to fight against those entities—and they can't even build their kitchen. A bunch of random, granola-smoking, acid-eating hippies go into a Dead tour, the kitchen is put up first and solid. So we got an environmental activist group who's trying to overthrow the world, who aren't smart enough to build a kitchen.

The hippies were better than that. They knew, when you got there, everybody had to eat, so the first thing they built was a kitchen, a comfort station, and a first aid, and it got built in the most permanent structure they could construct, and then everybody else could have their anarchy. These people have insisted that we're going to have anarchy, and nothing's going to actually be accomplished. But we're going to take over the world this way. Shut up!

Tell me what your ideal winter plan would be.

The smallest tent you can get will keep you warmest. You want that air pocket. You don't want to just be laying there wrapped up in tarps on the ground. If you're working in a restaurant in the dish room, you're in hot water and steam all day long. If you wear a baggy shirt, you will steam yourself to death. If you wear a shirt that fits all the way to your skin, the water leaches through, the wind blows it off of you, and it keeps you cool.

Reverse that: If you're wrapped up in your sleeping bag, you don't have an air pocket. If you have a little bit of an air pocket around you, your body heat warms that air and gives you a little better chance of survival. If your tent is too big, there's no retention of the heat. It's the difference between sleeping in a closet or sleeping in a warehouse.

Right. I used to live in a loft, and we were freezing. I mean, we never were warm.

Bedsheets. Make yourself, like, a four-poster room, and it holds the heat for your bed. You come out, and there's a temperature change. Well, imagine that on a smaller scale. You got a two-man tent with one person and their backpack, and it keeps them warm. Or you can put them in a sixteen-by-sixteen warehouse, and you don't have enough blankets to keep them alive.

You're envisioning that the big tents should be used more for infrastructure, and then with little ones surrounding them.

They want to have anarchy and this and that and the other, but this is very simple. We have an encampment that's planning to make it through the winter. You have to enclose your permanent facilities. That is a no-brainer. That's something that doesn't even get voted on. We need the kitchen, Info, LiveStream, Comfort and First Aid. You don't vote on that crap! You build them a tent, and you work from there. But people here are like, "Oh, we don't need any central whatever!" Break your leg and tell me that! Have a heart attack! We're going to leave you laying here because we don't have First Aid. Come up there to get some food and there isn't any. So how you feel now about not having any infrastructure to this movement?

People don't want to use the big tents for the infrastructure?

The special interest groups have decided who the tents go to. They've taken their own funds, and allocated funds from the movement, to buy tents for the most ridiculous reason. "We need to consolidate a little better, so we'll get rid of the two-man tents, and we'll put up these monstrosities that still only sleep nine people." In an eleven-by-twelve, you can fit nine people. Actually, in a ten-by-twelve, you can only sleep five, and that's if they want to snuggle.

How big did you say those were?

They're eleven-by-sixteen, give or take. These two are different than that one, and I'm not sure what's coming next, but the general statement is: It's eleven-by-sixteens. So okay, eleven-by-sixteen, and then we're going to go ahead and pretend we get to pick where the door is, just for the sake of doing this. A person is six feet long. So if you've got sixteen feet, you put them end-to-end, and it leaves a three-foot channel in between. A six-foot person, a three-foot channel, a six-foot person—that's fifteen feet, with room to walk between them. You got the eleven feet sideways. A human body's at least two and a half feet. So four people makes ten feet, and it only leaves you three inches between each cot. They are not going to sleep that way.

Oh, are they doing cots?

Oh, yeah. Now even if they weren't, you still need two and a half feet for a human, so say they're laid straight out. That fits . . . let's say five because we're all friends. Ten people in an eleven-by-sixteen. You can fit twelve people in four four-man tents in the same space, and they'll stay warm. So their entire reason for doing this is not-thought-through and wrong. "Oh, let's save space!" You're actually taking up an extra foot in each direction to house less people.

Was there a meeting today? This is on everyone's minds.

Yeah, this was their idea, because I go there and tell them they're going to freeze to death, and they go, "Oh, but the tents are so nice! In the summertime, you can roll the flaps up." I said, "Are we getting any kind of heat?" Basically, there's some theory about a whole bunch of them hand warmers. Oh, that's got to be environmentally friendly, yeah, which is something else they haven't thought through. What are the chemicals in them hand warmers? And you're putting out a thousand, two thousand of them a day, and then throwing them in the trash! Dumb-ass! But we can't have any kind of heat source. If you could have a wood stove in them tents, yes. Move in. Put in bunk-bed cots and move in.

That would be kind of nice and comfortable.

Yeah, we can't have any of that in the park. No generator. We don't have enough electric to make electric heat, which is wasteful anyway. We can't run propane, we can't run pellets, we can't run wood, we can't run oil. What else is there for heat? We are not going to have any heat sources. So you put people in the two-man tent. If you could actually get them little slender one-man tents and talk people into moving into them . . . couple of fleece blankets over the top, and you still better have four or five sleeping bags, and a pallet to get you off the ground.

I live in the woods. I've lived in the woods for a large chunk of my adult life, and they're going to freeze to death. They don't know what they're doing, and they won't listen to me. "Oh, brother man, I read a magazine article. I know everything about this." I just spent the last three winters living in the snow in a tent. I think I know a little more than you do.

Did you have a heat source?

No, not really. You turn the tongue of your shoe down because it will be frozen when you get up, and that's the only way you get your shoe back on. They don't get this. Just your breathing causes condensation. If it's cold for more than a week, your tent is frozen. It's crystallized on the inside. If you touch it, it might shatter or rip. Your zipper is going to give out. After it freezes up, you can't zip your tent anymore. You have to lay some kind of blankets over the doorway so you can get in and out of your tent, and after about four days, it turns into a flap because it's frozen. They don't get this. They think, "Oh, we'll move into the tent. Oh, we'll sit there in our t-shirts. It'll be a good winter." You will freeze to death, and they don't want to listen to me.

The only thing I would say, though, is that there is a difference between being out in the woods—where you don't have recourse to go inside—and being in the city.

Yeah, so everybody files out and goes into the subway or McDonald's or whatever. That's going to be great!

I'm just saying.

Well, no. My other thing is: I was smart enough that I was down in a hollow. You always try to build halfway up a hill because heat rises, cold sinks. The sun hits the top of the hill first, and moves down to the coldest spot, so you don't want to be at the bottom; it will be cold longest, all that. And I built it in the trees, so the wind never hit me. Out here, the wind never stops. If you have a five-mile-an-hour wind, you need two more sleeping bags. If you have twenty-mile-an-hour wind, you need five more sleeping bags. It took eleven loads of laundry to wash my bed, and I wasn't warm this winter.

This was upstate?

I live in Maine. It wasn't that bad a winter. About six, seven o'clock in the morning some days it was down to zero, five degrees, stuff like that. Most of the time, it was in the teens. You know, like, somewhere between five and twenty degrees was the nighttime temperature, and I had that much bedding.

Now they're trying to put people on a cot with a sleeping bag "because we got you an army tent!" Retard! The people are already cold now. In their tents, with a couple of sleeping bags, they're already cold sleeping here. But they want to move them into a warehouse that doesn't have any protection or heat retention.

And this is the biggest problem with this park. The movement as a whole isn't organized enough to have any of these problems. But in this park, that's the biggest problem is: The people who don't know anything are the ones trying to run everything. And the most ignorant amongst us are the ones that get on the T.V.

Well, that I've seen.

That's Jeff Foxworthy. He said: "You have a hurricane or tornado or something in the South, they don't find a doctor or a lawyer. They find Shirley, in the muumuu and the sponge curlers, worrying about her casserole dish." Everybody thinks people from the South are stupid, you know? "The most ignorant amongst us gets on the news." Well, we got the same thing here. The photo op comes down to that corner, where that ignorant crackhead was there yelling, "You're the one!

You're the one! You're the one!" That's front page in tomorrow's newspaper, and they don't see the people up there taking care of things.

◆

I'm an innovator. I'm a child prodigy with poor parents and a public school system. I should've entered Harvard when I was about thirteen. My father's the only man I ever met anywhere in life who tried everything he could to make sure his children did not succeed.

My sister was working at Gino's, which is—you know what that is? It shows your age! [Laughs.]

I don't care.

Trying to get through George Mason University, paying her own way. My father wouldn't give her a cent, and announced at the dinner table he started a college fund for some little girl we baby-sit.

Oh, my God.

That's my father. My brother played team sports from the time he was six until he got out of school and went in the military. My father ranted and raved, "You're a dumb-ass! You can't follow orders! You've never been able to follow orders! You're going to suck in the military! Blah, blah, blah!" But he'd been in team sports his entire life. He knows how to follow orders; he just doesn't listen to my father. [Laughs.]

You know some of my background. I am a contractor of everything except HVAC. I know everything they need. Plus, I'm an innovator. I can't buy anything new because I'm going to cut a hole in it and duct-tape something to it. I'll go to the hardware store for pulleys, go to the plumbing shop to get them to bend a piece of pipe, and I'll build a T.V. stand that swings to both rooms. That's what I do. I'm wearing a-hundred-and-eighty-dollar shoes. They were seven bucks at Goodwill. That's how I do things.

I should be running this government. I should be running this. They're spending thousands and thousands and thousands to accomplish very little, where I could've taken a tenth of that money and done twice as much. And they won't give me finances. My ideas will work, but that doesn't affect them. They don't care if it works or not. They want the credit. "No, I did all this. I'm going to go on my blog and tell everybody I saved New York."

That's what we're fighting against is people's ego. I keep telling people, "I'm not even here. Just make it work, and I'm leaving. This is how it should work. Please put it together. You take all the credit you want to." And then you got somebody else, "I've had a committee for four weeks discussing this." Yeah, and you've accomplished nothing. We got to finish in two days. You won't let it happen because you didn't get the credit for it. Welcome to O.W.S. And you go to people—actually, the ones that rushed over to make me quit screaming are the ones that do get shit done. They are sick of that internal anarchy that gets a whole bunch of money to do nothing, and they can't get money to do what's right. The tech room—they're over there with P.V.C. pipe and duct tape trying to save all of our electronics. At a thousand dollars a laptop, there's fifty thousand dollars worth of electronics in that tent, and they're trying to fix it with duct tape.

They should have a good tent.

Well, like I said, the transgender population, which I'm not prejudiced against them at all, but they've got the sign that says, "Treat us equally, but we get our own tent." And that's a large part of this movement, too, is, "Oh, no! We want equality, but I want a little bit extra, actually," you know? "Don't call me out of the crowd like I'm special, even though I got a tent, and I eat first, and this and that and the other. I made sure everybody knows I'm special; don't treat me like I'm special."

It's so tricky. I mean . . .

[Laughs.] There is not an adjective to describe the trickiness of this!

Well, I think the other thing is, it is really stressful.

What's going on right now with the tents and the park is a bunch of scared little suburbanites who've never been exposed to anything. I've spent a little over nine years in jails, prisons, and penitentiaries—along with the rest of my education—for being a bad driver, or tour-related injuries when I was following the Dead. If you're on a Dead tour long enough, you'll go to prison. [Laughs.] But you got these people who grew up a suburbanite, and they went to their little college, and they studied with their little soft-spoken little clique. And they come out here, and they're living with the homeless and the junkies in the street, the people that drink every night. I grew up in the South. Everybody drinks. They get loud and obnoxious, and you go, "Shh, baby's sleeping," and they calm on down.

They're like, "He's getting loud!" and then they're like, "We don't want that! We need to get a tent and just move them out!" Shut up! Stay out of the area! You know, it's like having a bad neighborhood. Do you wander through at two a.m. and complain that it shouldn't be so bad? No! Get the hell out of the neighborhood! If you don't like it, don't go there.

They're trying to pretend in this movement that that element isn't actually part of America or the world. We are a very good snapshot of the cosmology of this country. The drunks and the junkies and the peaceniks and the rich people and the dumb-asses and the mentally impaired and the bad people . . . that's America. But we got this little clique on the inside who's decided that they're going to create social change at the same time as the political change, and guess what? No junkie ever wants to quit; they want to quit getting arrested.

They don't want to. They want their dope every day. And even after they've gone through drug rehab and this and that and the other, and they're out there going, "Yeah, man. I'm clean," you talk to them and they're like, "I sure would like a slam. I just . . . I'm not going back to jail again," is why they quit. Know what makes people decent? Fear. If you have nothing to fear, you act like an asshole. If you're afraid of something, you learn manners really quick.

Send them down there to the Tombs on a bad Friday night when, like, the Irish bar got arrested. Let one of these little hippies sit in there. He isn't going to spout his political shit because there's a bunch of big, angry, drunk Irishmen who would stamp him up and hurt him. So he'll sit in the corner, quiet. And then he'll come back out here and think he knows everything about the world. He'll start telling people what to do, because in this crowd they would nag him, but they won't punch him in the mouth. ❖

November 7

King

I don't watch T.V. at all. I don't watch T.V. I don't listen to the news. I don't listen to the media. I just go by my spirit forces. If it's going to rain, I look at people around me; when I see them preparing for the rain, I just fall in line. I just put up my top or my umbrellas or whatever.

But back to the issue at hand. What led me to this movement was that I was in Harlem one day, and a friend of mine says they're trying to give you a hundred fifty or two hundred dollars in panhandling or some junk. I didn't know what was going on down there. They were saying it's, like, a little political movement, things of that nature. That's when I became involved, because I majored in political science and law. I went to Morgan State University, like, 1992, so I've been active in the movement—in any type of political-related issues dealing with oppression, anything pertaining to humanitarian.

So I came out to the park. I started getting flyers and leaflets—you know, finding out what's going on here. I didn't understand the science of the movement at first.

Then I created a table. I put up flyers and leaflets. Whoever was a protester, I put their information on the table. And then I came up with a concept called International Grassroot Media, because I started feeling everybody's pain and struggle was from different ethnic backgrounds and different regions of the world. I want their message to get out to the general public, that we all are struggling. It's not just a national issue, it's an international issue.

My message is: Listen to the people who are struggling. It doesn't matter where they come from, what origin or religious background. I feel that we all came here to voice our opinion on one landmass, you know? Let the people know. Let the world at large know.

How long have you been occupying?

I've been down here for about a month, and I seen myself develop over the month. There are people who have their little bizarre way of expressing themselves—a little hostile, a little bit of rage—and I've seen people who want to get physical with these guys. I've been blessed with the spiritual barometer to become the mediator of different issues. And I must say, I'm an expert on it. I have a little charisma to communicate with those who are hostile. I know how to calm them down, make them feel good, motivate them to be here on a movement, not out here on rage. I try to get people to understand and respect one another, no matter what background they come from, even if they're hostile, or they have a little psychological disorder, whatever. We all are God's children, and that's why we all need to be protected.

So that's the message I'm bringing to people out here. You have a point of view, even if you've got a little psychological issues that need to be addressed.

But we're not here to really fully address it. We are not no psychologists or anything, but we do our best. We get people to understand the issues that they have in the park. Accept it, and don't hurt them.

What are some of your ways of getting through to people?

I embrace them. I try to be, like, a little wall, or a human bridge to join people together. I don't know . . . I had law enforcement come through with me to help me mediate issues. The law enforcement seen that I have a way of communication with people. And they say, "Well, you know, just walk with him. Make sure he's all right." I'm like, "Yeah, that's what I do." I walk with them . . . walk with them out the park. Walk two, three blocks with them, calm them down. I don't try to keep them away because we all have rights to this park.

One thing we all have in common in the park is that we are rebelling against a system of authority who exceed their rights. From the mayor on down, they exterminate movements from different political backgrounds. So I don't believe in people from the park trying to police people in the park. This is what we are against: policing.

What do you mean, policing? Like, kicking people out?

Yeah. Not that they get physical, but they try to push you out a little bit. They try to surround you, you know? I'm for that if you're, like, a rapist, and you're a threat to people here. You know, there was a rapist here one night. A couple of times, they keep showing up to the park. But we join forces and push him out the park. I pull out my camera; I take pictures of him. I go, "Wasn't he here two nights ago?" I say it to him in a sarcastic way so he understand, like, get the message: "Please leave." And then he just left, and that's it. And that's it. They just run away, certain cats.

But not someone who's just voicing their political opinion about the government or this or that, because everybody voices their opinion about the government. I'm not supporting with some of their opinions, but everybody's got a voice. They've got to be heard.

Are you planning on being here for the winter?

Yes. I plan to be here, yes, until the last day.

How are you going to stay comfortable?

Just bundle up, and just maybe doubling sleeping bags. That's it. It's not that bad. It's not that bad. It's all psychological. You've got military troops doing it all year every year, camping out, and nobody's talking about them, so . . . ❖

Catherine

My name's Catherine. I'm a singer/songwriter. I ordinarily live in Portland, Oregon. My husband and I came to the occupation about a month ago. We saw online that it was happening. About ten days into it is when we found out about it. And then we didn't have the money to come, but some folks that we knew contacted us and said that they wanted to help us get there, without us asking or indicating that we wanted to go. Sebastian probably told you this story . . .

No, I don't think so.

We do house concerts a lot. We played at these folks' house in Idaho. It's, like, sort of a fledgling intentional community, and they live part-time in Portland. They basically contacted us and said, "We think you should be there." You know, "We think your music should be there."

Out of the blue.

Yeah, we hadn't indicated to anyone, like, we wish we could go but we can't. They said, "We have a gold coin that we want to sell, and give you the money so you guys can go," which they did, and so that paid for our airfare and part of our rent. Yeah, so that's how we came to be here, and we've been here about a month.

It's been a mixed experience, you know? Really inspiring some-times, really difficult other times. The practicality of sort of camping on concrete is not ideal, but . . .

Do you have pallets now?

Yeah.

Is that helping?

Yeah. It hasn't really rained since we put the pallets under there, but it's nice to be off the ground a little bit, anyway.

Do you have a background in activism?

I was involved in a protest in Los Angeles against the Iraq war before it started, and I have been active online, you know, forwarding peti-tions and things like that. I was interested in MoveOn dot org at the beginning of their sort of thing. And I also have written a few political songs, being a singer/songwriter, but I haven't been extremely active before now.

So what was the difference in this movement for you?

I think much of the activism or the issues that came to the fore previ-ously—in my view, anyway—were more special-interest. Not that they weren't important, but they were very specific, where this was sort of this cry that *everything's* fucked up, and that's how I felt.

I've been really opposed to fracking and other similar environmen-tal choices, but haven't particularly found specific forums in which I could be useful in resisting something like that. There hasn't been any fracking where I live yet, thankfully. Hopefully there won't be. So yeah, this just felt like something that was really important, really broad, and I don't feel like that sort of protest has been seen for a long while in this country.

I find it interesting. The appeal of the occupation seems to be very broad, but then that's what people criticize it for.

A lot of people I talk to say, "Yeah, but what are you protesting? What are your practical solutions?" The first couple of times, I answered that question, but now it's kind of like . . . at this point, I'm tending more towards: "The corporate media is feeding you this line that we don't know what we're protesting."

Of course we don't have all the solutions; it's just starting out. But there are certainly solutions being talked about. That's where you start. You can't fix a problem without understanding what it is and hearing a lot of voices, so that's where we are right now.

What I have noticed is that the experience of occupying the park partly explains why for a lot of people.

Um . . . yeah, I think some people feel that the park is the answer and some people don't. I think the park being the answer is both hopeful and also really scary, because things don't always happen here in the most logical, well-thought-out, democratic way.

My experience is that we've built a small community in our little area of tents, and we've all realized the need to be protective of that little community and of those relationships. That has been the only way that we really could have stayed, and I think a lot of the problems in the park and in the larger society basically stem from a collapse of community, even of family, to a certain extent.

We don't totally have it figured out here, but we're trying. It's difficult because we've all grown up in a dysfunctional society—one where oftentimes, community is not valued, is not fostered. So we're having to learn how to do that, and it's under not ideal circumstances. We're really close together, we're on a relatively unforgiving terrain . . . but we also have a lot of wonderful advantages. There's no-cost food available to us, no-cost medical care and things like that, and constant conversation—an openness to conversation, which is important.

What's going on with this tent?

I wasn't here at the beginning, but Town Planning has been putting together a plan to make the camp operate more efficiently, and one of the things that was part of their plan, as far as I know, was to move Medical up to here, further up in the park so that it had street access and maybe was a little more central. There doesn't seem to be a forum by which those sorts of plans are communicated, so they basically just came in this morning and said, "We need you to move your tents because we're putting the Medical tent here."

There wasn't warning.

There wasn't warning. While I was laying in my tent last night, I heard someone talking about this plan, but they weren't talking to us. They were talking to someone else. [Laughs.]

[Laughs.]

So yeah, there was no consulting the people that would be affected. As I was saying to Joey, we're choosing to live here—at least, most of us are not truly homeless. Most of us in the community where we live are not truly homeless, so we could go elsewhere if we needed to. I understand that Medical needs a space. It's important to a lot of different people to have that service available, but yeah, lack of communication is an ongoing problem within the movement. So we moved our tents, but there were three different guys who all were saying, "I know what's going on. Don't listen to the other guy," and all giving us different information about how big the tent was, where it was going to be placed, how it was going to be placed . . . so it just gets silly.

So this is your new spot for tonight?

I don't know. I am not sure whether Medical is planning on being open at both ends. If they're planning to have people come in through the back door, there is not room for that as the tents are now. And also, that would be, I think, pretty disruptive to be right on the path where people are coming and going constantly throughout the night. So I'm not sure what's going to happen.

Anything else you'd like to put into the record?

I guess just that it's easy to get caught up, as in life, with the minutiæ, or even just the practical problems and challenges of living in the park.

It's really necessary to maintain positivity, and a broader view of the significance that this is happening at all, and that we've come as far as we have come. One of the guys who's here—his name is Shen—was at Tiananmen Square back in the day. He often facilitates the working group coordination meeting that happens at nine a.m. every day. At the end of every meeting, he says, "It's another beautiful day in the occupation," and it's so important, because it's often a meeting that has a lot of bitching, like, sort of inherent to the process. It's a really good reminder at the end of it: "We're still here." That in itself is awesome, even though it's hard and frustrating. ❖

November 8

Marsha

Well, I saw something about Occupy Wall Street on Facebook, and I was really curious. I don't live that far away—midtown on the West Side—so I came down a couple of evenings. It was the first weekend that they were predicting the weather was going to be getting cold at night. I had a few hats at home that I had knitted, and I thought, "I'll bring them down and donate them so people can keep warm." But after being down here a few evenings, I felt compelled to participate.

This is really important. I think people here have the right idea, and what we're trying to accomplish is good for the country and good for the people. That's what America's all about: for the people, by the people. I think we've lost that along the way. It seems like our government is now bought and sold by the corporations. They serve the corporations, and that's got to change. They're talking once again, this morning on the news, about cutting social services for the people that need it the most to help fund the wars that we don't need.

I have five grandchildren. That began as my main focus of why I want to be here. Their future, right now, looks very bleak. The oldest one is sixteen, and only two years away from college. I don't see her ever being able to achieve her goal of becoming a doctor without going into extreme financial debt with student loans. Her parents, between the two of them, have three jobs off and on, and a lot of part-time jobs just to help make ends meet. They have four other kids at home that they need to take care of, so how are they going to help her pay for college? She's so bright and so ambitious, and she really has focused goals in her life. I would love to see her be able to achieve those.

I grew up on a farm in Michigan. Farmers don't make a lot of money, but back in the sixties and seventies, my parents were able to afford to send all five of us kids to college. That doesn't happen anymore. So if we could end the war and funnel some or all of that money into education, we wouldn't have to worry about our lower-income children being able to get a higher education and a good job.

But then we have to worry about the job market because so many of our jobs have gone overseas. Even if they do get a good education, where are they going to get a job?

There's so many things that are wrong right now. It's because a lot of Americans have been asleep for the last twenty, thirty years, and just let these things occur. Little by little, they snuck all this in on us, with the whole trickle-down theory way back from Reagan's time.

So you know, when I first came down here forty-one days ago and started knitting in the park, I was mostly talking about, "I want things better for my grandkids." But now that I've talked to so many people, and heard a lot of different issues and a lot of information about what's going on . . . to effect those changes that I want, people have to vote.

We've just got to take back our country. Half the people in this country that are eligible to vote, don't vote. If all those people got together, that would be more voters than the Republicans and Democrats put together, who are not doing us any good right now because all they can do is fight about the issues. So I have become a huge advocate for voting. Registration, information . . . it's very important you're an informed voter, and then you just have to go vote.

All the politicians that have been there for years and years—that have gotten out of touch with their constituents—they've got to go. Vote them all out! People say, "Well, what if the people you get are worse." Then you vote them all out. Eventually, the politicians will get the idea. If they're not serving us, the people, they will lose their job.

It's the only job I know of in the world where you can get elected and you're pretty well set for the next four to six years. There's hardly any chance at all of you getting fired. Most people, you get a job and you work really hard to keep your job by the person paying you. We pay for them, but they're not working hard for us right now, so that has to change. I think, if we vote enough of them out, they'll finally get the message that they're there to serve the people. We are the people. The people have the power, and that power is in our votes.

The more information we can get to voters so they're an informed voter, the more we can really start to effect change, if not within this particular round of elections, then definitely the next one. The country's been going downhill now for more than a generation, so it might take a generation to fix it. When I say things like that, some of the younger people I talk to—this has become such a country of now, now, fast food, instant 4G Internet, this and that—they go, "I want change now. That's why I'm here." I say, "It's going to take some time, and a lot of people, and a lot of effort."

So that's why I'm in this park.

How many items have you made so far?

Oh, I've been able to make and donate over fifty items to the Comfort station, or to the individual people I've met since I've been down here. It's becoming more and more an individual thing for me because I've met so many wonderful people here that are so dedicated to this cause and have been here from day one, practically. They need to be taken care of, and kept warm, and appreciated. So I like to appreciate them with a gift of something I made for them.

Okay. So you came down . . . you've been here forty-one days—not since the beginning, but quite a long time—

Well, I don't sleep here. I have a warm place to go home at night—a warm bed. I really appreciate that because some of these people here don't have that. There is definitely a wide contingent of everybody in this park right now: all ages, all races, and all levels of economic status.

I happen to be unemployed at the moment, which allows me to be here during the day, but there are people with chronic unemployment problems here. They're fighting in the job market. There are a few homeless people here, and they're fighting for better benefits.

One person put it really well: The people who deal with him in the system have a job because he's homeless and out of work. If they get him a job and get him a home, they're out of a job. The system is set up to make it very hard for you to get out of that cycle of joblessness and homelessness, and get back into what most people consider a normal lifestyle. It's just built that way, because if you get a job, they're out of a job. That's his main focus is changing the way that people who are in dire straits like that are dealt with and treated.

I was on food stamps once. I depleted my savings. I depleted my retirement account that I had built up. I waited until I was in dire straits before I applied for help, and I just felt so badly treated. I just wanted to eat, and I wanted to get some help with my medical bills and my medications I take. I'm type-two diabetic, and I have high blood pressure and arthritis.

It's completely demoralizing to have to ask for help, and I've been working on and off since I was seventeen years old. I have paid my taxes. I have given a lot of money to this government, and the one time I ask for it back in over forty years, it's hard to get it. That's just not right. People should not be treated like that. I'm a human being just like you are, even if I'm applying for help from you. It makes you want to not go back, and I think that's their goal. If you don't go back and ask for money again, they get to keep it.

It's so hard, once you get down to that level, to get back out of it. People go, "Well, don't you have any family who can help take care of you?" I've got plenty of family, but they're in almost the same straits as I am. They're working really hard; they're barely making their bills. Their jobs are disappearing, so how are they supposed to help me? *You're* supposed to, because I paid my taxes all these years.

And now they want to cut all those services. That's another reason a lot of people are in this park. For every person you talk to, they're going to have more than one issue.

I also would like to see them abolish the death penalty because I don't think we have that right to kill someone. I don't care what you did, I don't have the right to kill you. God will take care of you when that time comes. Put them in prison for the rest of their lives. Don't let them out if they're that bad of a person, but I don't have the right to kill you. Two wrongs don't make a right. If you killed someone, that was wrong. I'm not now going to do wrong against you.

And of course, end the wars. Take that money, put it in education. It would help a lot of things. It all boils down to money. That's why people are here in the Wall Street area. This is where the money is. ❖

Max

Why don't you start by telling me about your many roles here?

Well, technically I'm with Facilitation and Organization. Organization is recently-formed, and we do inter-group coordination. Now, most people in Organization are involved in getting office spaces for Press and Media and Information, stuff like that. What I've gotten really involved with is coordinating the on-site groups around safe spaces.

Safe spaces?

Safe Spaces is its own group, and I'm not saying I'm part of that. I just mean lowercase. What I mean by that is nothing vague. I mean communal tents where no one is going to get sexually assaulted.

Honestly, I kind of look at this as "What's the most important and most urgent issue at any given moment?" and that's what I'm trying to tackle. But of course, each of them takes a lot of work. So we met for the first time about eight days ago. About three or four days ago, we put up that thing. [Points.] And so women's safe space has gone up.

This happened through Organization?

Capacity is in Organization.

[Pho approaches.]

Max: Hey, Pho. How are you?

Pho: I'm good.
   [To Olivia.] This is the man right here.

Max: Thank you.

Pho: We got them up!

Max: That's awesome.

Pho: We got them erected, and ... what's next? I guess Comfort? I don't know what's next.

Max: Um, I think we have one or two more to go up. There's a trans tent, and it's not clear where that's going or even who's going to run it. It was going to be Razor who was going to be our point person, but Razor's very frustrated with stuff that's happened, so I don't know what his plan is. And then we have one more eleven-by-eleven that's going to either co-ed or intentional community, depending on which ones those are. We do need to do more outreach for the next batch. We've already ordered, apparently, twenty more.

Can you fit those all in here?

Max: No.

Fair enough.

Pho: [Laughs.] I love that answer.

Twenty more of these, like, the army-style?

Max: Ten big, ten little. So we have to do outreach to get buy-in for all of that.

Pho: And that's next week, right?

Max: We were going to be doing it this week, but I've honestly been putting out so many more sudden fires . . . we had a two-hour emergency meeting about that today that was the most inefficient meeting I've sat in on in a while. I walked out of it.
[To Pho.] You know what? I don't have the paperwork right now.

Pho: Give me the gist. I'm taking the day off.

Max: Cool. I'll tell you about it tomorrow.

Pho: All right.

Max: Have a good one.
In my capacity as a member of Organization, this is my solo project. Solo only because I'm the only person from Organization involved. There is a team . . . it's something rotating, but there's, like, you know, maybe seven or eight core people who have been involved in this, and we're trying to expand it out now and get more buy-in.

Passer-by: Are you one of the core people?

Max: I suppose I am, yeah.

Passer-by: Because I never met you. [Walks away.]

Max: Not the movement . . . I don't mean the movement. Sir! I was talking about something else!

They're really desperate to find those leaders.

I think he thought I was claiming to be a leader when I'm not.

Well, I think the leaderless-ness is to be upheld at all costs.

I agree. I think everyone's pretty committed to that, but this was a situation where we felt we needed to move very quickly.

Winter-wise?

No, safety-wise. And in some ways, we moved too quickly. We pissed some people off—moved some stuff that shouldn't have been moved without getting permission. That's what happens. But there's nothing like precedent to convince people. "It's happened. It's through. Get over it. Stop complaining about it." I don't want to do it that way. We're trying to get a lot more buy-in for the next batch.

Like I said, I'm looking at the biggest issue, and the biggest issue is camp culture. That's one of the biggest issues, anyway. This is an attempt to address camp culture; it's not just about security. It's getting people in communal spaces where you don't have closed doors. You can't be doing drugs, you can't be committing crimes, and you're living with other people. You're interacting with other people. You're sharing spaces, maybe getting served meals together. Your space is communal in the daytime, so it's not, "This is mine!" It's like, "I sleep here, and I go out and do stuff there."

We want to get the G.A. area cleared out. There's a whole bunch of projects in that regard.

So that you can have a cleaner meeting?

So that we can have a meeting. There's no space to have a G.A. We've been having them, but they're really small. They used to be much bigger. It's down to about a little over a hundred people. It used to be, like, five hundred a night.

Out of how many people in the park?

In the park? I don't know, but that's not all the people in the movement. I don't live in the park. The estimates are around maybe one fifty, two hundred. Maybe a little more like two fifty.

Pho: I'd say there are more than that. I'd say it's probably, like, four.

Max: Really? That's not the estimates I've heard, but I don't doubt it.

Pho: It's at least two hundred, three hundred.

Max: Yeah, I think you're right. But I'd say there's probably a thousand people working on the movement. At least.

Pho: At least.

Max: Just on O.W.S., not counting other occupations.

Pho: It would be cool to get a whole movement-wide tally, but that would be impossible.

Max: That would be hard, but it would be awesome. Well, you know, who's in the movement? Someone who shows up once every three weeks?

Pho: Yeah, that's true.

Max: But the thing about the G.A. is: It's largely a tourist attraction. Of the people who are there, a lot of them are just there to watch.

They're not participating?

Well, no, they might participate, but they're not actually on working groups. They're not actually committed to the movement. It's still a decision-making body, but it's just become a little bit of something no one wants to go to. We have trouble finding facilitators because no one wants to stay for the whole thing. It's a big mess.

How long does a General Assembly last?

Anywhere from two to five hours. I mean, five is rare, but it happens. We're moving towards a Spokes Council—you've probably heard about that—so hopefully, that will improve things. We also need to streamline the G.A. There's a group that's getting together to work on that.

How would you streamline the G.A.?

Well, I think you'd set time limits on agenda items, and table them or go to vote when you get to the time limit. And therefore, there would be a time limit on the whole thing. There's probably a couple of other things, but that's the main idea.

Anyway, so there's seven or eight people who were heavily involved in getting the tents coordinated and organized and up—figuring out the process for that—and there are a lot of really good people. It's a great, great team of people. The people who were actually involved with planning the whole thing were really solid, and continue to plan the whole thing, try to get buy-in, try to get people to sign up.

We were talking about trying to change the whole park culture. One of the things we're doing with the tents is asking people to sign on to our community guidelines. They're all basically legal things, I mean, you know, no drugs and alcohol . . . it's pretty obvious stuff, but I think if people have buy-in when they go in, it'll help.

Is it normal to have high-ranking police officers walking through?

No, I don't know what's happening.

How do you know they're high-ranking?

They look it.

They sure do.

They have medals.

Do they? Oh, yeah.

People's Mic: We have two high-ranking officers in the park! That's all I have to say!

Pho: Looks like we have three, because one's not in his uniform.

Max: Oh, yeah. The guy in the suit.

All right, well, as long as everybody else feels relaxed about it, I too am going to feel relaxed about it.

If they were going to clear us out, this isn't how they'd go about it. There was a bomb scare earlier. It might relate to that.

Let's move on. Can you tell me about your beginnings in the movement? How long have you been here?

I got here three weeks ago, and I've only been full-time for, like, a week and a half, but I've been doing a lot in that time. I've been pretty disillusioned with political movements for a long time. I went to some protests when I was younger. I just felt like they weren't effective ways of making change. When this got started, I thought similarly about it. And then when it stuck around, I started to think there was something else going on. I came down here—it was pretty exciting. I came again, saw the General Assembly in Washington Square Park on the Saturday night of the Times Square protest. I was really . . . moved by that, the way people got together and cooperated to make a decision under very pressured circumstances. Without a microphone, it was three thousand people with a deadline—deciding whether to stay in this park and get arrested—and they listened to each other. People got to speak. There were moments when it wavered, and you thought, "Is this going to become a mob?" But it didn't. It stayed a movement, and that was incredibly exciting. ❖

Kyle

I work in the kitchen. I do a lot of community outreach for the kitchen, like, talking to people in the camp. You get the concerns. We talk to a lot of people who donate stuff. I do little prep work in the kitchen nowadays. I'm mainly just taking donations, and talking to people who have concerns and issues, and trying to coordinate volunteers and stuff like that.

How long have you been here?

I came the first day. I was here a couple of hours the first day. I left for a week, came back, and it was, like, every three days, every couple days, now it's every day. So it just gradually progressed to me being here every day.

Are you sleeping here, or just working?

I work, and I sleep here occasionally. I'll sleep here some nights, but I'll go home some nights.

Are you from New York?

I'm from L.A., originally. I lived in San Francisco for five years, too, before I lived here. I just moved here a couple of months ago, actually. I guess it's almost three months now.

So you didn't come here specifically for the occupation?

I was here two, three weeks before it happened. I moved just in time, as I like to say.

How did you hear about it?

Well, the first day I came, I just stumbled upon it. I was going to see the World Trade Center, and then I came here. I walked through the park on the way to the subway. It was like, "What the fuck is going on?" And I was like, "This is cool!" And you know, I've always liked going to protests. I've always liked stuff like that, so I stuck around for a little while, talked to people about it. And then I left to visit my ex-girlfriend for a little bit, and it blew up, you know, exponentially. It's awesome.

Can you tell me a little bit about your experience day-to-day?

I work a lot, honestly. I'm always doing something in the kitchen. There's always something that has to be done. I used to like going on marches more, and just being out there and talking to people about politics, but now I just really don't even have the time for that. I'm just trying to make sure everything goes smoothly here, so . . .

Is there anything that you'd like to put on the record?

I mean, I think it's beautiful. It's hopefully going to really change some things in our society. I hope we just completely flip the table on the entire United States government and start it again. So hopefully, that's what we're going towards. It would be kind of amazing to be one of the only nonviolent revolutions to succeed. [Laughs.] So that'd be cool, but we'll see. That still remains to be seen. We're still babies, you know?

What's your game plan for the winter?

I just got a brand-new North Face sleeping bag. Hopefully, we'll get a new tent for the kitchen staff.

Do you guys sleep in the kitchen?

There's a tent right behind the tree over there that all the kitchen people who sleep here use. Some people sometimes sleep in here. [Points.] We'll let some people slide and sleep in here, but it's mostly just us.

There's one more thing, but it slipped my mind . . . it's hard with the noise.

I know, dude! Those drums annoy the shit out of me sometimes.

Do they?

Yeah. It's like, all right, I mean, I get it, but they're so offbeat!

[Laughs.]

It sounds like fucking banging pots and pans on New Year's.

It's good to have the drums on the marches.

Yeah, the people who lead at the front of the marches are cool. I like that.

So what happened with the bomb threat this morning?

I woke up, like, right for the tail end of that, but there was a bomb in the subway station, so they made everyone get back.

Was there actually a bomb?

No! There's never actually a bomb! New York's just like that. They're like, "Oh, my God! There's a brown box! There's a bomb in it!" If there's any bag or package that someone is not just right next to, they think it's a bomb in this city . . . which is understandable. There's been a lot of bombs that have gone off in this city. Anyway, it's over now. It wasn't that big of a deal, I thought.

People's Mic: The Think Tank is about to begin! The topic of the day is mental health in Occupy Wall Street!

Kyle: That needs to happen!

[Laughs.]

There's a lot of fucking crazy-ass people here. Like, I thought I was crazy, and then I moved here, and now I'm just like, "Oh, yeah . . . no, I'm not." ❖

Clementine

I'm Clementine. I come from Paris, France. I study photography in New York. Originally, I came to just check it out, and I stayed—it was two and a half weeks ago—because . . . I fell in love with the community, and also with their fight. I don't know . . . there's something about this place. I wanted to be a part of the fight.

Can you tell me a little bit about what your day is like here?

Well, it's between here and school. Occasionally, I go back to my place in Brooklyn, shower and all that. And I admit that when it's too cold, I also go back home. But most of the time I'm here.

I'm working on this photo project with the community and for the community. A big part of my day is to talk with people about the project and get them to participate. And then a big part of my days here is just to interact and have great conversations with people. Sharing ideas, you know? A lot of that, yeah.

Is there anything specific that you'd like to put on the record about the movement?

Yeah, well, coming from France, which—the system in France is not perfect, either, but it's a lot more social. Personally, I'm hoping to see the U.S. copy the European systems, so the people here have a better access to health care and education. That's my main concern, and what I would like to see changed in America.

What has been the reaction in France?

Since I've been here, I haven't been so much on the Internet, but I checked a little bit and my parents told me. Right now in Europe, they're so preoccupied with Greece and the European Union . . .

Oh, those issues. [Laughs.]

Right, those, you know, big issues. It's not that they don't take it seriously, but it's not a big topic right now in France. And I see that there are some movements, apparently, growing in France, but they're . . . a little shy, which is very surprising because there are a lot of protests in my country. I thought that they would follow right away and start, like, burning cars and stuff—the French way, you know?

[Laughs.]

[Laughs.] But it's been pretty shy in France. It's really surprising! They just love going in the street and shouting, protesting, you know, for any reason!

[Laughs.]

I'm still waiting for it to happen.

What do your parents think about your involvement?

Well, my dad was involved in May '68, so . . . he was young, though. He was sixteen back then, though he did spend the night in jail, and my grandma was very pissed off! [Laughs.] But no, he understands. He understands that being young, I have a revolutionary spirit. Rebel. Having lived that himself, he gets it, you know? And he respects it.

I think they're a little concerned about my balancing my involvement here and school, but I'm at school for photography, and as I said, I'm working on a photography project with the people, so it's okay. It's still doing pretty much what I'm here for: photography. At first, they were a little concerned, but they're starting to get that this is, you know, not a very dangerous place to be. I mean, when you're away, you don't really know. They're parents, so they freak out, but no, they're okay with that now. They were very curious about all this, actually. ❖

Colin

My name is Colin. I'm from Pennsylvania. I'm twenty years old. I was a student before I came here, but now I'm here.

Were you a student up until you came here?

Yeah.

Okay, so you dropped out to do this?

Yeah. I mean, I was just going to community college—just kind of going for the sake of going.

How did you hear about Occupy Wall Street?

I heard about it because I saw the video of the girls being pepper-sprayed. I started looking into it after that. I just thought it was an amazing thing that this was actually happening. I mean, it was, like, the Revolution.

What's your day-to-day life like here?

I kind of just float around. I try to experience a little bit of everything. I mostly came here to try to learn as much as I could, because I don't really know about all the subjects that people are angry about. I mean, I know that things are bad. I don't know how to fix them, but I'm going to try to get as much insight as I can.

What are some of the things you feel like you've learned since you've been down here?

I've learned a lot about fracking, a lot of little specific things about stuff that's going wrong with the banking and economics in general, the justice system in this country, people going for profits in places where compassion would be better-suited.

How would you describe the experience of occupying?

It's changed a lot. The first time I came was about six weeks ago. It was a whole different beast here. I feel like I've watched it go downhill a little bit.

In what way?

It just seemed more free and open to everybody. It seemed like a more welcoming environment then. It's kind of closed up now. It just feels more . . . more instruction, I guess, which a lot of people were looking for, but it feels like it's kind of made us deviate from our course.

I'm just odd. I become kind of disenchanted with the whole thing. Well, I mean, like, just being in the park; the movement is still a beautiful thing. I think it's going to happen regardless of what happens in this park. It's already started, and it's going everywhere. It's with everybody now.

So I'm not going to stay here much longer. Yeah, I'm just here for little while longer.

Are you sleeping in Sustainability?

Yeah, I mostly hang out with these guys. I try to help out where I can.

What has Sustainability been up to lately?

They're trying to make our existence in this park more sustainable. The society we come from is very, very unsustainable, so we're trying to bring some good practices into here. It hasn't totally caught on yet. There's still a lot of things we're doing that aren't sustainable, but . . .

We have these bike generators now, with power to the whole park.

They power the whole park?

Yeah. It's the only power we have here now, because they took the generators that we had.

So there's no chance of getting them back?

No, we're not allowed to have them in the park. It's kind of a blessing, though, because generators are really dirty anyway, so if we can do it this way, we ought to.

How much biking does it take?

I think it takes about four hours to power a battery.

You don't need to have people on there all the time?

We have a whole bunch of batteries, so they kind of cycle them out whenever they're needed somewhere. But it helps to have people going so you can keep them charged.

What are the batteries powering?

They're powering everything that you pretty much see running off electricity here. Everybody can charge their computers and phones, their cameras. They run the Internet and everything out in Media. Everything they have to do up there is powered by the batteries. Also, all the lights in the kitchen.

Who set up the system?

It was a couple of guys from M.I.T.

Really? They came down here for that?

I think they're involved, anyway. They're involved, and there's a group called Time's Up!—I'm not exactly sure what they are, but I think they donated a lot of stuff, and they really put some time and effort into building these things. They kind of brought the know-how.

That's huge. How's the composting going?

They send it out to somewhere . . . I think they bike it out whenever we have a lot. They ride it out there on a bike. Also, we're collecting all the recyclables, and they want to start getting some wind turbines in here—little ones.

Is that something that people would crack down on, or do you think you'd be able to do that?

No, I think we'd be able to do that. I mean, it's clean. It's efficient. It's compact.

And it's passive, right?

Yeah. It's basically just another form—like the bike—for generating electricity: Harness the wind. We have a lot of it in here.

Yeah, it's kind of a wind tunnel down here.

We're, like, the garage here. We have all the tools. A lot of the tinkerers come around and try to fix things. That's sustainable practice in itself, because you just get more life out of things if you fix them instead of getting new stuff.

What kinds of things are people needing repaired?

People have brought, like, tables and stuff. Everybody just kind of brings their crap here, like extra wood and stuff. We've got to try to deal with stuff like that. There are a lot of people that are building shelters. They're kind of hoping we have all the tools and stuff here, but I think they're going to tear all those down to get tents now.

Now that they have the fancy tents.

Yeah, now we're getting the really big tents, so that's our next step.

Are you going to get a big tent over here?

I think I'm going to be leaving. He's leaving today. [Points.]

Balance is leaving?

Yeah. I'm going to be leaving before they actually get the big tents here, so I won't be here for them. ❖

November 14

Stefan

My name is Stefan. I'm twenty-two. I live half in the park, half in Brooklyn. I've been here since the beginning.

The first time I was involved with this was in August. I went to one of the first pre-General Assembly meetings, and then I had to take a big step back. I was here day one, and on and off for the first two weeks, but I was recording an album. Then I went on tour for three weeks, so I was kind of being involved, and then cutting out a chunk of the life here. Then I came back three and a half weeks ago or so, if my math serves me well, and have been on the ground, entrenched, pulling, like, twelve plus hours every day since, and that's kind of an indefinite thing.

I do Facilitation and Structure. I help with the tents, as well as a few other side projects here and there, as needed. Generally, just existing here means that you're doing a lot of other work in a lot of other places.

I don't have a real set tent here. I'm just kind of floating around under the good will of others who might have space on the night, you know? It's a tricky process, but I find it's important to sleep here because then I can get to the nine a.m. coordinators' meetings. I can be entrenched in the culture of the park, and I can help switch the culture to something that's beneficial and healthy and sustainable, as opposed to just . . . like, it's a little leery right now. Some of the people in the park don't quite have a long-term vision. So I'm just trying to be here, to be an entity that is ready to work in the long haul.

Could you talk about some of the changes you're seeing?

On a physical level, things are very different. It actually looked like a park once upon a time, and the General Assemblies were around one of these potted-plant things. There was, like, two hundred people. It was way tiny, and this whole west side of the park was almost completely empty. It felt weird. It felt like the park was really big at that moment. If you imagine nothing else is in this, this is kind of a large-size park. But now it's completely filled to the brim, literally. We're having police confiscating tents because they're just spilling over into the sidewalk. They're trying their hardest to be in the park, and they can't be here.

When I went away to play music—when I went on tour—before then, there were no tents. And when I came back, all the tents were here. So that was the biggest change, the biggest shock for me. I'm trying to adjust myself to this world, where there are all these tents and the tents are really disorganized. So that's a big one.

Culturally, I've seen a lot of shifts, too. Before I left—and maybe this has to do with the tents—the people who were here were, by and large, either the people who were in it for the long haul, or tourists who wanted to see what was going on. There was no middle ground. And now I see a lot of people on the west side of the park that are involved in their own microcosm of culture. They have their own ways of organizing or not organizing that don't work in tandem with the larger Occupy Wall Street movement—the reason why we have actually come here in the first place.

That's something I've noticed. It started occurring the past month, maybe, and it's a little upsetting because it doesn't help us clarify our vision of why we're here. It doesn't help us think about things in three-month, six-month, year patterns. I don't think that maybe what they want is what we want here. I think what they want is very rooted in the spatial here. Not to create this divide, like us and them, but the people who are in working groups have affinities that are action-oriented, that are radical. We're trying very hard to come together, and that's a difficult process, too.

I have noticed a lot of splintering and fragmentation since I first started here. Before, it was like, "We need to do the things we need to do because they need to be done." We didn't come in with the intention of having a million working groups. They came out of necessity, and I understand that, but now they've all become these little cultures in and of themselves. I just see them rocketing off in their own directions without this consciousness of the whole, and that's really dangerous in terms of collective liberation.

Town Planning can do the best they can to make tents available for everyone, but if we're not—and I'm on Town Planning so that's the reason I'm saying this—but if we're not taking into consideration sexism, racism, homophobia, and real consent policies and things like that—if we're not looking at all of these other things that should be interwoven to all that we do—then we're just building another destructive culture like the one we're fighting against. We're just building a microcosm of the culture we're fighting against, which is really hard for us to get our minds around.

But there's good things happening, too; I don't want to focus on the negative. On a positive end, our allies are coming in full force. We have a ton of people who are providing lots of support. We have people from Egypt coming in. There are trainers from all over the world, sitting down with us to try to tell us these things that are so vital, trainers for forty years that are sitting down and spending weeks on end here, just conferencing with us, trying to drill into our heads how to do this and how to do it well. So that's awesome. We're totally lucky.

It's like going to college for free. Every day, you're just learning from your peers, learning by your actions, learning from mentors and elders who've come in, who can provide resources to you, not to mention the physical resources we have that are almost endless. It feels almost endless, to some degree. I mean, everything has an end, but . . .

There's a lot to offer, there's a lot of potential, and there's a lot of issues. A lot of bridges need to be built, and there are ways to do it, and we'll find out which ones are effective.

I've been running around with my head cut off for a few weeks, and that's an issue. In the past few days, I'm realizing that what we need to be focusing on isn't so much the urgent, but the important. And while we can find things that are both urgent and important, we should be focusing on the important, but not urgent. And that's our vision.

What's the distinction?

An important, not urgent thing would be why we're here in the first place, why we came to this park. Take ourselves out of our context of this park, and look down at what are we doing and what are we building and why we are building it. Those are the important things. What we build in six months isn't urgent, but it's important, and it needs to be talked about now.

The urgent and important are the things that are in this park that we need to address immediately because they directly link in with our views. So if we're splintering as groups, that's urgent and important.

But the urgent non-important are these things that happen day-to-day that we freak out about because we're so entrenched in our own mindset in this park. We're like, "Oh, my God! This person slept in this tent!" or, "This person said this thing!" or, "The police acted in this way today!" as opposed to saying, "How can we get into the mindset of police in relationship to here? How can we get into the mindset of this culture?" The urgent non-important are specific things, and we focus so much of our efforts and time on it that it's exhausting. We're so exhausted, we can't focus on the abstract important things that need to happen, and that's dangerous. But we can overcome these issues.

Last week people were starting to do Spokes Council. Has that been answering the issues at all?

It's been addressing the issues; I don't think it's been answering them yet. Again, people are in this urgent state. As someone in Structure who helps organize the Spokes Council, I know that the Spokes Council is our strongest weapon. It's the best information-sharing warehouse we have. Anyone from any of the operations groups that have been consented upon can share their information with each other. We can pool our abilities together. We can use that as a model to build things. That's awesome. But what we keep seeing is less and less consent, more and more airing of issues that people have. I think that they are urgent issues. However, some of them are important and some aren't.

We are trying to push forward the Spokes Council because we do think it's a model that works. We've been told by many people in many contexts that it does work. We've seen it work in other Occupys. It works in a lot of anti-fracking movements in upstate New York. It worked to end the U.S. invasion of Nicaragua. It worked to end building nuclear plants in the United States. It's done a lot. It's the best information clearinghouse that any radical, non-hierarchical organization could use. It's great, and it's time-honored. So we're not reinventing the wheel. We're just trying to replace a bad wheel with a good wheel.

The Spokes Council, when and if it gets up, will be awesome, but right now, just having everyone in the same room together is volatile. We have to understand that, and it might take a while for us to air that out before we can sit and really work. A lot of people have issues with each other, and we need to feel out how we can overcome this urgent obstacle to get to the things that are really important in the macro.

Which just leads me to a really quick statement that a lot of people are taking this movement personally, and I think that's very toxic. I think what we need to realize is that when we're here, we're building as parts of this movement, not as our personal selves. We need to take care of our personal bodies and our needs, but those can happen both in the park and outside of the park. People should feel welcome to take a step back for a night or two and just decompress, get their head straight, as opposed to throwing their needs out to the movement. That gets very heavy and very crazy. And personal arguments need not happen here. They can happen elsewhere. This needs to be a space for the movement to build and grow.

Do you think that's the answer to defusing tension? People taking better care of themselves?

Yeah, I think that that's a huge part of it. If we take care of our needs, then we impose a lot less on other people, and we have a better focus and sense of self. One of the skill sets that I've been learning here a lot is nonviolent communication, which just says that if we recognize our needs, and recognize that we're the only people who can satisfy our needs, then we can be a lot less detrimental to other people and to ourselves. I think that it's good to have Wellness, N.V.C., De-Escalation, lots of people on-site to help with that, but it's also personal accountability and self-facilitation.

There is one day when I first came back here that I just wasn't eating or drinking, and I was working a lot. And then I wound up snapping at someone. The second that I did that, I pulled back and said, "Wait a minute! Red flag! I'm not taking care of my body. I'm not taking care of myself, and because of that, I'm starting to be detrimental to other people. I'm going home tonight. I'm going to cook a big breakfast in the morning, and I'm going to pack a lunch, and I'm bringing water. I'm going to fix this right now, before I dig this hole," you know? I think, if we all recognize where we are at physically and mentally and spiritually, then we can create this system that's better.

I understand that not everyone can go back to an apartment, but we're slowly building up an infrastructure of people who have spaces and can offer them. I'm trying to pass along the information that several people from upstate New York have offered log cabins for anyone to go up to for retreats.

That's really nice.

There's a whole network of support all over the world that's willing to take care of us and get into a head-space where we can push and build, but we have to be accepting. We have to be accepting of the fact that we, as individuals, need space from this park sometimes.

But as a movement, we need to focus on what's important.

Could you explain to me a little bit about how Structure works?

Well, what Structure does right now is mostly focused on the Spokes Council. We do some of the spatial stuff, like, we try to get the actual spaces for Spokes Council. We send out the emails to all the working groups, letting everyone know where the Spokes Councils are, what time they are, because the times fluctuate a little bit. They're usually seven to ten or seven thirty to ten thirty, but that really depends on the space and their needs, so it fluctuates.

Also, it's kind of a very intense brainstorming session for how we're going to try to set the spokes. We had, like, an eight-hour conversation one day just about, "How are we going to get the spokes consented upon?" because that's not the G.A. process. That's not the traditional consent process. How can we do it in a way where everyone is validated, recognized, and there's reducing the amount of back-and-forth for personal conversations and personal arguments to come in?

We want: "Is this group an operations group? Yes? Or does it need further discussion?" And if it's, "Yes, they're consented upon," that's it. We can flesh out personal grievances or tactical issues later, but we have to get these groups in now. There are other spaces and forums to handle these grievances. You can come to these working groups and say, "Hey, I think you're having these major issues in these ways, and we need to talk about it." I think that there should be other forums for this, and that's maybe a piece of the puzzle that hasn't been fleshed out as much but needs to happen more.

How many working groups are ideally involved in Spokes Council? All of them?

It's operations working groups, and I can't speak on how many because that's not up for me to decide, but it's any group that logistically or financially contributes to the operations of Liberty Park. That's what we are building here.

Okay. So Comfort, Library . . .

Yeah. I'm trying to think of who's already been in. Medic is in. Sanitation is in. Kitchen is in. I think N.V.C. is in. I think Comfort is in. Finance is in. Anyone who's handling the tactical everydays—those people are the ones that we're mostly talking about.

There are other groups that might get in, like Facilitation and Training—things that do provide services, but maybe it's slightly more up for debate whether they're operational or logistical. And then there's groups that a lot of people want to discuss because we're not sure. A lot of those might be movement groups.

Also, note that caucuses are welcome, caucuses being a body of people who have a common affinity, usually around marginalization. So there's a women's caucus,[1] there's a People of Color Caucus, there's a Queering O.W.S. caucus . . . the women haven't quite found their way in yet. Every time they're ready to speak, something goes wrong in the Spokes Council, and the Spokes Council deflates.

Wow, that is so horrifyingly true-to-life.

I feel so bad. To take off the Structure hat for a second: We really, really need the women's caucus in.

That really bums me out, I have to say.

Yeah, it bums me out, too. It's really important that they're there. I think that the caucuses are really healthy in these Spokes Councils. The caucuses are threading into these meetings that which is really important to all of us. So when a group acts in a sexist way, the women's caucus can say, "I'm standing up and I'm going to directly address this." It's great to have a forum. Like, "This spoke will handle these issues. And while we all can feel empowered to deal with them, this spoke has a lot of knowledge about this, really understands the issues, and can speak concisely on it so that we're not all going back and forth."

---

[1] Women Occupying Wall Street (WOW).

The models that work the best are: Small groups with common affinities get most of the shit done. Then bring in larger groups, like a Spokes Council, to share information and to draw more people to those affinities. We're here as autonomous collectives. Occupy Wall Street is a movement, but each group should be entitled to make its own decisions. I can't tell the kitchen what kind of food to get or how to organize their structure or when their hours are. I accept the fact that they are based on what's best for them because they have a much better knowledge, in the same way that I don't complain to Medic about what kind of medicine they have or how they practice it. But if there's a serious issue that could compromise the movement, then we can discuss it. There are working groups that might have these larger issues, but by and large, we need to respect autonomy of working groups. These larger movements, like the General Assembly and Spokes Councils and things like this, should really just be information-clearing and asking for things that are larger than themselves.

What is a General Assembly issue as opposed to a Spokes Council issue?

Once we have the Spokes Council in place, the Spokes Council will handle all financial things that are operational to the movement. General Assemblies, we are trying to have more of an open invitation for people to brainstorm and popcorn—which is a style of brainstorming session where anyone just calls out things—or breakout groups about ideas, theories. Like, "We want to talk today about our relationship with the neighborhood." Or, "We want to talk about Occupy Wall Street in relation to the other Occupys." Or, "What are we, as the Occupy movement, doing in this macro picture? Let's just talk about it." They could have breakout groups and small information, and then harvest it and bring it back to this wider community. That's really healthy because that's a way for us to be self-aware. So that's what I think a General Assembly is good for. And that should be open to anyone and all people.

I do think a Spokes Council should be open, but the most important people in the Spokes Council are the spokes themselves, conferring with the other spokes. If all the spokes are there, legitimately speaking on behalf of their working groups, I think that that would be an acceptable Spokes Council to me. I do like having other people from working groups come in to back their spokes, so that they can confer with each other on issues that they might not have addressed in their internal working groups. I think it's healthy. But it's not an open meeting for tourists and for people . . . like, you can audit it if there's space, and I'd love to find a large enough space for that, but we do have to accept the reality that we are in Lower Manhattan. There aren't five-hundred, six-hundred-person meeting spaces that are friendly with Occupy Wall Street and available in two days at a price we can afford.

You guys have to rent space for it?

Yep.

What kind of spaces are you getting?

Well, we were in a high school cafeteria over by the Brooklyn Bridge for two days.

Oh, were you in Murry Bergtraum? I used to teach there.

I think it was. It's right by the police precinct?

Yeah. I know that cafeteria well.

It was very hot.

It's unpleasant.

Yep, didn't create the best atmosphere.

But I think Murry Bergtraum, the guy whom it was named after, was some sort of old-school socialist.[2]

Cool. Maybe that's one of the reasons they were down for us.

Then we were at a really nice area, although it was a little bit too small. We were at a Trinity Church reception area that fit two-twenty people. We had about three hundred people in the space, and they were still letting people in and out. They weren't harassing us about it. They were really actually really, really awesome and welcoming. But there was some controversy about Structure putting out this email to everyone, asking each working group to only bring, like, three or four people backing up the spoke. That isn't super all-inclusive.

Isn't the spoke rotating?

---

[2] Murry Bergtraum (1916–1973) was an accountant for the fur industry who presided over the New York City Board of Education in 1970–71.

Yeah.

So I mean, they'll be included eventually, right?

Yeah, and I think that's fine. The spoke has to rotate every time. It keeps working groups of one—which do exist here—it keeps them from being able to be present at the meetings, because you're not a working group of one. That's not a working group. That's not even a group. To take us out of Occupy Wall Street world and into the dictionary, that's not a group. The dictionary will argue that this group has no validity in this space. It's not a personal bias, it's kind of an objective thing.

How many working groups of one are there?

I think two, maybe three.

I'm not going to ask what they are.

I'm not going to tell.

No, no. Keep moving.

So the Spokes Council is here for information-clearing, because no one has time to sit in on every group. I have no clue what goes on in the groups that I'm not involved with. It's like blind spots in my vision, you know? I can see where Structure is. I can see the future of Facilitation. I can see where the tents are now, and where the tents will be in the future, hopefully. And I can also see some of the larger "where we as a movement are going," just because I'm involved with a lot of the network here. But I have no idea what's going to happen with a lot of these groups. Being able to sit in on the Spokes Council is awesome. It's really empowering.

What would you say is the direction now?

I'm not completely sure, but what I see is us transcending this physical space. We need to, and we need to soon. And although we never know where we are, I'd like to see us really fleshing out what's important to us, networking with other people who've already been doing it, and doing it a long time. Kind of going glacial, in many ways, although still maintaining this really strong vibe. Having really good campaigns, like, "We're going to shut down this!" in a spirit of direct action, while also being an entity in our community, and taking this model and bringing it to other places. So it's not about . . . I don't know how to describe it . . . I think physical occupation is really good because it is a clearinghouse for information; it roots us in the spatial, it's symbolic, it's theatrical. But what I see is our ideas going forth.

As an occupier, I'd like to see a lot less government, a lot less corporatization. Mostly, I just want to see people feel empowered, and empowering themselves.

What we're doing here isn't a reactionary movement. That's why we don't have demands. We're here because we're a non-hierarchical community-building movement. We're testing out how communities can get together, and if we can find a way that works, that's going to go everywhere. That's going to spread like wildfire, and it already is, to some degree. That's why everyone is talking about consensus, and I couldn't be happier. If we're talking about consensus, then we should be talking about consent—personal consent—and if we can all take in personal consent, we're going to be much healthier.

How are you distinguishing between consensus and consent?

Consent is a personal thing. I can consent to this interview. Occupy Wall Street doesn't need to consent to me having this interview because it respects that I'm an autonomous individual with decisions. Consent is an individual saying yes to something. It always comes into it in terms of sexuality, but a good consent policy applies to everything that we do in our lives. It's being held personally accountable to make decisions, and then empowering ourselves to vocalize those decisions so that we're not put in situations that we don't want to be in—we're not put in these coercive combinations, as Utah Phillips would say.

Consensus is: As a movement, as a body of people, we all agree this is something that can happen. So consensus is a large-scale thing, a way of groups deciding things. Consensus is the idea that we don't have to take votes. We don't have to marginalize people and step over people in our way of progress.

Which is happening, and we do need to be aware of that as an issue. That's part of the urgent and not important. We need to consent to things as a movement, and we need to feel empowered horizontally to speak up, to raise issues, to raise questions and concerns. And also, we need to know that just because someone has an idea that we may not agree with fully, we should be respecting it's autonomy unless we really feel like it's compromising us as a whole. Consensus is an individual speaking on behalf of a part of the movement, as an entity of the movement.

How do you empower people in the greater world toward an ability to consent?

The biggest way it seems to be happening is just by everyone being plugged into what's going on here and watching. Watching us in the media and coming to the park and just seeing everything that we've built here. We've built a lot, and it's very impressive. We should celebrate the victories that we've already accomplished.

I think that people want that world that we want. It's a pretty common idea. We want that world, and we're providing a model. Whether that model's perfect or not . . . it's certainly not, but I think it could be really good. And we're still building it, so it's a work in progress. But we're providing a rubric for people to base their own community on, and that's really cool.

Everyone comes to Facilitation meetings and says, "We're from all these other Occupys. You need to help us." We're not, like, the parent occupation, but it feels like we are, and we do have to take that in the back of our minds. In all that we do, the whole world is watching us. Not just the media and all these people, but all the other occupations, all the other activist movements.

And we're looking to Greece, looking to Spain, looking to Egypt in the same way that they're looking back at us. We're learning from each other. In this consensus model, we're both saying yes to our movement-building, and we respect the autonomy of the other one. We can't have the same tactics that Greece has; it doesn't work here. But we can learn from the Greek model.

I've spoken to a lot of people from other Occupys who told me that they came here to learn what's going on, and are taking it back home with them.

I hope that they're sharing what they've learned, too, because that's the other part of it. I just hope, because we're looking to other Occupys for certain models ourselves.

What are you learning from the other Occupys?

Some already have effective Spokes Councils. Some know how to handle destructive, toxic people in ways that we don't know.

What are some of the ways?

There are evictions in some parks. If someone is time after time disruptive and dangerous to themselves and to others around them, there are people who've been asked to leave and forced to leave. Years ago, I would have thought that was a horrible thing. Now, I don't think it's a horrible thing; I think it's a necessary thing. I feel really bad saying that because it doesn't create this air of all-inclusiveness, but if you're a danger to yourself and to the others around you, there's no justification that these people should be here, especially if other avenues have already been explored.

It's a very dangerous route because it's hard. People want everyone to be here, and I want everyone to be here, but we have to take care of our needs. If we're not taking care of our needs, that's really detrimental to everyone around us, including ourselves. That's really dangerous. We need to build the safest space possible for ourselves and for the world. It's hard.

It's very exciting at the same time.

Yeah. I'm nervous and optimistic, working really hard, and trying to not just spin my wheels when I'm working, which takes perspective, too. That's my personal challenge right now is: How can I be more efficient and doing less busy work? ❖

November 16

Luis

I'm here specifically for school. I think it's ridiculous to treat our kids, the future of this country, like complete garbage.

I think this is a country that was based on ideas. And revolution? That's the only reason why we're the United States of America.

And I think it's completely ridiculous that they just go in and kick us out like that. They're treating us as if we're convicts now. Look at the security; they're watching our every move. Like I said, I was questioned about a schoolbag. You know, that's not the way you treat . . . people. We're here in peace!

I've been here for a month. I have yet to see any of us pick a fight with a cop. I've always seen it the opposite. Everyone who talks all of that—that we're not here for a specific reason, you know, and they talk badly about us—they haven't been here for more than ten minutes. I can guarantee that.

We're down, but we're not out.

What's their plan for the park? Are they going to open it all the way, or is this it? Is this the best you get?

Well, I think what they're planning to do is just to annoy the hell out of us until we decide, "Okay, it's time to leave." So I'm guessing it's going to be like this until the last protester leaves. But mark my words: We're not leaving. We're not going anywhere.

Do you think there's going to be a move to another park?

No. I mean, it might spread out to other sects, I guess—other Occupy movements—but this is the main one. We're not leaving. ❖

Paul II

I've been sleeping here for a month now. I went home this weekend to get some rest. I was kind of sick and needed to get some energy back. I wasn't really paying attention, but I found out about it yesterday, and I rushed here. I had a tent. I had a crew here, but when I came, everything was gone. I have been up all night, making sure that there's a presence here until we figure out what's next.

What's going on tomorrow?

I don't know about everything that's going on. I know that there's plans to block the subway lines. We're going to do all kinds of direct action. They're expecting something, but they don't know what. Direct Action has been planning all kinds of things, you just wait and see.

And in the meantime, you're holding down the fort.

Right now, yes. That's what I've been doing. That's my short-term agenda, but in the long term, we can't know yet what the outcome of this is going to be. Can we come back? Can we not? What retaliation can we do in terms of legality, or in terms of civil disobedience? We'll see. Who knows what the future will bring?

This movement is not just about the park. The park is a symbolic thing that we have to defend, but it's bigger than the park, and they're not going to just shut it down like this. If they chop off this head, millions will grow. We have, like, B-C-D-E-F-G-H-I . . . you know, the whole alphabet beyond. It's so dense. This movement is so dense. You can't just sum it up in a few words.

For example, I went to a meeting last week about planning for occupiers to squat empty buildings owned by banks in the neighborhood. Squat buildings could be a good road we could explore, just to keep things going having this community. That's what Occupy Wall Street was engined by, this little town square where people met, where you could come and actually express your ideas, meet people who disagree, agree. Networks of ideas—networks of political action—keep that energy going. We're going to have to do that if we want this movement to survive and go somewhere.

It's important to have a place to go.

Exactly. So I think we could try, also, to fight using the law, continue occupying this park, have a presence in Lower Manhattan, try to see other places we could occupy, and continue to support the Occupy movement overall, in the U.S. and in the whole world.

Yeah, you shut down Occupy Wall Street, which is the symbolic epicenter, but there's Occupy all over the world, so it's not like this is the end of it. Just look at what happened in Oakland, what's happening in Europe right now. We're unstoppable. We're unstoppable. They're pulling their hairs out right now, you know. It's not like it's a relief for them. They're still scared. ❖

Mike

All right, Mike follow-up. Tell me what happened to you.

As much as I remember.

I'd just gotten back from the Spokes Council. It was fun for me because the group I'm with, O.W.S. en Español, got through into the Spokes Council. We have a spoke. [Laughs.] "Great!" you know?

[Laughs.] I want to say, "Great!" but it's more like, "I'm sorry!"

It was sort of funny. We just got back. I was like, "Okay, fine. Let me just step into my tent and get, like, fifteen minutes." Actually, way before that, when I was coming back from the Spokes Council, I did notice the cops dropping off barricades, but I just thought it was like, "Oh, they're preparing for the seventeenth. No big deal. They do that all the time." But as soon as I stepped into the tent, I just saw the whole corners of the park: Bam! Stadium lights, and I was like, "Wow!" Then people started freaking out, and that's when I kind of knew.

Freaking out how? Like, loud mic checks?

Yeah, mic checks, as well as, "Wake up! Wake up!" and what not. Just going from tent to tent, shaking it, waking people up. I mean, I just knew right away. I just kind of assessed whether or not I was going to lock down and get arrested or whatnot.

I had already started protecting the stuff I had, in terms of material I use to do what I do here. I started bringing them on- and off-site.

You were bringing it to the storage space?

No, I was just bringing it to—like, dumping it somewhere off-site where I could recover it. I've brought it to a couple of train stations, or I'll throw it behind some bushes.

So I left. And then when I came back, they were just not letting anybody in. I stopped right here, on Liberty, and then I pushed back all the way to Fulton. I tried walking around. I pretty much watched when they were starting to haul stuff away.

I went to a friend's house. I tried watching some of it on LiveStream, then went to bed, and I was here early the next morning.

Did you go to the G.A. in the morning?

No, I didn't. I helped facilitate the G.A. here, last night at seven.

People said it was very optimistic. You had it here in the park?

Yeah, it was right here. The G.A. was held right here in the park, as usual, seven o'clock. I think it was refreshing for people, because people were, you know, "What are we going to do now?" I think people got the chance to know that everyone they met—the faces they saw here—were safe, and they felt really better.

How many people were arrested?

I'm hearing a lot of conflicting reports. I know when I was leaving, there were probably between thirty-five to fifty people trained in direct action—who were willing to stay and get arrested—and I just saw those people preparing themselves for a direct action.

How do they do that?

Well, locking arms, and locking themselves around the kitchen, for example. People were trying to lock themselves around structures that are in place. That's pretty much it. Around trees or whatever, I don't know. But those are people—they have goggles, you know? They call their families, let everyone know, that kind of deal. They're okay with getting arrested, and they're okay with being pepper-sprayed and all sorts of cool stuff. And they did, by the way.

[Laughs.] They did get sprayed.

Yeah. [Laughs.]

Would you say some people were arrested who were not prepared to be arrested?

Yeah, of course, some people were probably not aware that these people are willing to get arrested. Some of these people panicked, you know? Yeah, there were random arrests.

Were a lot of people hurt?

Some. I'm hearing a lot of conflicting reports of that, too. I did see a video of a dog getting hurt. It got left behind, and it wasn't going to be picked up. So I know a dog got hurt. I've seen weird handcuff injuries, like, purple and yellow and whatnot. I think people's spirits are okay; some people did get kind of physically hurt. I don't know how much or what scale of injuries. I think, in general, people are doing okay.

It's good that things didn't turn out too violent. It was probably the most passive a raid could ever be. The people we know—we've called around and figured out they're okay.

It gives us some time to re-evaluate, refocus, and think about where we're going as a movement and what message we're sending.

Did you stay here last night?

Yeah, I did.

So you haven't slept?

Well, I got, like, an hour nap or so. The deal is: I'm going to try to maintain a position in the park as much as possible. I'm working in a lot of other working groups, and a lot of the stuff we're doing is off-site, anyways. For example, O.W.S. en Español—we have a lot of stuff geared toward Latin communities, so I definitely have to pick up energy in those areas. I want to hold up our presence, and we'll figure out how to do that systematically, but there's a lot of things we have to do, a lot of educational stuff we have to do, all over the place.

What about tomorrow?

I'm not too particularly concerned about tomorrow. I think people get it in general that we've been the most nonviolent we can be. People get it that we're a nonviolent movement. With that said, you never know what kind of provocations are going to happen, from cops or other areas where people get provoked. And again, the people who are willing to step out and do serious direct action—they have assessed the arrestability of the direct action they're doing.

There are direct actions that are a very low risk of being arrested. There's rallies, which will have the safety of our crowd. So I'm excited about it. I know it will be successful. I think, then, it will show people how hard we are.

Where are people meeting now? Where is everybody?

A lot of people are meeting in cyberspace, and that was always the deal. People are meeting here, and working groups are meeting wherever they usually meet. Sixty Wall Street is still open. Charlotte's Place—I go there every day to get my phone charged, and I eat there. A lot of people are meeting there. There's a meeting at twelve o'clock today. And to be completely honest, meeting here, too. Today I was talking to some other guys on the Facilitation team. We were thinking of probably doing some trainings here because we have the space now.

Will you read your sign?

It says: "Park rules: No constitutional rights allowed. All equal, but some are more equal than some. Yellow vests can be cops if they feel like.[1] Park rules can change any minute. Signed, Doomberg." ❖

Michael

What happened?

I was over here by the kitchen, and we had locked arms. They came up, and at first I thought all they were doing was checking the perimeter. I even talked to one of the police officers. I said, "Okay, you're going to do the perimeter, lock us up while you clean up the first half, and then

---

[1] Private security personnel wearing yellow vests patrolled the park in the days after the eviction.

you're going to do the back half." And they said, "Okay, that's fine." They cleaned up the first half, and then they came in like nothing I've ever seen before. They picked us up. They picked us up out of our locked arms. I was dragged out of my coat—you remember the coat I had? Torn to pieces! Shredded! I mean, it was a coat, but it was a coat I got here, you know what I mean? It meant something to me.

So I went to a paddy wagon. I'm going in the paddy wagon, I look to my left, I see tear gas bombs going off. It was like something I've never seen in America before in my life. It was horrible! It was horrible!

Bystander: It was horrible!

Michael: Terrorism at its worst!

Went to jail, stayed for a long time. The police are usually polite, courteous, respectful and responsible. They know what's going on here. But a police officer—maybe thirty, mid-thirties—looked at one of the girls—I mean, one of the young girls: eighteen-, seventeen-year-old girl—and said, "There goes another one of those Zuccotti hotties!" I almost lost myself! He said it more than once, about a few of the girls that came in. I didn't know what to do. I was like, "Really? This is what's happening?" I'm hearing stories about sexual assault with the N.Y.P.D., when the girls are booked and everything. I'm just beside myself now. I don't know how to fix that.

But I do know that we will be here. We will be here until the day arrives that we have peace in this country and throughout the world. We will! I'll die for it! I'll go on record to say that! I will! That's why I'm here. That's my purpose. Honestly, that's it.

What of my kids here in the park? They have no home! The homeless kids! I mean, that's when I really started weeping. What will they do? This is the first place where they really felt safe, and they really felt, "Wow! We do have a place in this world! We do have a purpose!"

They took it all away because they didn't know. They were doing what they were told, but they weren't doing what was in their heart. I believe that if any police officer came in here and talked to those kids, saw what they were doing, saw the change, saw the love, saw the hope, saw the everything that was happening in here, they wouldn't have done what they did last night. They wouldn't! I know that, because I believe, in spite of everything, that people are good. People are good. People are good. Anne Frank said that, not me.

I will try to believe with you that that's the case. So what's . . .

The next step? Occupy Together. November seventeenth.

Tomorrow.

Yes! Week before Thanksgiving, take a day off from work, from school. Be with your family. Turn off the television. Read the paper. Talk about what's happening.

I'm encouraging people who are working for companies like Walmart and Kmart, who don't pay their people for the amount of work that they do. I've been in these stores. I know people who work for these stores. It's not right! I'm saying: Let these people know that it's not right what they're doing. It's predatory, you know? I'm asking everyone—pleading—I'm getting on my knees and saying, "Please take that day off!" because the world will see that the power is still with the people. It always has been. It always has been. It's like Dorothy going to the Wizard: "It's always been with you. You've always had the courage! You've always had the heart!" That's it.

As somebody told me down here, "Without courage, there can be no other virtue."

There you go. Except for patience. You have to have patience . . . with the police, and with each other as well.

It's hard, right?

I don't know; I've never had a baby before! [Laughs.] I don't know how hard it is. I'm getting one now, and it's okay. It's a matter of reclaiming what's yours. It's not just the money, but it's the space! We belong here! We're here! Get used to it! ❖

Rafael

Cops came in and they did their job, I guess, which was to block the airspace so no one could see how bad they were. They stopped any helicopters from going above so that no one could film what they were doing. They arrested all the reporters who went in here, and they pushed them back—those who wouldn't leave the area—to a block or two radius away from here. They stopped the subway, and closed down all the bridges and tunnels, and then when they were sure that no one was looking, they came in and they simply mowed this place down.

Some people tried to tie themselves up in the kitchen, and those people were maced and thrown out of here. I was here until the last minute. When they came into the kitchen, I was getting my hands cuffed and I said, "I'm leaving! I'm leaving right now!" So when they were done, I walked over to the side and they let me go. They walked us up to the corner.

I left all my belongings here. They said, "Break down your tents!" So I did that, thinking that I could come back the next day to get my stuff. Kind of foolish of me to think so, but I already knew what time it was. I have nothing that I'm so attached to here that matters, you know? It's the long term that matters.

And they did what they did. They came back, went to court—though the judge that ruled in our favor was removed from the case because she worked for the A.C.L.U.[2]

Are you serious?

Yeah. So then the case had to be reheard again, and the decision had to be overturned. And then once that decision was overturned, another judge had it that we had to argue before him about whether we could be here or not. Now Brookfield Properties put up all these rules about people sleeping, about it being open twenty-four hours. They put these signs up saying you can only be here until ten o'clock. But that was a big mistake because it's in their deed. In order for them to get the extra floors that they got, they had to build this park and make it public twenty-four hours. So people stayed twenty-four hours regardless of the signs that say you can only be here until ten o'clock.

Did you stay all night last night?

Unfortunately, I didn't get a chance to stay because . . . since it was supposed to rain and we don't have any tents yet, there were some places that were giving shelter to the occupiers. They wanted security there

---

[2]The judge removed from the case on the morning of November 15 was Manhattan Supreme Court Justice Lucy Billings.

to make sure that if there was any disruption, our own security would handle it. So I went to a church around Seventh Street and Second Avenue, and I did security there. They told me they needed five or six people. We wound up with, like, eight people there doing security, but we only needed two people in the front, so we took shifts. So I got some sleep. That was my first sleep in two days.

The night before that, when they came, we all gathered and decided to march down Broadway. They made us turn on Fulton, and we all went down. Then, on the corner of the next block, they let a few of us go by, and then the rest of them they gathered and they started beating them. You know, there was a couple hundred arrested that night. They just kept the process going. We would be marching, and then they would stop and tell us that we had to go down another street, and they would do the same thing with the people that wouldn't keep going. They would start arresting them and making them go.

Eventually, by the end of the night—four something in the morning—we wound up at Foley Square, which is where we were all trying to meet. Some were on Pine and Broadway, and we were trying to get the two groups together. While we were in the process of that, the cops surrounded us in the park. Luckily, they used a bullhorn, and told us that if we didn't leave immediately, we were all subject to arrest. So everybody had to gather up again and start marching. We went through the same process of coming back, getting people locked up, and at five something, almost six o'clock, we wound up back at Foley Square.

They told us that we had to leave, but we had Norman Siegel from the American Civil Liberties Union with us by this time, and he went and spoke to the police. They decided—since it was only, like, twenty-five minutes to six—that they were going to allow us to stay. Finally, this walk of all night . . . I feel like I walked, like, eighty blocks, man, a hundred blocks, and all the stress of every couple of minutes about to go to jail, you know? That finally settled down. We went from there to a property that Trinity Church was supposed to be donating to us, but then the board of directors voted against it.

The church's board of directors?

Yeah. They had spoken about it, but they weren't prepared for it to actually take place. This emergency came up, and since we were in talks with them, we assumed that they were going to go through with it right away. They didn't want to have their hand forced. You know, they're going to do it, it just wasn't going to be that minute. So that gave the police a chance to go in. We had announced before that this was a new place, that we had already planned for this, that we're working on it. And then all of sudden . . .

Five hundred cops in riot gear show up, and you know, the tensions are between: They're on the phone with Trinity Properties, the board of directors are in the meeting and they're not answering the phone, somehow or other the cops got in touch with them and they're like, "Look, we're going to warn you guys before we go in." It was very tense. I was doing security for one of the reverends, and when it came down that cops were going in, I had to snatch him, and basically, carry him and shelter him through the crowd of people so that he didn't get mauled by the stampede.

Who was the reverend?

I don't know his name. I don't know if he's a reverend, or . . . I don't know what you call him. There's a bunch of different names of the people that dress like pastors, but . . . it wasn't "reverend." It's a congregation of clergymen that had organized this.

Then we made our way back here to find out that the park was still closed. We were waiting on the court for a decision. We got our decision, and then we walked around for a couple of hours, heard the G.A. I was so happy to see it was so big.

It was here?

Yeah, it was here. They finally let us in. It came all the way down to, like, the middle of the park—a little bit more than the middle of the park. It was an enormous G.A., and there were more people in the park now than there were before. Before it seemed like there were so many people, but it was because of the tents. Now there were no tents, and every inch of space was being occupied by a person.

Then I had to leave. Somebody came up: "Ralph, we need for you to get five guys together and do security." I was like, "Oh, my God! I haven't slept!" I was just hoping to go home for the night, like, "Finally, we got the park. Okay, I can go home to sleep." Instead, I was like, "All right, no problem."

Then I couldn't find no one from Security! So I started just pulling volunteers out the crowd. I had the address. We went down there, and luckily, I got some sleep.

Now I'm back here today, trying to look for, you know, the people, and see what the next step is to organize and get together. Tomorrow, we have a big event.

It's a general strike?

It's supposed to be a general strike and a march to Wall Street or whatever, but I have a feeling that for a lot of people—not for me, but for a lot of people—peace is over. The cops have demonstrated that. People are frustrated. There's no more freedom of speech. There's no more transparency. They did all this in the dark. They closed the airspace.

I hope it's not true that people are giving up.

No, they're not giving up; they're just giving up on the nonviolent part of it. You know, a lot of people actually attacked the police. They were throwing bottles. During those marches, they were turning over garbage cans in the street. Some people broke windows. But we're frustrated, you know? Our hands are tied.

I wonder about tomorrow, too.

I don't think it's going to be as bad as people think it is, but . . . it may get worse than we think. One little drop of negativity could turn into a whirlpool of it. So far we've been pretty peaceful, and there's a great deal of violence that has come against us. If you look at the big guy over there, he's got bruises on his legs, on his forehead. I spoke to another woman last night who—her finger . . . the girl who's pregnant? She lives in the Women's Tent? I don't know if you spoke to her, but they beat her in the hand, and—

They beat a pregnant woman?

See, this is not personal. These are soldiers, and they work for the one percent. They're just doing their job: removal. It didn't matter whether you were young or old. You had to be moved, and that's it. There's no talking to you. There's no sitting here trying to reason this out, you know? The order is: "You must move, and if you don't move in a timely fashion according to me, I will move you."

When I talked to you on Monday, you were like, "It's two weeks, tops." People in the library were like, "No way! It's going to be here forever!" but you called it.

I know the truth. I'm here. I'm in all these meetings. I know what's going on. I mean, there's still things that I'm not talking to you about that are going to happen, but . . .

If I turn the tape off, will you talk to me about it?

You can't help but to spread it. You'll ask other people about it, and before you know it, "I heard this!" and, "I heard that!"

You're right, you're right.
What's the next step for the park?

They might fight to put the tents up and to get looser restrictions on the park simply because of what the park represents to the rest of the world. You know, it's like if we're taken down, then it's understandable how another occupation, maybe not as well-organized, can be taken down. It'll help people feel like the movement is dying or over. But as long as we keep this alive, as long as this is strong, then it'll keep hope up in the world. So we kind of have a responsibility to make sure it stays up. We can't allow them to win. ❖

David

Were you here the other night?

Yeah.

How'd that go for you?

Well, it wasn't pleasant. Basically, they took the tent down around us. We had a lot of medical stuff, which they said they would protect. First they said that by leaving, we were abandoning it, and we didn't want to do that. But then they said they would protect it. And I really don't know if—well, I know they didn't protect it well, but I don't know if we're going to recover any of it.

There were three of us, and we grabbed what we could, so we have a strange assortment of stuff left.

How long had you been working here?

Maybe about since the second half of October—October twentieth or something.

What drew you down originally?

Well, I was watching Operation Wall Street, and I first thought, "What is the point? Where is Occupation Wall Street going? What demands do they hope to realize?" But I came to feel that what we were doing was making people aware of the situation in this country.

People don't seem to be aware that one percent of the country owns thirty-five percent of the country. They don't seem to be aware that our rights are fast disappearing. They don't seem to be aware that environmentalists—people who know—tell us that too much carbon dioxide is going into the air. Not only is too much going into the air, but it's going into the air faster and faster.

They're going to have a pipeline from Canada down to the Gulf of Mexico, which they have a sample of in Canada which had fourteen leaks last year. And they're going through prime farmland. I mean, there's nothing going through desert or any land that where it's okay if we have a couple thousand gallons of oil spilled there. And besides that, that's the worst kind of fuel, which just shows that they're not really serious about the environment.

So that's part of it. Another thing is increasing secrecy in the government—ignoring laws, putting people who reveal law-breaking in jail instead of the people who break the law. I don't understand that.

People need to be aware that we've passed some kind of critical point in the United States. Things aren't really changing, and somebody needs to do something. Operation Wall Street is making people aware. There are a lot of conversations going on here about a lot of things, and there's a sense that things really need to change. There's a feeling that a lot of people are thinking about it and trying to put it together, trying to find something that will work.

Take medicine, for instance. Just working in the Medical tent, we had Western medicine—allopathic medicine, like me—and we also had herbalists and organic medicine people, and people who do alpha wave generation for relaxation and massage. Because people weren't in positions where they needed to look at the bottom line—at how much profit they were making—we found ways of working together where we really were doing better together. I mean, I learned a lot about herbal medicine that I never knew. And it was convincing because we had patients coming back and saying, "You know, that concoction really worked!" That's pretty convincing if people come back and say it, just independently. They weren't actors, you know? So I learned a lot, and they learned things, too. And I think that would be the way it would be if everybody wasn't looking for the profit.

I think the question really should not be "Why am I down here?" but "Why isn't everybody else down here?" you know?

Yeah.

So you have a sense that this is really, really important, and we really have to do something. I sense it. People have to do something, you know? I mean, I have grandchildren. I'd like to see them grow up in a decent world and live a full life. And you have a child, and you'd like, I'm sure, to see your child have a happy life.

Absolutely.

And I just don't see it happening if we're going the way we're going. It's like on the *Titanic*: They rang the bell and said, "Iceberg!" and then they sped up and headed toward it, you know what I mean? It would take a long time to turn a planet around. It took a long time to turn the *Titanic* around, but not as long as it takes to turn a planet around. And they're not even going in that direction!

So it doesn't seem weird for me to be here. I'm in a special position because I retired early. I was thinking that I like my job, and I was thinking I'd probably work until seventy-five or seventy-seven or something like that, but my partner had diabetes, and he became pretty disabled. We decided that he might be happier in a nursing home, so he went into a nursing home. He was absolutely miserable. He couldn't eat. He stared at the wall. He didn't do anything. And I thought I had to take him home.

So that was in 2008. I changed our apartment around: widened the doorways and took out the thresholds, and put a door into the bathroom that a wheelchair could go into. And I took him home.

After six months, he was so badly off that I had to take him to the emergency room. They diagnosed severe dehydration, severe anemia, and mental changes. He needed blood transfusion and a week on I.V. therapy before he could come home.

And then he didn't think that the apartment was actually the same apartment because of the changes I had made. He said, "No, we live at the other apartment!" So I took him out in his wheelchair to show him that it was his building, and he started calling to people, "I need to go home!" We went back in, and he told the doorman, "Could you call me a taxi?" and then he gave the address. The doorman thought he was kidding, so he said, "Oh, that'll be twenty dollars to go that far."

Then he called 9-1-1, and the people talked to him for about half an hour. The E.M.T.'s talked to him, because he was very rational in explaining why he knew it wasn't [his apartment]. They finally said, "We have news for you: This is your apartment." And he was just quiet for a while. Then he said, "That's hard to believe." And they said, "Yes, and that's why we're going to take you to the hospital, because we want to find out why it's hard for you to believe that."

So we went to the hospital, and his primary physician took him off the psychotropic medication that he had been receiving at the nursing home. In about a week, his confusion totally cleared and never returned.

Wow. That nursing home was—

It was a good nursing home. The people were trying—he was not a good patient—but they didn't realize they exhausted him. They did physical therapy because he was walking on crutches. They were into improving his mobility, but he ended up in a wheelchair.

He didn't realize the extent of his disability. He had diabetes since the age of eight, and he was sixty-nine years old. He had four injections a day. He had been on crutches since forty. He was in the hospital with osteomyelitis. He was in the hospital innumerable times with complications from diabetes. You can't be a brittle juvenile diabetic and be in good shape after sixty years of that. So they exhausted him, and they were just a little angry at him all the time and he knew it.

But he wasn't happy, anyway. He wouldn't even listen to the radio, which he loved to do. He had C.D.'s and everything. So I'll never regret taking him when he was . . . he was home for over two years, and we did a lot of things. He got a three-wheeled scooter. He got a big twenty-four-inch iMac computer. He took lessons at the Apple Store, and learned to be really adept with YouTube.

He came from the Bronx, and back in the Bronx they have old Bronx things. He went to William Howard Taft High School—P.S. 75—and they have pictures of it—how it looks now. He found all these things, and he found old Gertrude Berg—*The Goldbergs*—which he loved. And he found a movie. She had a full-length movie that showed in theaters.

Snippets on YouTube. He put it all together, and it was really nice. It's a nice movie. It's a good movie. He did lots of things like that. He put together shows from T.V. that he recorded.

We went out to eat. We got a wheelchair van and a three-wheeled power scooter so that we could. Once he called me—he went out, and he called me from Broadway and Sixty-Eighth Street. He said, "Meet me because I want to go to the library." He had been in bed about to die in the nursing home, and he was going out to eat. We went to Washington. We went to Maine. We went to Vermont. And you know, stayed at disabled-access motels. We had a good time, and he did okay.

His previous partner had died in 1997. He moved from the Bronx in '79 or '78 because his previous partner, Paul, lived somewhere else. Paul died after they were together for twenty years. He had a bad heart. And then Eli was alone for a few years until we got together, and we were together after that.

We were not at all polite, but we really got along together, and we never went back to the nursing home, either. He couldn't stand. He had to have a stand lift to stand, but then he wasn't able to use the stand lift. He wasn't able to sit up by himself. And so I called Adult Protective Services. They said we needed a lift that you didn't have to do anything, and we couldn't get it without him being in the hospital. You need a hospital just to get that.

And then the day when I was going to take him home—we had gotten permission—I came in, and he had aspirated food into his lungs. He was unconscious. They expected him to die. They had him on two antibiotics. He was breathing with a mask, and he was unconscious.

But he recovered, slowly. After he recovered, he wasn't able to keep food from going into his airway when he tried to eat. He gradually got better at it. But [his doctor] checked him and said, "He's dying. He needs hospice care." I asked if we could go home, and he said we could.

So we came home, and we had home hospice care, and he only lived eleven days. So he died on February twenty-seventh.

I'm so sorry.

The visiting nurse people explained to me that he had been dying for a while and I didn't realize it. His appetite had been decreasing, and he had been sleeping more, and the weakness; these are all signs that he was dying already. When they got him home, they said, "He has two or three days to live." But he lived eleven days. I had sort of started hoping that he would be better.

So anyway . . . since then I've been thinking about going back to work. I feel able to. But this [Occupy Wall Street] has been pretty good, actually. You know Shakespeare's comment, "Conscience doth make cowards of us all"? I raised two children—family to raise and people to support. And when I was an intern and resident, I was involved in the same kind of thing: medical, and getting better medical care for people. I worked in the covered hospital system in Washington. I did things only sporadically, because you just get too busy.

Some of the kids don't understand that the cops—they have families to support. Somebody tells them to do something, they're going to do it because it's not easy to get a job these days. And they can be very much in sympathy with us, but they still are going to be here with their riot helmets on and their billy clubs out. It doesn't mean that they hate us; it just means that they're doing their job, the policemen and the firemen. So I keep reminding people of that, because it was a mistake that we made. We used to call the police "pigs," and saw them as enemies, and it was stupid. We all gradually realized that, so . . .

It would be better to start out with that awareness.

Yeah.

Maybe I told you too much.

I understand. It's difficult to lose someone.

Well, it takes a while to get over it.

Yeah. If ever, right?

I guess I'll get a job eventually. I get Social Security, and I get some retirement money from the state, so I can sort of get by without working. But this . . . I mean, I feel like I'm doing something worthwhile, you know? ❖

Appendix A: Distribution

The People's Mic is based on a simple principle: If you copy, say again. Relay the message so that everyone can hear it. Accordingly, *Why We Occupy* is free literature—free as in freedom, that is, as stipulated in the GNU Free Documentation License (Appendix B). Everyone is free to read and redistribute this book. The License guarantees that all copies of the book and all derived versions remain freely redistributable in the same way.

Consequently, if you have access to *Why We Occupy* in any format, you are free to make copies of it by any means and give them to anyone. What the license says is that you do not need permission to share this work. You are even free to charge money for reproductions that you create, regardless of motive.

The License also gives you the right to make modifications. One might object to this freedom on the grounds that it encourages vandalism, but since the original remains freely available, marks of defacement are easy to identify, and reflect wholly on the vandal.

Of greater importance is what we have to gain by encouraging openness, trust and dialogue. Public space, a resource that is as vital as it is difficult to cultivate, depends upon the willingness of the people to use their voices. The occupiers put themselves into many hostile situations to make their voices heard; we couldn't presume to now contain them. No one can claim ownership over the conversations that happened in Liberty Plaza in the fall of 2011. Occupy Wall Street was and is all about free conversation, free as in freedom. ❖

Appendix B: GNU Free Documentation License

Preamble

The purpose of this License is to make a manual, textbook, or other functional and useful document "free" in the sense of freedom: to assure everyone the effective freedom to copy and redistribute it, with or without modifying it, either commercially or noncommercially. Secondarily, this License preserves for the author and publisher a way to get credit for their work, while not being considered responsible for modifications made by others.

This License is a kind of "copyleft," which means that derivative works of the document must themselves be free in the same sense. It complements the GNU General Public License, which is a copyleft license designed for free software.

We have designed this License in order to use it for manuals for free software, because free software needs free documentation: a free program should come with manuals providing the same freedoms that the software does. But this License is not limited to software manuals; it can be used for any textual work, regardless of subject matter or whether it is published as a printed book. We recommend this License principally for works whose purpose is instruction or reference.

1. Applicability and Definitions

This License applies to any manual or other work, in any medium, that contains a notice placed by the copyright holder saying it can be distributed under the terms of this License. Such a notice grants a world-wide, royalty-free license, unlimited in duration, to use that work under the conditions stated herein. The "Document," below, refers to any such manual or work. Any member of the public is a licensee, and is addressed as "you." You accept the license if you copy, modify or distribute the work in a way requiring permission under copyright law.

A "Modified Version" of the Document means any work containing the Document or a portion of it, either copied verbatim, or with modifications and/or translated into another language.

A "Secondary Section" is a named appendix or a front-matter section of the Document that deals exclusively with the relationship of the publishers or authors of the Document to the Document's overall subject (or to related matters) and contains nothing that could fall directly within that overall subject. (Thus, if the Document is in part a textbook of mathematics, a Secondary Section may not explain any mathematics.) The relationship could be a matter of historical connection with the subject or with related matters, or of legal, commercial, philosophical, ethical or political position regarding them.

The "Invariant Sections" are certain Secondary Sections whose titles are designated, as being those of Invariant Sections, in the notice that says that the Document is released under this License. If a section does not fit the above definition of Secondary then it is not allowed to be designated as Invariant. The Document may contain zero Invariant Sections. If the Document does not identify any Invariant Sections then there are none.

The "Cover Texts" are certain short passages of text that are listed, as Front-Cover Texts or Back-Cover Texts, in the notice that says that the Document is released under this License. A Front-Cover Text may be at most 5 words, and a Back-Cover Text may be at most 25 words.

A "Transparent" copy of the Document means a machine-readable copy, represented in a format whose specification is available to the general public, that is suitable for revising the document straightforwardly with generic text editors or (for images composed of pixels) generic paint programs or (for drawings) some widely available drawing editor, and that is suitable for input to text formatters or for automatic translation to a variety of formats suitable for input to text formatters. A copy made in an otherwise Transparent file format whose markup, or absence of markup, has been arranged to thwart or discourage subsequent modification by readers is not Transparent. An image format is not Transparent if used for any substantial amount of text. A copy that is not "Transparent" is called "Opaque." Examples of suitable formats for Transparent copies include plain ASCII without markup, Texinfo input format, LaTeX input format, SGML or XML using a publicly available DTD, and standard-conforming simple HTML, PostScript or PDF designed for human modification. Examples of transparent image formats include PNG, XCF and JPG. Opaque formats include proprietary formats that can be read and edited only by proprietary word processors, SGML or XML for which the DTD and/or processing tools are not generally available, and the machine-generated HTML, PostScript or PDF produced by some word processors for output purposes only.

The "Title Page" means, for a printed book, the title page itself, plus such following pages as are needed to hold, legibly, the material this License requires to appear in the title page. For works in formats which do not have any title page as such, "Title Page" means the text near the most prominent appearance of the work's title, preceding the beginning of the body of the text.

The "publisher" means any person or entity that distributes copies of the Document to the public.

A section "Entitled XYZ" means a named subunit of the Document whose title either is precisely XYZ or contains XYZ in parentheses following text that translates XYZ in another language. (Here XYZ stands for a specific section name mentioned below, such as "Acknowledgements," "Dedications," "Endorsements," or "History.") To "Preserve the Title" of such a section when you modify the Document means that it remains a section "Entitled XYZ" according to this definition.

The Document may include Warranty Disclaimers next to the notice which states that this License applies to the Document. These Warranty Disclaimers are considered to be included by reference in this License, but only as regards disclaiming warranties: any other implication that these Warranty Disclaimers may have is void and has no effect on the meaning of this License.

2. Verbatim Copying

You may copy and distribute the Document in any medium, either commercially or noncommercially, provided that this License, the copyright notices, and the license notice saying this License applies to the Document are reproduced in all copies, and that you add no other conditions whatsoever to those of this License. You may not use technical measures to obstruct or control the reading or further copying of the copies you make or distribute. However, you may accept compensation in exchange for copies. If you distribute a large enough number of copies you must also follow the conditions in section 3.

You may also lend copies, under the same conditions stated above, and you may publicly display copies.

3. Copying in Quantity

If you publish printed copies (or copies in media that commonly have printed covers) of the Document, numbering more than 100, and the Document's license notice requires Cover Texts, you must enclose the copies in covers that carry, clearly and legibly, all these Cover Texts: Front-Cover Texts on the front cover, and Back-Cover Texts on the back cover. Both covers must also clearly and legibly identify you as the publisher of these copies. The front cover must present the full title with all words of the title equally prominent and visible. You may add other material on the covers in addition. Copying with changes limited to the covers, as long as they preserve the title of the Document and satisfy these conditions, can be treated as verbatim copying in other respects.

If the required texts for either cover are too voluminous to fit legibly, you should put the first ones listed (as many as fit reasonably) on the actual cover, and continue the rest onto adjacent pages.

If you publish or distribute Opaque copies of the Document numbering more than 100, you must either include a machine-readable Transparent copy along with each Opaque copy, or state in or with each Opaque copy a computer-network location from which the general network-using public has access to download using public-standard network protocols a complete Transparent copy of the Document, free of added material. If you use the latter option, you must take reasonably prudent steps, when you begin distribution of Opaque copies in quantity, to ensure that this Transparent copy will remain thus accessible at the stated location until at least one year after the last time you distribute an Opaque copy (directly or through your agents or retailers) of that edition to the public.

It is requested, but not required, that you contact the authors of the Document well before redistributing any large number of copies, to give them a chance to provide you with an updated version of the Document.

4. Modifications

You may copy and distribute a Modified Version of the Document under the conditions of sections 2 and 3 above, provided that you release the Modified Version under precisely this License, with the Modified Version filling the role of the Document, thus licensing distribution and modification of the Modified Version to whoever possesses a copy of it. In addition, you must do these things in the Modified Version:

A. Use in the Title Page (and on the covers, if any) a title distinct from that of the Document, and from those of previous versions (which should, if there were any, be listed in the History section of the Document). You may use the same title as a previous version if the original publisher of that version gives permission.

B. List on the Title Page, as authors, one or more persons or entities responsible for authorship of the modifications in the Modified Version, together with at least five of the principal authors of the Document (all of its principal authors, if it has fewer than five), unless they release you from this requirement.

C. State on the Title page the name of the publisher of the Modified Version, as the publisher.

D. Preserve all the copyright notices of the Document.

E. Add an appropriate copyright notice for your modifications adjacent to the other copyright notices.

F. Include, immediately after the copyright notices, a license notice giving the public permission to use the Modified Version under the terms of this License, in the form shown in the Addendum below.

G. Preserve in that license notice the full lists of Invariant Sections and required Cover Texts given in the Document's license notice.

H. Include an unaltered copy of this License.

I. Preserve the section Entitled "History," Preserve its Title, and add to it an item stating at least the title, year, new authors, and publisher of the Modified Version as given on the Title Page. If there is no section Entitled "History" in the Document, create one stating the title, year, authors, and publisher of the Document as given on its Title

Page, then add an item describing the Modified Version as stated in the previous sentence.

J. Preserve the network location, if any, given in the Document for public access to a Transparent copy of the Document, and likewise the network locations given in the Document for previous versions it was based on. These may be placed in the "History" section. You may omit a network location for a work that was published at least four years before the Document itself, or if the original publisher of the version it refers to gives permission.

K. For any section Entitled "Acknowledgements" or "Dedications," Preserve the Title of the section, and preserve in the section all the substance and tone of each of the contributor acknowledgements and/or dedications given therein.

L. Preserve all the Invariant Sections of the Document, unaltered in their text and in their titles. Section numbers or the equivalent are not considered part of the section titles.

M. Delete any section Entitled "Endorsements." Such a section may not be included in the Modified Version.

N. Do not retitle any existing section to be Entitled "Endorsements" or to conflict in title with any Invariant Section.

O. Preserve any Warranty Disclaimers.

If the Modified Version includes new front-matter sections or appendices that qualify as Secondary Sections and contain no material copied from the Document, you may at your option designate some or all of these sections as invariant. To do this, add their titles to the list of Invariant Sections in the Modified Version's license notice. These titles must be distinct from any other section titles.

You may add a section Entitled "Endorsements," provided it contains nothing but endorsements of your Modified Version by various parties—for example, statements of peer review or that the text has been approved by an organization as the authoritative definition of a standard.

You may add a passage of up to five words as a Front-Cover Text, and a passage of up to 25 words as a Back-Cover Text, to the end of the list of Cover Texts in the Modified Version. Only one passage of Front-Cover Text and one of Back-Cover Text may be added by (or through arrangements made by) any one entity. If the Document already includes a cover text for the same cover, previously added by you or by arrangement made by the same entity you are acting on behalf of, you may not add another; but you may replace the old one, on explicit permission from the previous publisher that added the old one.

The author(s) and publisher(s) of the Document do not by this License give permission to use their names for publicity for or to assert or imply endorsement of any Modified Version.

5. Combining Documents

You may combine the Document with other documents released under this License, under the terms defined in section 4 above for modified versions, provided that you include in the combination all of the Invariant Sections of all of the original documents, unmodified, and list them all as Invariant Sections of your combined work in its license notice, and that you preserve all their Warranty Disclaimers.

The combined work need only contain one copy of this License, and multiple identical Invariant Sections may be replaced with a single copy. If there are multiple Invariant Sections with the same name but different contents, make the title of each such section unique by adding at the end of it, in parentheses, the name of the original author or publisher of that section if known, or else a unique number. Make the same adjustment to the section titles in the list of Invariant Sections in the license notice of the combined work.

In the combination, you must combine any sections Entitled "History" in the various original documents, forming one section Entitled "History;" likewise combine any sections Entitled "Acknowledgements," and any sections Entitled "Dedications." You must delete all sections Entitled "Endorsements."

6. Collections of Documents

You may make a collection consisting of the Document and other documents released under this License, and replace the individual copies of this License in the various documents with a single copy that is included in the collection, provided that you follow the rules of this License for verbatim copying of each of the documents in all other respects.

You may extract a single document from such a collection, and distribute it individually under this License, provided you insert a copy of this License into the extracted document, and follow this License in all other respects regarding verbatim copying of that document.

7. Aggregation with Independent Works

A compilation of the Document or its derivatives with other separate and independent documents or works, in or on a volume of a storage or distribution medium, is called an "aggregate" if the copyright resulting from the compilation is not used to limit the legal rights of the compilation's users beyond what the individual works permit. When the Document is included in an aggregate, this License does not apply to the other works in the aggregate which are not themselves derivative works of the Document.

If the Cover Text requirement of section 3 is applicable to these copies of the Document, then if the Document is less than one half of the entire aggregate, the Document's Cover Texts may be placed on covers that bracket the Document within the aggregate, or the electronic equivalent of covers if the Document is in electronic form. Otherwise they must appear on printed covers that bracket the whole aggregate.

8. Translation

Translation is considered a kind of modification, so you may distribute translations of the Document under the terms of section 4. Replacing Invariant Sections with translations requires special permission from their copyright holders, but you may include translations of some or all Invariant Sections in addition to the original versions of these Invariant Sections. You may include a translation of this License, and all the license notices in the Document, and any Warranty Disclaimers, provided that you also include the original English version of this License and the original versions of those notices and disclaimers. In case of a disagreement between the translation and the original version of this License or a notice or disclaimer, the original version will prevail.

If a section in the Document is Entitled "Acknowledgements," "Dedications," or "History," the requirement (section 4) to Preserve its Title (section 1) will typically require changing the actual title.

9. Termination

You may not copy, modify, sublicense, or distribute the Document except as expressly provided under this License. Any attempt otherwise to copy, modify, sublicense, or distribute it is void, and will automatically terminate your rights under this License.

However, if you cease all violation of this License, then your license from a particular copyright holder is reinstated (a) provisionally, unless and until the copyright holder explicitly and finally terminates your license, and (b) permanently, if the copyright holder fails to notify you of the violation by some reasonable means prior to 60 days after the cessation.

Moreover, your license from a particular copyright holder is reinstated permanently if the copyright holder notifies you of the violation by some reasonable means, this is the first time you have received notice of violation of this License (for any work) from that copyright holder, and you cure the violation prior to 30 days after your receipt of the notice.

Termination of your rights under this section does not terminate the licenses of parties who have received copies or rights from you under this License. If your rights have been terminated and not permanently reinstated, receipt of a copy of some or all of the same material does not give you any rights to use it.

10. Future Revisions of this License

The Free Software Foundation may publish new, revised versions of the GNU Free Documentation License from time to time. Such new versions will be similar in spirit to the present version, but may differ in detail to address new problems or concerns. See http://www.gnu.org/copyleft/.

Each version of the License is given a distinguishing version number. If the Document specifies that a particular numbered version of this License "or any later version" applies to it, you have the option of following the terms and conditions either of that specified version or of any later version that has been published (not as a draft) by the Free Software Foundation. If the Document does not specify a version number of this License, you may choose any version ever published (not as a draft) by the Free Software Foundation. If the Document specifies that a proxy can decide which future versions of this License can be used, that proxy's public statement of acceptance of a version permanently authorizes you to choose that version for the Document.

11. Relicensing

"Massive Multiauthor Collaboration Site" (or "MMC Site") means any World Wide Web server that publishes copyrightable works and also provides prominent facilities for anybody to edit those works. A public wiki that anybody can edit is an example of such a server. A "Massive Multiauthor Collaboration" (or "MMC") contained in the site means any set of copyrightable works thus published on the MMC site.

"CC-BY-SA" means the Creative Commons Attribution-Share Alike 3.0 license published by Creative Commons Corporation, a not-for-profit corporation with a principal place of business in San Francisco, California, as well as future copyleft versions of that license published by that same organization.

"Incorporate" means to publish or republish a Document, in whole or in part, as part of another Document.

An MMC is "eligible for relicensing" if it is licensed under this License, and if all works that were first published under this License somewhere other than this MMC, and subsequently incorporated in whole or in part into the MMC, (1) had no cover texts or invariant sections, and (2) were thus incorporated prior to November 1, 2008.

The operator of an MMC Site may republish an MMC contained in the site under CC-BY-SA on the same site at any time before August 1, 2009, provided the MMC is eligible for relicensing.

Addendum: How to use this License for your documents

To use this License in a document you have written, include a copy of the License in the document and put the following copyright and license notices just after the title page:

Copyright © YEAR YOUR NAME.

Permission is granted to copy, distribute and/or modify this document under the terms of the GNU Free Documentation License, Version 1.3 or any later version published by the Free Software Foundation; with no Invariant Sections, no Front-Cover Texts, and no Back-Cover Texts. A copy of the license is included in the section entitled "GNU Free Documentation License."

If you have Invariant Sections, Front-Cover Texts and Back-Cover Texts, replace the "with ... Texts." line with this:

> with the Invariant Sections being LIST THEIR TITLES, with the Front-Cover Texts being LIST, and with the Back-Cover Texts being LIST.

If you have Invariant Sections without Cover Texts, or some other combination of the three, merge those two alternatives to suit the situation.

If your document contains nontrivial examples of program code, we recommend releasing these examples in parallel under your choice of free software license, such as the GNU General Public License, to permit their use in free software. ❖

Index

Colophon

Why We Occupy: Liberty Plaza 2011, v1.1

This book was typeset using TEX 3.1415926 by Donald E. Knuth, driven by X̣TEX 0.9995.2 by Jonathan Kew. The index and abbreviations were generated using MakeIndex 2.15 by Pehong Chen. In addition to the LaTeX macros written by Leslie Lamport, the following packages were employed:

- fontspec v1.18 by Will Robertson,
- graphicx v1.0f by David Carlisle and Sebastian Rahtz,
- hyperref v6.79a by Sebastian Rahtz, David Carlisle and Heiko Oberdiek,
- nomencl v4.2 by Boris Veytsman and Bernd Schandl,
- textpos v1.7f by Norman Gray,
- titlesec v2.8 by Javier Bezos,
- xeCJK v2.3.10 by Sūn Wénchāng [孙文昌].

All of the above are free software. TEX is essentially in the public domain, while X̣TEX is distributed under the X11 License. MakeIndex is released under a free license that conforms to the Debian Free Software Guidelines. All of the macro packages are available under the LaTeX Project Public License except for textpos, which is released under the GNU General Public License.

The text was set in Gentium, with bold letterforms provided by the Basic variation. Gentium was designed by Victor Gaultney expressly for the purpose of bringing diverse languages together in one typographic family. The potential of this project is barely hinted at by the appearance of pinyin accents in the present volume, but the spirit of radical inclusiveness resonates. Gentium is distributed under the SIL Open Font License.

Headlines were set in Adobe Frutiger 67 Bold Condensed, and the typewriter font is Adobe Prestige Elite Std. Both fonts are commercially available.

Chinese characters were set in AR PL UMing, a derivative of the Mingti2L Big5 and SungtiL GB fonts produced by Arphic Technology and released under the Arphic Public License. ❖